LATIN AMERICAN STUDIES
SOCIAL SCIENCES AND LAW

Edited by
David Mares
University of California, San Diego

A ROUTLEDGE SERIES

LATIN AMERICAN STUDIES

DAVID MARES, *General Editor*

INSURGENCEY, AUTHORITARIANISM, AND DRUG TRAFFICKING IN MEXICO'S "DEMOCRATIZATION"

José Luis Velasco

Routledge
New York & London

Published in 2005 by
Routledge
270 Madison Avenue
New York, NY 10016
www.routledge-ny.com

Published in Great Britain by
Routledge
2 Park Square
Milton Park, Abingdon
Oxon OX14 4RN
www.routledge.co.uk

10   9   8   7   6   5   4   3   2   1

Library of Congress Cataloging-in-Publication Data

Library of Congress Cataloging-in-Publication Data

Velasco, Jose Luis, 1970-
  Insurgency, authoritarianism, and drug trafficking in Mexico's
"democratization" / by Jose Luis Velasco.
     p. cm. -- (Latin American studies)
  Includes bibliographical references and index.
  ISBN 0-415-97209-4 (hardback : alk. paper)
  1. Mexico--Politics and government--1988- 2.
Democracy--Mexico--History--20th century. 3.
Insurgency--Mexico--History--20th century. 4.
Authoritarianism--Mexico--History--20th century. 5. Drug
traffic--Mexico--History--20th century. I. Title.
  II. Series: Latin American studies (Routledge (Firm))

F1236.V443 2005
320.72'09'04--dc22   2005019683

Contents

List of Tables

List of Figures

These figures can all be found in the Appendix.

List of Abbreviations and Acronyms

AC	Alianza Cívica (Civic Alliance)
AI	Amnesty International
ANAGSA	Aseguradora Nacional Agrícola y Ganadera (National Agricultural and Livestock Insurance Company)
ANCIEZ	Asociación Nacional Campesina Independiente Emiliano Zapata (Emiliano Zapata National Independent Peasant Association)
APN	Agrupación Política Nacional (National Political Grouping)
BANRURAL	Banco Nacional de Crédito Rural (National Bank for Rural Credit)
BOM	Bases de Operaciones Mixtas (Bases for Combined Operations)
CBS	Central European and Baltic States
CCRP/CJ-28	Comité Clandestino Revolucionario de los Pobres / Comando Justiciero 28 de Junio (Clandestine Revolutionary Committee of the Poor / June 28 Justice Command)
CECG	Coalición de Ejidos de la Costa Grande *(Coalition of Ejidos of the Costa Grande Region)*
CENDRO	Centro Nacional para el Combate a las Drogas (National Center for Drug Combat)
CEOIC	Consejo Estatal de Organizaciones Indígenas y Campesinas (Statewide Council of Peasant and Indigenous Organizations)
CFE	Comisión Federal Electoral (Federal Electoral Commission)
CIOAC	Central Independiente de Obreros Agrícolas y Campesinos (Independent Confederation of Agricultural Workers and Peasants)

CISEN   Centro de Investigación y Seguridad Nacional
            (Intelligence and National Security Center)
CJF   Consejo de la Judicatura Federal (Council of the Federal
            Judicature)
CNC   Confederación Nacional Campesina (National Peasant
            Confederation)
CNDH   Comisión Nacional de Derechos Humanos (National
            Human Rights Commission)
COCOPA   Comisión de Concordia y Pacificación (Legislative
            Commission for Pacification in Chiapas)
COFIPE   Código Federal Electoral (Federal Electoral Code)
CONASUPO   Compañía Nacional de Subsistencias Populares (National
            Company for Popular Subsistance)
CT   Congreso del Trabajo (Labor Congress)
CTM   Confederación de Trabajadores Mexicanos
            (Confederation of Mexican Workers)
DEA   Drug Enforcement Administration
DFS   Dirección Federal de Seguridad (Federal Security
            Direction)
ECLAC   Economic Commission for Latin American and the
            Caribbean
ENIGH   Encuesta Nacional de Ingreso y Gasto de los Hogares
            (National Household Income and Spending Survey)
EPR   Ejército Popular Revolucionario (Popular Revolutionary
            Army)
ERPI   Ejército Revolucionario del Pueblo Insurgente (Insurgent
            People's Revolutionary Army)
EVRP   Ejército Villista Revolucionario del Pueblo (Villista
            Revolutionary Army of the People)
EZLN   Ejército Zapatista de Liberación Nacional (Zapatista
            National Liberation Army)
FARC   Fuerzas Armadas Revolucionarias de Colombia
            (Colombian Revolutionary Armed Forces)
FARP   Fuerzas Armadas Revolucionarias del Pueblo (People's
            Revolutionary Armed Forces)
FDI   Foreign Direct Investment
FESEBES   Federación de Sindicatos de Bienes y Servicios (Federation
            of Good and Service Unions)
FFA   Fuerzas Federales de Apoyo (Federal Support Forces)
FGT   Foster, Greer, and Thorbecke Index

FLN	Fuerzas de Liberación Nacional (National Liberation Forces)
GDP	Gross Domestic Product
GFB	Grupo Financiero Bancomer (Bancomer Financial Group)
IFE	Instituto Federal Electoral (Federal Electoral Institute)
INCD	Instituto Nacional Para el Combate a las Drogas (National Institute for Drug Combat)
INEGI	Instituto Nacional de Estadística, Geografía e Informática (National Institute for Statistics, Geography, and Informatics)
INI	Instituto Nacional Indigenista (National Institute for Indigenous People)
INMECAFE	Instituto Mexicano del Café (National Institute for Coffee)
IT	Income Tax
NAFTA	North American Free Trade Agreement
NDI	National Democratic Institute
NGO	Non Governmental Organization
OCEZ	Organización Campesina Emiliano Zapata (Emiliano Zapata Peasant Organization)
OCSS	Organización Campesina de la Sierra del Sur (Peasant Organization of the Southern Mountains)
OECD	Organization for Economic Cooperation and Development
ONDCP	Office for National Drug Control Policy
PAN	Partido Acción Nacional (National Action Party)
PCM	Partido Comunista Mexicano (Mexican Communist Party)
PDLP	Partido de los Pobres (Party of the Poor)
PDM	Partido Democrático Mexicano (Mexican Democratic Party)
PDPR	Partido Democrático Popular Revolucionario (People's Revolutionary Democratic Party)
PFP	Policía Federal Preventiva (Federal Preventive Police)
PGR	Procuraduría General de la Republica (Attorney General Office)
PJF	Policía Judicial Federal (Federal Judicial Police)
PNCD	Programa Nacional para el Control de Drogas (National Program for Drug Control)

PRD	Partido de la Revolución Democrática (Democratic Revolutionary Party)
PRI	Partido Revolucionario Institucional (Institutional Revolutionary Party)
PROCUP	Partido Revolucionario Obrero Clandestino—Unión del Pueblo (Workers' Revolutionary Clandestine Party—Union of the People)
PROGRESA	Programa para la Educación, la Salud y la Alimentación (Education, Health and Nutrition Program)
PRONASOL	Programa Nacional de Solidaridad (National Solidarity Program)
PST	Partido Socialista de los Trabajadores (Socialist Workers's Party)
PSUM	Partido Socialista Unificado de México (Mexico's Unified Socialist Party)
SAGARPA	Secretaría de Agricultura, Ganadería, Desarrollo Rural, Pesca y Alimentación (Ministry of Agriculture, Livestock, Rural Development, Fishery, and Food)
SE	Secretaría de Economía (Economy Ministry)
SEDESOL	Secretaría de Desarrollo Social (Ministry for Social Development)
SHCP	Secretaría de Hacienda y Crédito Público (Finance Minister)
SIEDO	Subprocuraduría de Investigación Especializada en Delincuencia Organizada (Assistant Attorney General Office Specialized in Organized Crime)
SNSP	Sistema Nacional de Seguridad Pública (National Public Safety System)
SSP	Secretaría de Seguridad Pública (Public Safety Ministry)
UEDO	Unidad Especial contra la Delincuencia Organizada (Special Unit against Organized Crime)
UNDCP	United Nations Drug Control Program
UNDP	United Nations Development Program
UNT	Unión Nacional de Trabajadores (National Union of Workers)
UU	Unión de Uniones Ejidales y Grupos Campesinos (Union of *Ejido* Unions and Peasant Groups)
VAT	Value Added Tax

Acknowledgments

Many people contributed to this work. Outstanding among them is Prof. Irene L. Gendzier, from Boston University. While working on this project, I had the privilege of receiving not only her continuous intellectual support and encouragement, but also, and perhaps even more importantly, her friendship. My debt to her is enormous.

Professors David S. Palmer, Susan Eckstein, and Strom C. Thacker, from Boston University, also helped me at all stages of the research project. My deep thanks go to them.

This text would have never been published without the help of Mark Selden, Professor of history and sociology at Binghamton and Cornell Universities. His numerous suggestions on style and content greatly improved it. His personal support was equally decisive.

Dr. David Mares, from the University of California at San Diego, read the entire manuscript, correcting many mistakes regarding both style and facts.

I could never be eloquent enough to express my thanks to Kimberly Guinta, my editor at Routledge, for her kind, efficient, and warm professionalism.

Work on this project was made possible by two scholarships, one from Mexico's National Council for Science and Technology (CONACYT) and the other from the Regional Program of Graduate Fellowships in the Social Sciences, funded by the MacArthur, Ford, and Hewlett Foundations. The support provided by María Teresa San Román and Sandra L. Cervera, the administrators of this program, far exceeded their institutional obligations.

At the last, and critical, stage of the research process, I also received a scholarship from the project "Generación y transmisión de conocimientos en México" ("Generation and transmission of knowledge in Mexico") funded by CONACYT and carried out at the Instituto de Investigaciones

Sociales of the Universidad Nacional Autónoma de México. I owe a great debt of gratitude to Matilde Luna, the coordinator of the project.

As for contributions at the strictly personal level, they were so numerous, deep, bounding, and discreet that it is wiser to deliver my acknowledgments in person.

Chapter One
Anomalies of Mexico's Democratic Transition

In the late twentieth century, *democratic transition* emerged as the most influential model for the study of political change around the world. A vast literature applied it to dozens of countries in Southern and Eastern Europe, Latin America, Asia, and Africa. Ostensibly developed as a basic framework for describing, explaining, and predicting democratic change, this model is also an influential blueprint for political action and a powerful ideological tool.

From the late 1970s, but particularly in the 1990s, Mexico underwent democratic transition: its single-party dominated electoral system became competitive, its formal structure of power became plural; with limited success, many measures were taken to enhance the respect for civil and political rights. However, alongside this process there were changes and continuities that patently contradicted the expectations of the mainstream literature on democratic transition. Authoritarian practices and structures showed their capacity to interact with, and partially colonize formally competitive elections. A new and peculiar wave of insurgency started in 1994, contradicting the alleged moderating effect of democratic transition. At the same time, the illegal drug business became larger and probably increased its political influence, taking advantage of the weaknesses of the new political regime, undermining the rule of law, and reducing the scope of democratic accountability. This contradictory pattern persisted after the "culminating" elections of 2000. By 2003, after a brief interlude of optimism, disappointment with the first post-PRI president and with electoral politics became apparent.[1]

What accounts for this seemingly incongruous combination? How should one describe, in general terms, the process of political change that Mexico underwent in the late twentieth century? How firm and deep is Mexico's apparent move toward democracy? What does the analysis of the

Mexican case tell about the capacity of the mainstream literature on democratic transition to describe, explain, and guide macro-political change?

Because of its slow, contradictory, and indeterminate nature, political change in Mexico might seem a "deviant" case of democratic transition. In reality, this case is far from unique. The image of a worldwide move toward democracy depicted by the transition literature is misleading. The so-called third wave[2] of democratization includes two diverging processes: the establishment of a few stable democracies and the emergence of a large number of "other than fully" democratic regimes, in which democratic gains go hand in hand with potentially destabilizing contradictory elements.

The analysis made in this book seeks to be useful in two respects. First, by explaining the apparent "anomalies" of Mexico's democratic transition, it should present a more realistic interpretation of the process of political change in this country. Second, it should contribute to assessing the descriptive and explanatory accuracy of the mainstream literature on democratic transition.

These are urgent tasks. In Mexico, as in many other "new democracies," democracy remains weak and superficial. Under the legitimating mantle of democratic procedures, the real struggle for social, economic, and political power remains unsettled. It may take a long time before this situation, by its own inertia, degenerates into generalized chaos, escalates into a major violent conflict, or leads back into downright authoritarianism. In any case, unless decisive action is taken, stable democracy will remain unreachable. As the ensuing text shall show, taking a realistic view of macro-political change and building enduring democracy are closely interrelated goals: both entail transcending the narrow, misleadingly objective and "procedural" limits set by the mainstream transition literature.

1. DEMOCRATIC TRANSITION IN MEXICO

Deciding whether a specific country has undergone or is undergoing democratic transition has crucial analytical, normative, and ideological consequences. Yet, the term *democratic transition* has become strongly identified with a particular set of authors and texts. Thus, to avoid being caught in a debate about the meaning of the concept, this book uses the definition that has been put forward by the mainstream literature on the topic. According to this literature, democratic transition is a change in the "rules of the political game" that materializes in three practical processes: the establishment of competitive elections, liberalization, and state "pluralization."[3] To the extent that those phenomena take place in a given country, it can be said that such a country is undergoing democratic transition.[4]

Based on the above criteria, it is clear that Mexico underwent a democratic transition between the late 1970s and 2000. The "post-revolutionary" system, established in the late 1920s, was undemocratic, civilian-dominated, highly centralized, ideologically flexible, highly inclusive, stable, and enduring. It was a "one-party dominant regime" that never interrupted its electoral calendar and relied less on violent repression of dissidence than on its "substantive" legitimacy.[5]

With the "political reform" of 1977, the Mexican regime clearly intensified its reformism. Designed to bring the radical left into the electoral arena, the reform encouraged the formation of new political parties, increased official support to opposition parties, improved the opposition's access to the legislature, and took some steps to ensure the integrity of the electoral process. Between 1979 and 1997, there were seven rounds of federal elections, all of them under different electoral rules. Legal changes from one election to the other were particularly deep from 1988 to 1997. With only one exception, the proportion of the votes obtained by the official Institutional Revolutionary Party (PRI) systematically declined in the federal elections held between 1979 and 2000. By 1994, the country had a competitive three party system.[6] In 2000, the PRI lost the presidency. Overall, the Mexican electoral system became procedurally competitive and fair: an intricate web of legal and institutional safeguards ensures the integrity of the system; parties no longer question the electoral rules; defeated candidates usually accept the results; and disputes among contenders are usually settled through legally recognized means.

Paralleling this movement toward electoral competitiveness, a process of pluralization gradually transformed the formal structure of power of the country. In the post-revolutionary regime, the PRI directly or indirectly occupied most positions in all branches and at all levels of government. The PRI lost its two-thirds majority in the Chamber of Deputies in 1988 and its absolute majority in 1997. With some delay, a similar change took place in the Senate. As the PRI lost its monopoly on seats, the legislative branch overcame its subordination to the executive, actualizing its constitutionally mandated status as an independent power. Constitutional reforms in 1994 and 1996 significantly enhanced the Mexican judiciary. In 1989, the official party's monopoly on state governments was broken. In late 2000, parties other than the PRI ruled thirteen of Mexico's thirty-two states.[7] A similar process of pluralization took place in state legislatures and municipalities. On the whole, this process severed the partisan links that informally but strongly subordinated state and local governments to the president.

In contrast with its growing electoral competitiveness and formal pluralism, Mexico's record on liberalization has been ambiguous. In this, however, the Mexican case clearly conforms to the predominant pattern in the "third wave" of democratization.[8] In the 1990s, several legal reforms explicitly sought to enhance civil and political rights in the country. In practice, voting-related rights have shown great improvements. In terms of parties and candidates, citizens can now choose among several competing options; outright electoral fraud has all but disappeared. Nevertheless, progress with respect to other civil and political rights has been slow and uncertain. In spite of many legal and institutional reforms (including the creation of national and statewide human rights commissions), the country's record on human rights is even more dismaying. In the context of counterinsurgency, anti-drug campaigns, and the fight against common criminality, government forces continued to commit gross human rights violations, including extrajudicial executions, forced "disappearance," and torture.[9]

2. THE "ANOMALIES"

In the 1990s, as Mexico's democratic transition reached a decisive stage, the country was pulled in different directions. A general analysis of political change in Mexico should not—out of theoretical preconceptions, normative biases, or ideological expectations—discard seemingly "anomalous" phenomena as marginal, transient or otherwise irrelevant. Indeed, as this book shall show, the contradictory pattern of changes and continuities is emblematic of important and enduring political phenomena that affect the basic rules of the "political game" and interact in paradoxical ways with electoral competitiveness, liberalization, and political pluralization.[10]

Insurgency

The most influential contributors to the transition literature hold that insurgency tends to disappear as democratization advances and hard-liners from right and left become marginal.[11] If armed opposition to the new democratic regime persists, it takes the form of terrorism, with scarce legitimacy and eliciting the hostility of the democratic forces. The combination of relatively large armed opposition and democratization is seen as a logical and practical impossibility. The experience of Spain, the Southern Cone, and Central America apparently confirms this view.[12] However, the Mexican case (like that of Peru in the 1980s) evidently challenges the belief in the "moderating" effect of democratic transition.

Virtually all prominent students of Mexican politics agree that democratic transition was on course by 1994. However, that year the country also saw the emergence of its largest insurrection in the post-revolutionary period.[13] Insurgent organizations mobilized about five thousand armed people, and around fifty thousand civilian militants. The Zapatista National Liberation Army (EZLN) is by far the largest and most well known of Mexico's insurgent groups. It was also the first to appear publicly, through a well-coordinated offensive in southeastern Mexico, avowedly geared at toppling the president, "defeating the federal army," and achieving eleven social and political goals. In 1996, another organization—the People's Revolutionary Army (EPR)—emerged in southern Mexico. Several splits within the EPR gave rise to at least four more organizations. Guerrilla groups have been reported in twenty of Mexico's thirty-one states and in the Federal District. However, most of these groups, and particularly the most important ones, are concentrated in southern and central Mexico, especially in the states of Chiapas, Guerrero, and Oaxaca.

One peculiarity of this wave of insurgency is that actual fighting has been rather sporadic. Fatal casualties probably total less than one thousand. In contrast, there have been lengthy negotiations, several bilateral and unilateral "truces," and numerous military maneuvers. However, while avoiding direct military engagement, the EZLN and the government ignited local conflicts in the areas surrounding the main rebel strongholds. To a certain extent, the fight between insurgents and the government degenerated into the so-called paramilitary war—a protracted, often violent, conflict between their equally impoverished sympathizers.[14]

Since 1994, insurgency was a constant, if sometimes underestimated, companion of democratic transition in Mexico. It continued to exist after the "culminating" elections of the year 2000. The interaction of democratic transition and insurgency in several ways undermined the alleged democratic nature of the emerging regime: insurgency and counterinsurgency led to the militarization of several areas of the country, provoked numerous human rights violations, and legitimated anti-system (frequently violent and usually illegal) forms of political action.

How can one explain the coexistence of democratic transition and insurgency in Mexico? Why has the state, in spite of enjoying the legitimacy that only clean elections can bestow, been unable (and perhaps unwilling) to eliminate the insurgent groups? Why do these groups keep armed and maintain the threat of violent actions even though they are apparently unable (and perhaps unwilling) to launch an armed offensive against the state? How does insurgency affect the nature of the entire political regime? How does democratic transition affect the nature of insurgency?

A number of institutional and organizational factors contributed to the emergence of insurgency. Ultimately, however, it is impossible to understand it without referring to the socioeconomic conditions that made armed rebellion the alternative of choice to large groups of people. At the deepest level, removing the ultimate socioeconomic causes of Mexico's insurgency would require a substantial alleviation of poverty and inequality. However, the operating rules of democratic transition discourage political leaders from implementing even moderate redistributive programs that would affect the interests of the business elite. It is one of the main points of this book that democratic transition's inability to deal with fundamental socioeconomic issues largely accounts for the survival of insurgency even as elections become apparently cleaner and fairer.

Democratic transition contributes to the survival of insurgency in several other ways. The fact that the new regime enjoys electoral legitimacy and their limited military capacity prevent the insurgents from openly trying to overthrow it. The gross social inequalities of the country bolster the legitimacy of insurgency, deterring the government from undertaking decisive military action against it. Moreover, although widespread, the consensus on democracy is superficial and often negative: politicians openly proclaim their support for democratic rules, but they are unwilling to unite with their rivals in an unambiguous defense of these rules. All together, these factors in effect discourage both the insurgents and the government from seeking a negotiated or a military settlement of the conflict. This tacit agreement between adversaries to prolong the conflict easily degenerates into a "proxy" war between their respective sympathizers. Therefore, rather than a fundamental contradiction, there is an inherent connection between democratic transition and insurgency in Mexico.

Authoritarian Practices and Structures

Authoritarian corporatism, clientelism, *caciquismo,* patrimonialism, populism, and vote manipulation performed crucial functions in Mexico's postrevolutionary regime. These and similar forms of political mobilization and political control enabled the regime to survive without widespread use of violence. In different ways, all these practices violate or corrupt the basic democratic principle of one person, one vote, or encroach upon the autonomy of citizens—which lies at the core of pluralist politics.

The establishment of a competitive electoral system has not eliminated those authoritarian practices. On the contrary, they have shown their capacity to colonize the procedurally clean electoral system. The "authoritarian" PRI enjoys most support in the most impoverished areas of the country, precisely where it has most often resorted to authoritarian methods of political mobilization. Even more strikingly, in the late 1990s and early years of the twenty-first century, these practices also underwent a process of *pluralization:* as parties other than the PRI came to control public resources that can be exchanged for political support, they apparently began reproducing authoritarian forms of political mobilization. In sum, apparently "traditional" authoritarian practices have demonstrated their efficacy in times of tight electoral competition.[15]

The analysis of electoral patterns and party structures performed in chapter 4 shows the link between these practices and poverty. Large-scale electoral irregularities, usually enjoying the support or acquiescence of voters, have taken place precisely in the most "marginal" and impoverished areas of the country. How can this link be explained? Instead of explaining it away as the result of an undemocratic political culture or as an authoritarian vestige, this research shows the rational, if unequal and often tacit, agreement that makes this link possible. When combined with competitive elections, widespread poverty and extreme inequality shorten the time-horizon of electors and leaders; blur the distinction between public and private goods and between short and long term benefits; and increase the costs of autonomous organizing among the lowest sectors. In this context, the poor trade their votes or their political allegiance for immediate means of survival or for credible promises thereof, even if this means reproducing traditional authoritarian practices. For the poor, their vote and their political allegiance become one more tool for survival; for political leaders, public goods—delivered in a particularistic way—become one more tool for political mobilization. This tacit agreement corrupts formal democratic procedures, renders poverty functional in competitive politics, and discourages both political leaders and electors from seeking a decisive solution to the country's distributional problems.[16]

The evolution of poverty and inequality in Mexico during the 1990s confirms this view. By different estimates, between 31 percent and 79 percent of the Mexican population lived in poverty in the 1990s; between 15 percent and 29 percent of the total population lived in extreme poverty.[17] Most of this poverty comes not from general lack of resources but from the extremely unequal distribution of income and sources of income. Increased political competition and the pluralization of the Mexican state have not improved this situation. Pure economic factors do not explain this continuity: an analysis of the main social policies implemented throughout the 1990s and subsequent years shows that the new regime has adopted only timid and underfinanced anti-poverty programs. Democratic transition has coincided with a general decline in the "extractive" capacity of the state; and democratic leaders have consistently avoided any substantial modification of the tax structure of the country.

In general, this analysis shows that it is impossible to understand the survival of authoritarian practices without focusing on the "opportunity structure" that makes them desirable to both political leaders and impoverished citizens. Clientelism, authoritarian corporatism, and the like are rational responses of political actors in procedurally democratic but extremely unequal societies. As long as the socioeconomic structure that explains the survival of authoritarian practices and institutions remains in place, purely procedural political change is unable to eliminate them.

Illegal Drugs

In Mexico, the progress of democratic transition coincided with the growth of the illegal drug business. In the 1990s, as democratic transition took its most decisive steps, Mexico expanded its participation in the international drug market: it consolidated its position as a producer of cannabis and heroin, substantially increased its participation in global cocaine trafficking, and became a major producer of methamphetamine. The arrival of the first non-PRI administration in 2000 did not change this situation.

Although the income generated by illegal drugs probably amounts to less than 3 percent of Mexico's legal economy,[18] it is roughly comparable to such indicators as Foreign Direct Investment (FDI), total agricultural exports, and oil export revenues. Yet, its sheer economic value barely hints at the survival opportunities, profits, social costs, and political corruption that this business generates.

Regarding its political influence, there are two opposing views. On the one hand, the literature on democratic transition tends to deny or neglect the significance of the drug business. Top contributors to the transition literature rarely refer to large-scale organized crime; when they do so, they depict it as a law-enforcement problem, relevant for democratic "consolidation" but unimportant for democratic transition (Diamond 1999, 90; O'Donnell 1999).

On the other hand, many journalistic reports and even some government documents highlight the power of the so-called drug cartels, the large profits that illegal drugs generate, and the notorious cases of government involvement in the business. Opinion surveys showing that crime ranks among the top public concerns apparently support this view (Fernández Menéndez

2001, 21–2). Some analysts have even spoken of Mexico as a "narco-democracy" (Jordan 1999; Lupsha 1995; Paternostro 1995; Valle 1995).

What is the real political relevance of the illegal drug business in Mexico? How did it affect the process of political change that the country underwent in the late twentieth century and subsequent years? What can the analysis of this case tell about the analytical accuracy of the mainstream literature on democratic transition?

The "narco-democracy" view accurately stresses the importance of drug-related corruption, but runs the risk of overstating the problem. It relies too much on anecdotal evidence and does not seem to acknowledge that the illegal drug organizations' overriding goal is to earn money rather than seize political power. This does not mean, however, that the illegal drug business does not affect the nature of Mexico's political regime.

The analysis made in chapter 5 shows that illegal drugs significantly undermine the rule of law and democratic accountability. Because of their illegal nature, drug organizations cannot rely on the state to guarantee contract compliance. Therefore, they have to create their own "law-enforcement" apparatuses. Given the internal complexity of the drug industry, these apparatuses inevitably collide with each other. The relation between these illegal organizations and the state often entails different forms of collaboration, competition, and mutual tolerance. Whatever the specific combination, this interaction severely challenges the rule of law. Illegal violence, the existence of armed apparatuses outside the control of the state, corruption, and "cooperation" between drug traffickers and law-enforcement officials create an important economic and political area that is beyond democratic control. Due to the corrupting influence of drugs, some parts of the state become accountable to drug trafficking organizations rather than to the citizenry.

The illegal drug business and official anti-drug campaigns also undermine democratic change and democracy by fostering militarization and provoking human rights violations. Together with counter-insurgency, anti-crime policies have led to the worse human rights abuses in Mexico. Military involvement in Mexico's anti-drug campaigns has put key civilian functions into the hands of the military, reduced civilian control over the armed forces, and undercut democratic accountability. Militarization is at odds even with a minimalist definition of democracy as "elected civilian rule."

In all these ways, illegal drugs undermine democratic transition. However, there are also causal links in the opposite direction: in several ways, democratic transition creates new opportunities for the illegal drug business. Democratic transition decentralized formal political power but did not modify the distribution of real government capacities, which remain highly centralized. This created a "gray" area, full of opportunities for illegal drug entrepreneurs. Increased electoral competitiveness both augments the political costs of using "dirty" money and creates new incentives for illegal campaign funding. By so doing, it contributes to keeping the illegal business in operation and to the survival of drug-related corruption. Even more significantly, democratic transition dismantled several links between the state and important social groups—both legal and illegal—without replacing them with new and more democratic forms of political intermediation. Among other things, this made the links between criminal groups and authorities more fragmented and competitive; it also made criminal organizations more independent and confrontational. Finally, the superficial and often negative nature of the democratic consensus discourages the government from adopting an audacious, serious, and innovative approach to illegal drugs. In sum, as in many other countries, the illegal drug trade is deeply embedded in the overall power structure of Mexico.

3. GENERAL VIEW OF POLITICAL CHANGE IN MEXICO

In short, **Mexico's democratic transition is real—but it is also partial, weak, contradictory, and superficial.** Party leaders and candidates continuously engage in competitive electoral contests. The pluralized state remains underfinanced, nearly paralyzed by its internal divisions and its uncertain legitimacy. Traditional structures of power remain in place, legitimated by the gross socioeconomic inequalities of the country. Capitalizing on these inequalities and exploiting the weaknesses of the state, insurgent groups keep waiting for a major crisis, paradoxically unwilling and unable to mount a serious assault on the procedurally democratic regime. Criminal groups remain in control of a dilated "reserved domain," engaging in complicated (competitive and cooperative) dealings with the authorities. Presenting itself as the safest protection against criminal and anti-system threats, the military has taken over crucial government functions, interfering with civilian life and placing itself beyond the reach of democratic accountability. Strengthened by "market-oriented" reforms, the business elite became ostensibly tolerant of democracy, at the same time removing large distributional issues from the "vagaries" of electoral competition. Rather than raising a serious threat to the established socioeconomic order, the large number of people living in poverty or extreme poverty concentrate on the struggle for survival, fiercely competing among themselves, simultaneously believing in democracy and distrusting democratic politicians and democratic institutions.

This situation is complex and contradictory but it is not necessarily transitory. It might be "bordering on chaos"[19]—but it can remain so for a long time. Its very complexity and its contradictory nature could make the present stalemate surprisingly stable. Despite the rhetorical assaults on some facets of the current order, none of the actors involved seems to have a general, coherent, and publicly defensible alternative to procedural democracy and "free markets." Mutual toleration seems, therefore, the optimal strategy for each of them. Contrary to what a prominent forerunner of the transition model claimed, this equilibrium leads to a peculiar form of pluralism but not to enduring democracy (Dahl 1971). Not surprisingly, the ensuing "neutrality" of the Mexican regime and state ends up favoring the most powerful private agents.

In sum, that the country has become democratic is a partial truth—as partial and potentially misleading as saying that it is on the verge of insurrection, that it is in the midst of chaos, that it is a "narco-democracy," or that it is a neo-liberal dictatorship. Overemphasizing the democratic component inevitably leads one to covering the entire system with the legitimating mantle of democracy.

4. ANALYTICAL IMPLICATIONS

Putting forward a "procedural" and allegedly realistic view, the mainstream literature on democratic transition has made a systematic effort to free political change—and the study of political change—from socioeconomic factors. Instead, this literature underscores the role of elites, pacts, formal political institutions, political parties, and elections, and advocates moderate, market-friendly, and relatively rapid democratic change. This view is based on an influential definition of democracy, according to which democracy is a "procedure" to select and legitimize the governing elite through competitive elections, in a context characterized by respect for civil and political rights.

The analysis of the Mexican case highlights some central shortcomings of the procedural view of democratic change. In the first place, this analysis exposes the descriptive risks of seeing democratic change as mainly a matter of *procedures*. Because of its overriding concern with formal political rules, the mainstream literature on democratic transition is unable to account for the complex and paradoxical links among democratic transition, surviving authoritarian practices, insurgency, and the illegal drug business. The purely procedural view neglects the different ways in which these apparent anomalies undermine the alleged democratic nature of the emerging regime. Even more importantly, it also disregards the many ways in which democratic transition contributes to the emergence or survival of these phenomena. Simply affirming that the country is undergoing democratic transition is a partial truth that underrates the political significance of these apparent anomalies and makes one believe that the basic rules of the political game are far more democratic and institutionalized than they are in reality.

Further, the analysis of the Mexican case shows a peculiarity of the democratic consensus that is full of consequences. A central claim of the transition literature is that democratic transition takes place when all the "relevant" political actors accept the rules of democratic competition. It is argued that, while it does not eliminate programmatic and ideological differences, this agreement rules out anti-system political action. However, that all political actors proclaim their commitment to democracy does not mean that they are unambiguously bent on building and defending a democratic regime. In Mexico, the widespread but superficial democratic consensus in fact discourages political actors from undertaking fundamental transformations that would "consolidate" the initial agreement. In this way, the purely procedural consensus makes democratic "consolidation" unreachable.

Moreover, this analysis shows the political centrality of apparently "contextual" socioeconomic issues. It is impossible to understand the survival of authoritarian practices and structures, the causes of insurgency, and the complexity of the illegal drug business without referring to the gross inequalities of the Mexican society. In a more general sense, this shows the analytical futility of defining "political" democracy so as to deny the centrality of distributional issues.

Defining a "political" approach and identifying the proper object of political science are worthy academic undertakings. Striving for analytic and descriptive realism is the ultimate, if elusive, goal of social science. Denying, in the name of realism, the political significance of distributional issues is a stultifying endeavor, bordering on self-deceit or sheer ideological justification. The distribution of social and economic power is one of the top political issues of all times. It is impossible to understand politics at all—from totalitarian rule to anarchy, from municipal affairs to global struggles, from "primitive" social life to "post-modern" quarrels—without considering the different kinds of conflict and cooperation directly related to the distribution of economic power.

The analysis made here also shows that, as a blueprint for practical politics, *democratic transition,* understood as purely procedural political change, has a built-in corrupting device that activates itself in highly unequal societies with widespread poverty: the procedural view is based on the assumption that democratization should not modify the basic socioeconomic structure of a country.[20] In this way, democratic transition itself makes democratic "consolidation" unachievable.

This book shows that, in a country like Mexico—with huge socioeconomic disparities—the construction of democracy is impossible without far-reaching changes in the distribution of social and economic power. Regardless of the specific definition of democracy that one adopts, the path toward democracy is far more complex and conflictive than the mainstream literature would lead one to believe.[21]

International factors have strong influences on political change in Mexico. The international ideological context of the 1990s, which provided no support for armed insurrection but created some sympathy for a "peaceful" post-communist rebellion, certainly left its mark on the latest wave of insurgency. Mexico is but a link in the international illegal drug chain, its position being all the more subordinate because of its proximity to the United States—the main market for illegal drugs and the main promoter of the anti-drug "war."[22] By increasing the power of transnational economic elites and their domestic allies, economic "globalization" makes politicians more reluctant to alter the distribution of economic assets in a progressive way.[23] Closeness to the United States, reinforced by the North American Free Trade Agreement (NAFTA), reduces the autonomy of Mexican political forces and dissuades them from undertaking actions that would severely destabilize the country.[24] The worldwide ideological appeal of democracy, which became stronger in the 1990s, surely pressed the Mexican elite into adopting democratic procedures.

This book analyzes several of these influences. Nonetheless, for methodological reasons, the emphasis is placed on the domestic dimension. While strongly influenced by transnational forces, domestic power structures are not simply a reflection of them. Not all political regimes are equally vulnerable to foreign influences. As argued in this book, strong regimes and states, with firm institutions and enjoying the active support of the citizenry, may be more capable of asserting their sovereignty. This book endeavors to identify the main domestic obstacles to the creation of a strong democratic regime in Mexico and suggests some ways to overcome them.[25] Constructing such a regime would not only be desirable for the internal politics of the country; it may also make an important contribution to modifying the prevailing transnational structure of power. National changes are necessary steps in the path leading beyond the global predominance of purely procedural—that is, largely cosmetic—democracy.

5. BEYOND DEMOCRATIC TRANSITION

This book speaks primarily of Mexico but has broader implications. As argued here, the adoption of democratic procedures is but a part of the general process of political change in Mexico. Something similar has happened at the global level. What the mainstream literature describes as a single wave of worldwide democratization is in reality a combination of contradictory trends. A handful of "successful" democratic transitions coexist with a large number of weak, unstable, and superficial democratic regimes.[26] In many countries, electoral competition interacts with deeply undemocratic practices and structures: violations of civil and human rights, illegal political violence, "anti-system" forces, weak democratic institutions with fragile popular support,[27] politically corrupting organized crime, and disproportionately powerful economic elites.[28]

Facing these facts, contributors to the mainstream literature have shrunk the procedural definition of democracy to its minimum, claiming that the defining characteristic of democracy is electoral competition. Only in this way are they able to affirm that regimes with evident non-democratic characteristics are nonetheless democratic, that the process leading to those regimes is a "democratic transition," and that, together, these cases form a single "wave" of democratic change.

The analysis of the Mexican case sheds light on this contradictory global pattern. This book argues that the main reason for the weakness of democracy is the extremely unequal socioeconomic structure of the country. This seems valid beyond Mexico. Depending on the starting point, formal democratic change that does not modify the distribution of socioeconomic assets might entail preserving either a relatively fair socioeconomic structure or an unjust and politically disruptive social situation.

The list of "successful" transitions includes the most egalitarian and least impoverished countries that took part in the "third wave." Such was the case of the "exemplary" transitions of Southern Europe. In the former communist bloc of Eastern Europe and the Soviet Union, nations that managed to preserve relatively egalitarian societies had "successful" democratic transitions, while others that now rank among the most unequal in the world have either "concentrated" or "war-torn" political regimes (World Bank 2002, 98). A similar pattern is visible in Latin America: the relatively successful democratic transitions of countries like Uruguay and Chile, with the best social situations in the region, sharply contrasts with the experience of nations like Haiti, and Guatemala, which arguably have the worst democratic and social records. Thus, it seems evident that inequality and poverty have an independent and decisive influence on democratic change across countries and that, in societies with widespread poverty and high inequality, successful democratization necessarily requires substantial improvement of the distributional situation.

Further, in Mexico and many other countries democratic transition and "neoliberal" reform took place at roughly the same time. Because of this coincidence, it might be possible to attribute several problems analyzed in this book to neoliberalism rather than to procedural democratic transition. This view would imply that democratic transition has been the passive victim of an economic program that has undermined its legitimacy and reduced its effectiveness. Hence, a revision of the economic program would seem advisable, but a new approach to democratic change would not be necessary. The analysis of the Mexican case shows that such a view is misleading. Even in the absence of neoliberal reform, purely procedural democratic change in deeply unequal societies would tend to provoke problems like those analyzed here.

As said above, *democratic transition* functions as a potent legitimating tool. In this, as well, the Mexican case is far from unique. Most "democratic" regimes established in the late twentieth century fail to meet the standards of the procedural definition of democracy. By still calling these regimes democratic, the mainstream literature has contributed to legitimating them, underplaying their undemocratic components, their basic unfairness, and their potential explosiveness.

Finally, the analysis of a dependent country like Mexico—with its blatant inequalities, its weak state, and its shaky democratic institutions—reveals, in stark terms, the problems and contradictions that appear disguised or attenuated in "advanced" industrial nations. In these nations, economic inequality and poverty also undermine the practice of democracy; the economic elite exercises an unmatched degree of political influence, while the dispossessed sectors are politically marginalized. Large-scale organized crime also has politically corrosive effects in these countries. Here, as well, democracy often functions as a legitimating tool, covering up undemocratic practices. Moreover, the fact that these nations occupy a commanding position in the transnational power structure enables their elites to defuse domestic tensions. Political domination takes on an international character; to this extent, the relative strength of democracy in advanced industrial nations depends on the existence of a deeply unequal transnational structure. At the same time, this structure is a powerful obstacle to the establishment of enduring democracy in subordinated countries. This shows the link between the domestic and transnational struggles for democracy.

Democratic transition is put forward as a description and explanation of macro-political change. However, the preceding observations show that it accounts only for part of the changes that many countries underwent in the late twentieth century. This shows the need for a more realistic approach to democratic change, one that pays attention to the non-procedural elements of democratization. Such an approach must explicitly take account of the double nature of democracy, which is simultaneously a form of government and a powerful legitimating tool. It must pay attention to the interaction between socioeconomic and political power. It should also look beyond competition for government and legislative posts and analyze the general distribution of political power. Such an approach should question the idyllic image of democratic change put forward by the mainstream literature: democracy may be a regime that processes conflicts in a civilized way, but this does not necessarily mean that the path leading toward it is equally mild. The establishment of democracy through peaceful and democratic ways is indeed a historical rarity.

This last point has crucial practical consequences. Preaching a democratic agreement among all the relevant political forces of an extremely unequal country (where several legal and illegal forces coexist, following different sets of rules and pursuing ultimately incompatible goals) may be naïve or self-serving. In any case, it is utterly unrealistic. At best, such a program would result in a prolonged stalemate. As chapter 6 argues, implementing a firm and far-reaching redistributive agenda might provide a way out of this situation. This would inevitably produce some level of conflict, but it seems the safest way for creating the socioeconomic basis of enduring democracy. This, again, is valid not only for Mexico but for other countries as well.

Chapter Two
Democratic Transition in Mexico

According to the mainstream literature,[1] *democratic transition* is brought about by explicit or implicit pacts among members of the political elite and results in three practical changes: liberalization,[2] the establishment of a competitive electoral system, and the "pluralization" of the state.[3]

By these standards, Mexico has long been in the process of democratic transition: since the late 1970s, the country progressively established a competitive electoral system, underwent an ambiguous process of liberalization, and pluralized its state structure. All three processes accelerated in the 1990s. At the beginning of the 21st century, the legislative branch has become plural and more assertive in its dealings with the executive. The judiciary is now more independent. Electoral competition has modified the distribution of power at the state and municipal levels, thereby actualizing the federal structure of the country. With the gradual elimination of electoral fraud, citizens' electoral rights are better respected than before. Many procedural restrictions on the freedom of speech, information, organization, and the like have been removed, although violations to these rights persist in practice.

Usually, democratic transition is presented as a characterization of overall political regimes. The mainstream literature claims that the establishment of competitive elections, liberalization, and pluralization modify the "basic rules of the political game."[4] Allowing for some temporary incongruence, this implies that the "secondary" rules of the game would necessarily evolve in the direction followed by their "basic" counterparts. The Mexican case has not lived up to this expectation. Many "basic" and "secondary" political rules are not moving in a democratic direction. Nonetheless, democratic transition has brought about important changes, modifying, often in paradoxical ways, the context in which social and political forces interact.

This chapter analyzes, in a summarized way, Mexico's democratic transition. After observing some "peculiarities" of this transition, it focuses, in turn, on each of the three processes identified above: the increased competitiveness of electoral processes, the diversification of the formal power structure, and the evolution of civil and political rights.

1. "PECULIARITIES" OF MEXICO'S DEMOCRATIC TRANSITION

In several respects, the Mexican case defies the descriptive and explanatory capacity of the literature on democratic transitions. Since the Mexican regime never interrupted its electoral calendar and opposition parties always participated in electoral contests,[5] no "foundational election" marked the change of regime.[6] Moreover, since the Mexican Constitution and laws formally guaranteed civil and political rights, the "authoritarian" elite never had to openly proclaim its willingness to grant or extend typical liberal rights. Given the already inclusive nature of the regime, democratic transition did not require lifting prohibitions on political participation; it rather entailed progressively widening up existing channels for political participation and making them more independent from the PRI. As a result, it is hard to identify the beginning and characterize the development of "liberalization" and "democratization" in Mexico.

The most famous analysts of Mexican politics agree that the country underwent democratic transition in the late twentieth century. Yet, they disagree on when the transition began. Some authors affirm or imply that democratic transition started with the political reform of 1977.[7] Others hold that it began in 1988, when, according to the official tally, the PRI presidential candidate obtained less than half of the votes cast and the PRI barely won a majority of seats in the Chamber of Deputies.[8] Still other authors think that Mexico's transition was clearly on route in 1994, when the country held its first truly competitive presidential contest.[9]

In the Mexican case, it is hard to identify the main actors depicted by the transition literature. On the government side, it is not clear who played the role of "softliners" and "hardliners"; within the opposition camp, it is also difficult to pinpoint the "opportunists," "maximalists," and "democrats" (Whitehead 1994).[10] This case also fails to conform to any of the paths identified by the transition literature: there was neither a transition pact nor a collapse of the "authoritarian" regime.[11]

According to Linz and Stepan (1996, 55–65), democratic transitions from authoritarian regimes are easier and shorter than are those from totalitarian and "sultanistic" regimes. Mexico clearly belongs in the authoritarian category, but despite numerous reforms, the institutions of the post-revolutionary regime have proven extremely difficult to eradicate. The Mexican regime did not simply collapse as soon as electoral rules were transformed. On the contrary, although its power declined significantly, the PRI was able to survive in the context of procedurally clean elections.

The incongruities between some definitions provided by the mainstream literature and the evolution of the Mexican case show some descriptive limitations of the former. Because several of those definitions fail to give precise indications for the analysis of this case, Mexico's regime change appears as a peculiar or problematic democratic transition.[12] Yet, these ambiguities do not affect the basic fact that, by the standards of the mainstream literature, Mexico has undergone a transition to democracy.[13]

2. ELECTORAL RULES AND COMPETITION

Since its inception in the late 1920s, the post-revolutionary regime changed its electoral rules many times.[14] This reformism intensified in the late twentieth century. Between 1977 and 1996, the electoral legislation was substantially reformed six times.[15] The first and last of these reforms were particularly consequential: the 1977 "political reform" encouraged the formation of new political parties and gave the opposition greater opportunities to gain seats in the Chamber of Deputies. The 1996 "definitive" reform—approved in its fundamentals by all political parties—consolidated the competitiveness of the electoral system.[16]

Since 1986, the Chamber of Deputies has 500 seats, 200 of them allocated on a proportional basis; since 1996, no party may hold more than 60 percent of these seats or may be "overrepresented" by more than 8 percent.[17] In 1993, proportional representation was also introduced in the Senate.[18] The Federal Electoral Institute (IFE), created in 1990, became fully autonomous in 1996, with authority to organize elections, oversee party finances, and allocate public financing to political parties. A series of measures—like creating a professional bureaucracy within the IFE, expurgating the electoral registry, allowing foreign electoral observers, establishing complicated voting procedures, and setting up a Special Prosecutor Office within the Attorney General Office (PGR) to deal with electoral crimes—have sought to eradicate electoral fraud.[19] By 1994, these changes had "created the conditions, for the first time in Mexican history, for a fair election" (Domínguez and McCann 1996, 193).

These reforms have had important practical effects. From 1979 to 1997, there were seven rounds of federal elections, all of them under different electoral rules. Legal changes from one election to the other were particularly deep between 1988 and 1997. In the last quarter of the twentieth century, the only elections based on the same electoral rules were those held in 1997 and 2000.

The PRI share of the votes in federal elections declined systematically from 1979 to the year 2000.[20] Correspondingly, there arose a competitive three party system.[21] The PRI remains the most important member of this system: after losing the presidential contest in the year 2000, it still has the largest number of seats in the Federal Congress and retains most of the state governments.[22] The second most important member is the National Action Party (PAN), which, after six decades in the opposition, won the presidential election in 2000.[23] The Party of the Democratic Revolution (PRD) is the third important member of this system, even though internal disagreements and lack of ideological definition have made its electoral performance highly volatile.[24]

Electoral competition among these parties is usually fierce. However, traditional descriptions that place the PAN on the right, the PRD on the left, and the PRI on the center right of the political spectrum tend to exaggerate ideological divergence in the Mexican party system. While some divergence exists on specific points (especially in formal party documents and campaign speeches), there seem to be no substantial ideological or programmatic differences among Mexican parties. On the issue of regime type, all parties have come to accept the validity of procedural democracy. As Woldenberg (1997, 39–41) argues, the unification of the left, which eventually led to the foundation of the PRD, coincided with its "conversion" to electoral democracy. The PAN has shown its longstanding commitment to electoral politics (Loaeza 1989, 1997). The PRI's discourse never denied the desirability of democracy; often reluctantly, in the last decades of the twentieth century, it gradually came to accept competitive politics in practice.

Mexican political parties also converge on a second critical dimension—that having to do with socioeconomic issues. Contrary to some popular beliefs, the main political parties have come to accept the neoliberal economic model. Traditionally, the PAN has held a "market-friendly" ideology. Since the 1980s, the PRI moved to the right, converging with the PAN. While its economic program is "loosely nationalist and popular," the PRD has also moved into that direction (Craig and Cornelius 1995, 277; see also Domínguez and McCann 1996, 186–7).[25] The analysis of debate within the legislative confirms this convergence (Martínez Rodríguez 1998).

In sum, in the 1990s, and especially since 1994, the Mexican electoral system became more competitive and fairer.[26] Yet, while competition among candidates and parties systematically increased, the Mexican party system has become largely homogeneous in ideological and programmatic terms.

3. PLURALIZATION OF ELECTIVE POSTS AND SEPARATION OF POWERS

In the post-revolutionary regime, the PRI directly or indirectly occupied most positions in all branches and at all levels of government. Since the president controlled the PRI, real power was concentrated in his hands. As politicians from different political parties came to occupy key positions in the formal structure of the state, the separation of powers started to become real. Legal reforms aimed at strengthening the legislative, the judiciary, and the state and municipal authorities further contributed to this process.

Changes have been most visible in the legislative branch. As table 2.2 shows, in 1976 the PRI clearly predominated in the Chamber of Deputies, opposition seats being few and dispersed among several small parties. Not surprisingly, the chamber's main function was to rubber-stamp the initiatives of the executive. Since 1988, when the PRI lost its two-thirds majority, any constitutional reform needs the agreement of at least two parties. Finally, since 1997, when the PRI lost its simple majority, any decision in the chamber needs the support of two or more parties.

Pluralization of the Senate started later and was more rapid. Until 1988, the PRI held all seats in this chamber. As table 2.3 shows, with the exception of 1991, the PRI's share of seats steadily declined in the 1990s. In 1997, for the first time it lost the two-thirds majority needed for amending the Constitution and for many other important decisions.[27] In the year 2000, along with the presidency, the PRI lost its majority in this chamber as well.

Greater pluralism within the legislature had effects on the general state structure. Only when the PRI's monopoly on seats was broken did the president need to negotiate with the legislature. At that moment, the legislative branch actualized its constitutionally mandated status as an independent power. At the same time, legal reforms in the 1990s enhanced the competences of this branch.[28] However, the ban on consecutive reelection—which, according to critics, prevents lawmakers from accumulating experience, developing endurable links with societal groups, and pursuing a legislative career—has not been lifted.

Changes have also affected the judiciary. In the post-revolutionary regime, the Supreme Court systematically shunned political issues, thus giving up two of its key functions: preserving the distribution of power among different branches and levels of government, and ensuring the constitutionality of laws and government actions.[29] Virtually the only way to challenge the legality or constitutionality of official decisions was the *amparo:* a peculiar suit that does not affect the general validity of the contested resolution but only its application to a particular case.

Constitutional reforms in 1994 sought to enhance the Mexican judiciary, changing the procedure for appointing members of the Supreme Court,[30] increasing the judiciary's capacity to settle controversies between different organs of the state, and enabling the Supreme Court to review the constitutionality of laws passed by federal and state legislatures. The reform also enhanced the financial autonomy of the judiciary and created the Council of the Federal Judicature (CJF), intended to improve the internal administration of the judicial branch.[31]

The 1994 judicial reform explicitly excluded electoral matters. The "definitive" electoral reform of 1996 addressed them. It integrated the Federal Electoral Tribunal into the nation's judicial power, thus making it supreme authority in almost all kinds of electoral disputes.[32] Among other things, the Federal Electoral Tribunal is now entitled to assert the validity of elections, review the legality and constitutionality of actions and resolutions of electoral authorities, and protect the electoral rights of citizens.[33] Together, these changes might set the basis for "a more politically active and publicly engaged" judiciary (Domingo 2000, 733).[34]

Increased pluralism also affected Mexico's federal structure. In the early 1980s, the PRI ruled an overwhelming majority of municipalities and held all thirty-one state governorships, plus the mayoralty of the Federal District. The federal structure only existed in paper, as the president had *de facto* power to appoint and dismiss state and municipal authorities. The PRI's monopoly on governorships was broken in 1989, when a candidate from the PAN won the election in Baja California. In 1995, four states had opposition governors, all of them from the PAN. In late 2000, parties other than the PRI ruled twelve of Mexico's thirty-one states and the Federal District.[35]

This process necessarily severed the partisan links that informally but strongly subordinated state authorities to the president. A second process also affected this situation. Until 1988, the PRI held at least two-thirds of seats in every state legislature. This near monopoly steadily eroded in the 1990s. By mid 1999, the PRI had absolute majority in only eighteen legislatures. Moreover, at least for some years in the 1990s, twenty states had "divided governments," defined as those cases where the governor's party has a minority of seats in the legislature (Lujambio 2000, 62–8).

In 1988, the PRI ruled 98.4 percent of Mexico's municipalities. This situation changed in the 1990s. In August 2000, the PRI controlled less than six out of each ten municipalities. In terms of population, the change was even more remarkable: total population under PRI municipal rule dropped from 98 percent to 44.4 percent over the same period.[36]

In practice, the pluralization of Mexico's formal state structure progressively took power away from the presidency. Thus, in a sense, the triumph of a non-PRI candidate in the presidential election of 2000 was the culmination of many opposition victories in municipal, state, and federal legislative elections.

4. CIVIL AND POLITICAL RIGHTS

In contrast to those dealing with electoral matters, analyses focusing on civil, political and human rights in Mexico are scantier and less conclusive. This is largely a reflection of reality: respect for those rights is the weakest part of Mexico's "democratic transition." In this, however, the Mexican case clearly conforms to the predominant pattern in the "third wave" of democratization.[37]

In part, the rather ambiguous evolution of these rights has to do with the starting line of Mexico's transition. The post-revolutionary regime was evidently milder than most military dictatorships. Apart from occupying a prominent place in the Mexican Constitution, civil and political rights also existed in practice, especially for some privileged social groups. In case of violation, the *amparo* suit provided a "relatively effective" way to seek redress (Domingo 2000, 726).

In the 1990s, several legal reforms explicitly sought to enhance civil and political rights in the country. Since 1996 citizens can sue any authority that violate their rights to vote, run for office, and join legal political organizations. The 1996 electoral reform also prohibited collective affiliation to political parties. Since 1996, the Supreme Court has ruled against compulsory affiliation to one union and against mandatory affiliation to business chambers (Domingo 2000, 732; Cervantes 2002, 48). Together, these measures removed the most visible legal foundations of the PRI corporatism.

In the 1990s, civilian organizations explicitly devoted to promoting clean electoral processes in Mexico also flourished. Acting as electoral observers; lobbying government agencies, parties, and candidates; and promoting public awareness, those organizations have played a crucial role in several federal and statewide elections. Their role was particularly important in 1994. The 1996 electoral reform also authorized the registration of National Political Groupings (APNs), designed to provide non-party channels for political participation. APNs receive public funding and—allied with political parties—may nominate or support candidates to public office.

In practice, voting-related rights have shown great improvements. Outright electoral fraud has all but disappeared, and votes are fairly counted and translated into posts.[38] Nevertheless, other civil and political rights have not improved as much in reality. This is evident, for example, in the Mexican section of the Freedom House country ratings. With many fluctuations, political rights clearly improved in the period analyzed here, with the score moving from 5 in 1972–1973 to 2 in 2000–2001.[39] In contrast, civil rights remained essentially unchanged throughout the period, the score often swinging from 3 to 4 (Freedom House 2002b).[40]

The record on human rights is even more dismaying. Many legal and institutional reforms have been clearly positive. In 1990, the National Human Rights Commission (CNDH) was founded; constitutional reforms in 1992 and 1999 made it autonomous. A constitutional reform also mandated the creation of statewide commissions modeled on the CNDH.[41] Furthermore, since the early 1980s but especially in the 1990s, a large number of non-governmental human rights organizations sprang up. Often acting in concert with international or transnational groups, these organizations have played an increasingly important role in denouncing human rights violations and seeking redress for the victims (Cleary 1995; Reding 1995).

All these changes notwithstanding, "Mexico's general record on human rights has contradicted many of the goals implicit in democratization" (Camp 1999b, 239). As chapters 3 and 5 will elaborate upon, in several respects, the human rights situation of the country worsened in the 1990s. The situation did not improve in the early years of the 21st century. The renewed incidence of "disappearances" and the persistence of torture are among the most notorious trends. The poor remain the most frequent victims of such abuses.[42]

CONCLUSION

The formal political institutions of the country have undergone unprecedented changes. Two diverging trends are clearly distinguishable. On the one hand, there is strong electoral competition. The formal structure of the state has become plural. Political leaders have apparently come to accept the desirability of democratic competition. On the other hand, however, the room for choice has narrowed: citizens can choose among different candidates and parties but, in practice, programmatic and ideological differences across parties are all but inexistent. Moreover, efforts to improve the respect for civil, political, and human rights have met with uncertain success.

These changes have interacted with a persistently unequal distribution of social, economic, and political power, leading to some disruptions and several unexpected continuities. The following chapters analyze this interaction.

Chapter Three
Transition and Insurgency

"Where government has come into power through some form of popular vote, fraudulent or not, and maintains at least an appearance of constitutional legality, the guerrilla outbreak cannot be promoted, since the possibilities of peaceful struggle have not yet been exhausted." With this warning, *Che* Guevara—surely the most prominent promoter of revolutionary insurgency in Latin America's entire history—seemed to postulate the basic incompatibility of democracy and armed rebellion (1997, 51).[1]

On the other extreme of the ideological spectrum, Huntington concurs. Apart from approvingly quoting Guevara's "democratic corollary," he adds that, in the modern world, "democratic systems tend to be less subject to civil violence than are non-democratic governments. Democracies . . . provide accepted channels for the expression of dissent and opposition within the system. Both government and opposition thus have fewer incentives to use violence against each other" (1991, 28–9).

Recent developments in Latin America have shown the limits of the alleged incompatibility between procedural democracy and insurgency. In democratic Colombia, guerrilla groups (with around twenty thousand armed members) are one of the four protagonists of that country's protracted conflict (the others being the big drug trafficker groups, the "paramilitary," and the government itself).[2] In Peru, a pioneer in Latin America's latest wave of democratic transition, the return to elected civilian government virtually coincided with the beginning of civil war. Although subversion in Peru is extremely weak today, it is noticeable that it took a government with strong authoritarian practices (which went so far as to "temporarily suspend" democracy in 1992) to defeat rebellion.[3] Virtually all the well-known students of Mexican politics agree that democratic transition was on course by 1994; the analysis made in Chapter 2 clearly confirms this view. However, that year the country also saw the emergence of its largest left-wing insurrection in the seven-decade old post-revolutionary period. Since then, some other insurgent organizations have arisen, bringing the estimated total number of armed rebels close to five thousand.

What accounts for this unpredicted coexistence? Why has the state, in spite of enjoying the legitimacy that only clean elections can bestow, been unable (and perhaps unwilling) to eliminate the insurgent groups? Why do these groups keep armed and maintain the threat of violent actions even though they are apparently unable (and perhaps unwilling) to launch an armed offensive against the state?

This chapter does not seek to provide a general explanation for insurgency, but rather focuses on the link between insurgency and democratic transition. By its very nature, armed political action aimed at fundamentally overhauling the political and social structure of a country contradicts central components of *democratic transition,* as defined in the mainstream literature.[4] Therefore, the coexistence of insurgency and democratic transition provides a unique opportunity to assess the analytical accuracy of that literature. More specifically, by focusing on the interaction between "democratic transition" and armed insurgency, this chapter seeks to answer four basic questions: What explains the coexistence of democratic transition and insurgency in Mexico? How does insurgency affect the nature of the entire political regime? How does democratic transition affect the nature of insurgency? What does the analysis of this coexistence tell about the descriptive and analytical accuracy of the transition literature?

The central argument of this chapter is the following. Insurgency was a central component of Mexico's process of political change in the 1990s. By coexisting with competitive elections, liberalization, and state pluralization, insurgency and counterinsurgency in several ways undermine the alleged democratic nature of the overall political regime.[5] Ultimately, insurgency responds to, and finds justification in, the gross socioeconomic inequalities of the country. Democratic transition did not create these inequalities, but it has failed to address them. In this and other ways, democratic transition prevents a negotiated settlement of the conflict. The electoral legitimacy of the government, the military weakness of the insurgents, the peculiar fragility of the democratic consensus, and the glaring social disparities of the country combine to discourage both the insurgents and the government from launching decisive attacks on each other, thus in effect preventing a military settlement of the conflict. Hence, democratic transition paradoxically contributes to reproducing a form of political action that fundamentally contradicts it.

After outlining a framework for understanding the coexistence of insurgency and transition, the chapter presents basic data on Mexico's current wave of insurgency. Afterward, it analyzes the socioeconomic, institutional, and organizational causes of insurgency. Then, it addresses the impact of insurgency on democratic transition. Next, the chapter focuses on how democratic transition discourages the authorities and the insurgents from seeking a negotiated or military settlement of the conflict. Right before the concluding remarks, it analyzes how and why insurgency has degenerated into a limited civil conflict in some regions of Chiapas.

1. EXPLANATORY FRAMEWORK

According to the most influential contributors to the transition literature, insurgency tends to disappear as democratization advances and hard-liners from right and left become marginal (O'Donnell and Schmitter 1986, 67–70). If armed opposition survives after the adoption of the "democratic rules of the game," it tends to take the form of terrorism, with scarce legitimacy and eliciting the hostility of the democratic forces. The combination of relatively widespread armed opposition and democratization is seen as basically improbable.

The passage by Huntington quoted above suggests that democratization has a moderating effect. The case of Spain seems paradigmatic in this respect. Linz and Stepan argue that nationalist or revolutionary violence progressively lost legitimacy as democratic rules and institutions began to take root (1996, 96–108).[6] Some aspects of Latin America's experience with democratization also seem to confirm this view. As one famous text put it, in the 1980s, with the advent of democracy in the region, the Left abandoned its revolutionary methods and utopia became unarmed (Castañeda 1993). Authors focusing on Central America have also seen a "mutually reinforcing relationship between processes of democratic transition and peace" (Arnson 1999, 6).

As mentioned above, events in Peru, Colombia, and Mexico lead one to question the moderating effect of democratization. Realizing that the hypothesis put forward by the main transition literature did not materialize in these cases, some authors have proposed new and more specific explanations. One argument suggests that the coexistence of democratic transition and insurgency is the result of "violent opportunities" existing in regions where the democratic state is weak and there are financial havens that illegal organizations can exploit (Kay 1999; Collier 2000).

For the specific case of Mexico, numerous authors who question the accuracy of the transition literature have affirmed that the Zapatista National Liberation Army (EZLN) that rebelled in 1994 represents a radical (and, for some, a desirable) alternative to procedural democracy and neo-liberal economics.[7] According to this view, the Zapatista movement is a creative response to the economic and political elitism now in vogue in Mexico. Rather than seeking to seize power, the EZLN would be trying to establish a more participatory kind of democracy, along with a more equitable economic order. In this view, violence fulfilled only a symbolic function to awaken civil society, becoming marginal afterward. Thus defined, the radical nature of this peculiar armed opposition lies on the fact that it proposes a radically different form of political and social organization, rather than on its use of weapons. One fact cited to support this view is that the actual war between the EZLN and the Mexican government lasted only twelve days, but the former has remained an important political actor ever since its emergence in January 1994.

However, these two explanations have important drawbacks. The "violent opportunities" view cannot account for the fact that, in the Mexican case, insurgent groups have appeared precisely in some of the poorest regions of the country, where there is no financial haven to be exploited. On the other hand, viewing armed groups as a radical but peaceful alternative to procedural democracy and neo-liberal economics can at best explain the existence of the EZLN but not other, more radical groups that have not proclaimed any intention to give up the use of weapons. Moreover, affirming that insurgency takes place at the margins of the democratic regime or seeing it as a radical alternative to "elitist" democracy prevents one from analyzing the possible connection between democratic transition and insurgency.

Other authors have seen Mexico's recent wave of insurgency as the latest episode of a long history of indigenous rebellions. Seen as an intrinsically Indian phenomenon, insurgency has little to do with democratic transition.[8] Although it rightly focuses on the cultural oppression and economic deprivation that have led some Indian communities to rebel, this view also has important deficiencies. In the first place, it is noteworthy that most Mexican Indians did not rebel. As table 3.1 shows, Yucatan is the Mexican state with the largest indigenous population, but no insurgent movement has developed there in recent years. Oaxaca, the other state where Indians represent more than one-third of the total population, has been an important base of current Mexican insurgents, but not as much as Chiapas and Guerrero (where Indians are less numerous). In Chiapas, where most of the insurgents are Indians, rebellion has been strongest in the *Cañadas* region, where Indians are certainly numerous but not as predominant as in the Central Highlands (where support for insurgency has been more ambiguous). Moreover, not all rebels are Indians. Indeed, insurgent groups other than the EZLN are not based on Indian populations. Similarly, most of the demands made by insurgent groups are of a national, rather than "Indian" character.[9] Even in the case of the EZLN, the top leadership is not, either racially or culturally, Indian. Finally, and most significantly, the EZLN's decision to emphasize its indigenous component and its cultural demands was largely a strategic choice, rather than something predetermined by the intrinsic nature of the movement.[10] As explained below, Mexican insurgency should be understood not as the protest of an Indian minority but as a movement rooted in the enormous inequalities of the entire society (many of which are particularly hard on the Indian population) and responding to a peculiar political context.

Still other authors have presented a suggestive approach, according to which Mexico's current insurgency is a radically unprecedented phenomenon. Fuentes (1994) defined the Zapatista uprising as "the first post-communist rebellion in Latin America." Another author has affirmed that the EZLN has contributed to creating a "new modernity" (Le Bot 1997, 19). More specifically, authors have seen the newness of Mexican current insurgency in that it is a product of the "information age," in which local struggles link with global conflicts through a complex network structure (Ronfeldt et al. 1998; Cleaver 2000). This view successfully depicts the links between insurgents and widespread networks of international supporters, in which information technology has played a crucial role. However, it can explain neither the origin nor the internal structure of the insurgent organizations. Moreover, although it provides an explanation for the survival of the EZLN, it has little to say about Mexico's other insurgent groups. Of course, by stressing the newness of recent insurgency, this view could make one disregard the connections between rebellion and democratic transition.[11]

Given the limitations of the above views, in order to explain the coincidence of armed rebellion and democratization in Mexico, this chapter needs to draw on some older theoretical and comparative works. While doing this, it is important to keep in mind that, for the purposes of this research, the central question is why substantial numbers of people, in some of the most impoverished areas of the country, embrace insurgent options precisely when electoral competition supposedly provides them with more peaceful means to express their grievances.

Partly drawing on Gurr's study of the causes of rebellion, this chapter will take the notion of *deprivation* as the underlying cause of armed political action (Gurr 1970). This will allow it to focus on the particularly deteriorated socioeconomic conditions of most people participating in Mexico's current insurgency. From Skocpol (1979), it will take the idea of *institutional variables*, especially those related to the state, as factors that might allow underlying discontent to take the form of armed rebellion. Drawing on Tilly (1978), it will stress the importance of *organizational factors*, and will see them as the active element that actualizes the opportunities for insurgency created by socioeconomic deprivation and institutional variables. From Dix (1984) and Ryan (1994), it will take the notion that the capacity to build an "anti-system" coalition is crucial to the insurgent groups' potential to grow and eventually succeed.

Other authors have focused on the relative importance of land ownership as a cause of rebellion (Midlarsky 1988; McClintock 1984; Muller and Seligson 1987). By so doing, they have also analyzed the role of economic inequality, subsistence crises, and types of agrarian structures. These factors are certainly relevant to the study of Mexico's case, but it seems possible to integrate them into the range of conditions that contribute to *socioeconomic deprivation*.

The foregoing discussion has suggested that a complex explanation is necessary to grasp the multiple dimensions of so complex phenomenon as rebellion. For the interests of this research, it is crucial to resist the temptation of seeing democratic transition and insurgency as necessarily separate or incompatible phenomena. As the chapter shall show, it is more accurate to see insurgency as a part of the broad process of political change that Mexico is currently undergoing. On the one hand, this broad process has given rise to more competitive elections and, on the other, has provoked the emergence of radical "anti-system" groups. Moreover, it is necessary to keep in mind that the factors that explain the emergence of insurgent groups are not necessarily the same as those that explain their capacity to survive and expand in the context of a "democratic transition."

In light of *deprivation* theory, to find the causes of insurgency this chapter looks at the socioeconomic conditions (especially poverty and inequality) that make armed rebellion attractive for relatively large groups of people. Democratic transition has not created these conditions, but it has been patently unable to address them. Thus, it has contributed to making some important social groups believe that electoral participation cannot bring about economic redistribution and that a more radical form of political action is necessary or acceptable. Following the *institutional variables* view, this chapter also focuses on social and, above all, political marginality (including relative state weakness, and geographical isolation) that facilitate the emergence of insurgent groups, providing "sanctuaries" where they can initially develop. However, the chapter also underlines the importance of *organizational factors*, which include previous experience with legal but independent organizing in the regions involved, and especially the existence of a nucleus of armed struggle promoters.

To explain insurgency's capacity to survive in the context of democratic transition, the chapter focuses on elite divisions, the nature of the democratic consensus, and the economic marginality of the regions involved. The notion of "superficial" (or "negative") consensus, explained in section 5 below, is crucial to understanding the peculiar weakness of the state that prevents it from launching a decisive military campaign against the insurgents, and at the same time precludes it from seeking a definitive negotiated settlement of the conflict.[12]

As the chapter shall also show, along with their capacity to survive, Mexico's current insurgent groups have also demonstrated their incapacity to fundamentally challenge the existing political elite or the political regime as a whole. Factors that explain this limited character of insurgency include: the insurgents' "strategic" and programmatic adaptations to the opportunities and risks created by the recently established democratic regime; their deficient military and economic resources; and the lack of international support for armed rebellion.

As the chapter shall stress, rather than a fundamental contradiction, there is an inherent connection between democratic transition and insurgency in Mexico's process of political change. Only in this context is it possible to explain a peculiar situation in which rebel groups are unable and unwilling to seize power (even though they openly proclaim their radical opposition to the state), but are capable of surviving because the state is also unwilling to eliminate them (even though it proclaims its earnest commitment to peaceful competition for power).

2. MEXICO'S INSURGENCY IN THE 1990S

Mexico's current wave of insurgency began on January 1, 1994, exactly when NAFTA went into effect. It is difficult to calculate the number of people participating in it. A report by Pentagon analysts leaked to the press in February 2000 estimated as many as 7,500 armed rebels, with at least 45,000 active sympathizers. More conservatively, Mexican military sources put the figure slightly above 2,000 combatants and little more than 15,000 sympathizers (Cordoba 2000). From the review of the sources, it seems reasonable to conclude that the real number of combatants is close to the average of those two estimations—that is, nearly 5,000 combatants—supported by tens of thousands civilian collaborators.[13]

The EZLN, by far the largest and most well known of Mexico's insurgent groups, was also the initiator of the current wave. The Popular Revolutionary Army (EPR) arose in June 1996, two and a half years after the Zapatista uprising.[14] Two years later, it was publicly known that a large breakaway faction from the EPR had formed the Insurgent People's Revolutionary Army (ERPI). Since then, several smaller groups have separated from the EPR, creating new organizations, among them the People's Revolutionary Armed Forces (FARP), the *Villista* Revolutionary Army of the People (EVRP), and the Clandestine Revolutionary Committee of the Poor (CCRP/CJ-28). Apart from these, different sources have mentioned between ten and seventeen lesser groups.[15] Some of these might be genuine, but several others might have been concocted by the press or the security offices, and still others might be real but very short-lived organizations.

Guerrilla groups have been reported in twenty of Mexico's thirty-one states and in the Federal District. However, most of these groups, and particularly the most important ones, are concentrated in Southern and Central Mexico, especially in the states of Chiapas, Guerrero, and Oaxaca. The EZLN has operated almost exclusively in Chiapas; the EPR, the ERPI, and the FARP have had a more diffuse geographical basis, but have been particularly active in Guerrero and Oaxaca.[16] On a list of twenty-three insurgent groups compiled by CIEPAC (2000), thirteen such groups had their main bases in Guerrero. Coincidentally, these are the most impoverished regions and states in Mexico.

All of these rebel groups have left-wing ideologies and programs. They all denounce poverty and extreme poverty, and claim to fight for a more egalitarian social and economic order.[17] Indeed, most of their combatants come from very impoverished areas of the states and regions involved. While they have made occasional references to socialism, they all affirm to be fighting also for democracy.

The label *insurgent* seems appropriate to describe these groups. Apart from underestimating their considerable social bases, calling them just "armed groups" would downplay their explicit political aims and tactics, making it difficult to tell them apart from criminal gangs. The label *terrorist* is also evidently inappropriate. In some rare cases, they have performed violent actions that clearly sought to frighten or hurt the civilian population.[18] Most of their actions, however, have had a more conventional political or military character. Finally, although calling them "guerrilla groups" would seem more appropriate, it would overemphasize the military component of these organizations, a component that has not been very active during these years.

3. CAUSES OF INSURGENCY

Seen as a goal in itself, explaining the emergence of Mexico's current wave of insurgency goes beyond the limits of this research. However, it would be impossible to understand the links between democratic transition and insurgency without at least a brief look at the factors that led to the rise of armed leftist groups with considerable support in several Mexican states.

Insurgency has multiple causes. However, to explain the emergence of insurgent movements in Mexico it is possible to distinguish three sets of factors: socioeconomic deprivation, institutional weakness (including relative state weakness), and organizational factors. Roughly speaking, socioeconomic deprivation makes armed political action acceptable or desirable for the affected people, institutional weakness allows armed opposition groups to develop, and independent organizing is the active element that creates the complex structure on which rebellion is based.

Socioeconomic Deprivation

The next chapter will analyze Mexico's high levels of inequality and poverty. As will be mentioned there, poverty in the countryside is several times higher than urban poverty, the situation being even worse in the states of Chiapas, Guerrero, and Oaxaca. It is interesting that the recent wave of insurgency in Mexico has developed mainly in the countryside, which starkly contrasts with the relatively ampler urban footing of the previous wave (from 1965 to the late 1970s).[19] Its main leaders come from urban settings, where many of its civilian supporters also live. However, most of its combatants come from rural areas, and all its known strongholds are located in the countryside.

Nevertheless, in a strict sense, current Mexican insurgency is not a rural rebellion. While its main social and geographical bases are rural, its demands, ideology, program, strategy, and actions go beyond those of typical peasant armed movements.[20] In this respect, the Mexican case is similar to recent insurgent movements in Peru and Colombia, also based on the countryside but with national (and therefore predominantly urban) agenda, leadership, ideology, and program.[21]

The rural character of Mexico's current rebellion might come from the fact that, geographically, rural areas are the most isolated, and hence less subject to state overseeing. While this is certainly an important contributing factor, its explanatory value is limited by the fact that insurgent groups did not develop in the remotest populated areas of the countryside. Similarly, this rural character might also come from strategic and tactical calculations, as it might have resulted from the founding leaders' decision to operate mainly in the countryside. However, evidence shows that these leaders have also attempted to develop an armed basis in urban areas, but their success has been almost negligible.[22] Therefore, to understand why considerable numbers of rural people have supported insurgency, it is necessary to look at the socioeconomic conditions of the countryside.

Some basic data illustrate what one might call "the structural weakness" of the countryside and that of the Mexican states most affected by insurgency. Throughout the 1990s, agriculture (including forestry, hunting, fishing, crop cultivation, and livestock production) generated 5.7 percent of Mexico's Gross Domestic Product (GDP). However, people living in rural areas comprised around 25 percent of the country's population. This means that, from a purely quantitative standpoint, the countryside's economic contribution does not match its social importance. The same mismatch is evident if one looks at workforce data: the number of people working in agriculture amounted to 20.7 percent of Mexico's whole workforce, but the value of their production represented only 5.7 percent of the country's total GDP.[23] The great disparity between urban and rural per capita incomes is an obvious result of these asymmetries.

Similar imbalances are evident if one sees the Mexican states most affected by insurgency in comparison with the entire country. Four percent of Mexico's people live in Chiapas, but their contribution to the country's GDP from 1993 to 2001 was only 1.8 percent. Data for Guerrero and Oaxaca are similar to those of Chiapas.[24] Accordingly, Chiapas, Oaxaca, and Guerrero are the three states with lowest GDP per capita in the country. Finally, Chiapas and Oaxaca—closely followed by Guerrero—are Mexico's most rural states; in the 1990s, Chiapas was the only state with most of its workforce in agriculture and related activities.[25]

These imbalances have also affected the political relevance of the countryside. Virtually any analysis on the subject agrees that urban electoral competition has become more important since 1988.[26] In 1988, the opposition beat the PRI in several crucial urban settings; the PRI's resurgence in the cities was crucial to its electoral victory in 1991; subsequent federal elections also showed that the decisive party contest was located in the urban areas. Parties have courted urban inhabitants more intensely than they have sought the support of rural people. The ultimate reason for this is that rural voters represent less than one-third of Mexico's total voting population.[27] The problem is that, even if they are not decisive for the national political competition, rural voters still represent an important part of the Mexican population.

Apart from the ideological inclinations of Mexico's top policy-makers, the economic and political imbalances described above surely explain why it was possible to mistreat the rural economy so openly during the economic reforms that the country underwent in the 1980s and 1990s. At the same time, the fact that the countryside still holds an important part of the

Mexican population explains why armed rebellion promoters have been able to use it as the main basis for insurgency.

Partly as a reaction to the successive economic crises that have haunted the country since the early 1980s, the government has implemented several consequential reforms in the agricultural sector.[28] One central goal of the reforms was to make agricultural production contribute to controlling inflation and reducing the country's foreign trade deficit—both central components of the stabilization package implemented in the late 1980s. The other goal, which would harmonize the countryside with the reinforced market foundation of the economy, was to bolster private property and competitiveness in the agricultural sector. In many cases, the most visible result of these reforms has been to increase inequality in the countryside.

Specific policies included the dismantling of several state institutions, among them the state-owned company that marketed basic food products (CONASUPO), the agricultural insurance agency (ANAGSA), and the National Coffee Institute (INMECAFE), as well as the adoption of strict market criteria in the government's rural development bank (BANRURAL). By 1990, price supports (or "guaranteed prices," in the official Mexican jargon) were eliminated for all agricultural products except corn and beans. Something similar happened with tariffs on agricultural goods. In the early 1990s, guaranteed prices for corn and beans failed to keep pace with inflation and were eventually eliminated when NAFTA came into effect (Harvey 1998, 181). In 1992, the government also promoted an audacious reform of the landownership system. The main component of this reform was the amendment of the article 27 of the Constitution—a milestone of the Mexican revolution that in several senses symbolized the alliance between peasants and the government. The reform's main objective was to privatize the *ejido* sector[29] and eliminate the legal basis of land redistribution, thus making private landownership safer.

Implemented in a "chaotic" way (Pastor and Wise 1998, 64), these policies had contradictory results: grain (especially corn) production has been severely damaged, while a selected number of crops (especially fruits and vegetables) have become much more efficient and competitive. The problem is that most of the rural population works in the losing sectors, whereas competitive production is highly concentrated in both economic and geographical terms (Godínez 2000, 395–7). As a result, living conditions in the countryside have deteriorated dramatically, provoking among other things a remarkable increase in out-migration.

The cases of corn and coffee deserve special mention. In terms of workforce, corn production is Mexico's main rural activity. Traditionally, corn growers occupied a fragile position in the Mexican rural economy.[30] The crisis initiated in the early 1980s severely affected them. This situation worsened after 1994. NAFTA established a fifteen-year period to phase out the quota system intended to protect domestic corn production. Yet, the Mexican government largely disregarded this system, allowing the free importation of corn in excess of the established quota (Public Citizen 2001, 28). Low productivity and nearly unmitigated foreign competition have had almost fatal consequences for the corn sector and therefore for the entire rural economy (Levy and Van Wijnbergen 1995).

Coffee was the main crop in the areas of Guerrero and Chiapas that later became rebel strongholds. Most participants in the coffee sector are extremely small-scale producers. In 1989, international coffee prices dramatically dropped off and at the same time the government privatized INMECAFE. For coffee growers, the consequences were terrible. It took three years for the government to implement an emergency program for the sector (Harvey 1998, 178; Paz Paredes and Cobo 2000).

The reform of the land-ownership system also deserves special mention. Amendment to article 27 of the constitution has not led to the disappearance of the *ejido* sector. Nevertheless, it had a deep symbolic impact, destroying the expectation of future land distribution among peasants. Abundant evidence shows that it provoked angry reactions among peasant organizations (Harvey 1998, 186–90; Jones 1996; López Monjardín 1996).[31]

To substitute for its dismantled rural structure, the government resorted to two programs: the National Solidarity Program (PRONASOL) and the Program of Direct Support to the Countryside (PROCAMPO). Rural components of PRONASOL included support for agricultural day laborers and small coffee growers, and efforts to develop rural micro enterprises. Created in 1993, PROCAMPO is a fifteen-year income support program for basic grain producers. While these programs have somewhat mitigated the effects of the rural crisis, they are poorly financed, their funds have been often misallocated or misused, and they fail to deal with the basic causes of the crisis (Pastor and Wise 1998, 68–70; Harvey 1998, 183–6).

Most peasant and rural organizations unsuccessfully opposed the policy changes described above (Gramont 1996). In this context, the armed struggle promoters' ostensible stance against economic inequality and social marginality in the country could not fail to attract sympathy or acquiescence from relatively broad social sectors. It certainly allowed the armed groups to obtain the active support of many people living in some of the most impoverished rural areas of the country.[32]

Institutional Weakness

Socioeconomic deprivation alone can produce bitter resentment and frustration, but it does not necessarily lead to rebellion.[33] Several deprived Mexican regions have not taken part in insurgency. Institutional factors, especially those related to the state, were also decisive in the emergence of Mexico's current insurgent groups. Evidence shows that, seen from the standpoint of many people living in current insurgent strongholds, the state has simultaneously been weak, repressive, and illegitimate. This mixture, which at first sight might seem paradoxical, lies at the core of the institutional factors that contributed to the emergence of insurgency in Mexico.

Insurgent groups developed in relatively isolated areas with rather dense populations. The *Cañadas*, the EZLN's main stronghold, is a rather isolated zone. On the east, it borders on the relatively sparsely populated Lacandon jungle; it takes a long trip through bad-quality roads to reach the towns located on the other cardinal points.[34] Seventy percent of the *Costa Grande*, the main stronghold of the EPR-ERPI's, is mountainous, while coastal plains occupy only 10 percent of the region. Government surveillance in these areas has been evidently weak, thus providing a haven for the initial development of insurgency; the regions' rather numerous populations meant a large number of potential supporters.

By weakening the economic and political institutions that linked the countryside with the central authorities, the "reform of the state" carried out in the late 1980s and early 1990s further debilitated the state presence in those regions.[35] The National Peasant Confederation (CNC), the PRI organization that traditionally controlled the countryside, underwent a profound crisis that further deteriorated its already weak presence in the future guerrilla strongholds.[36] Political maneuvering and the state's withdrawal from the rural economy debilitated the economically oriented social organizations that had previously worked in association with state institutions in those regions.[37]

The reform of the state and elite infighting also weakened Mexico's intelligence apparatus. The EZLN uprising caught the government off guard, even though military encounters between Zapatista and government troops had occurred seven months earlier. Some authors have affirmed that this was not an intelligence failure, but rather the product of a political decision. The Mexican government feared that confirming the existence of guerrilla groups in Chiapas might endanger the passage of NAFTA in the U.S. Congress. While this was indeed an important factor, it is also evident that Mexico's intelligence agencies underestimated the threat, failed to identify the EZLN leadership in advance, were unable to deactivate the planned uprising, and did not anticipate the date and related circumstances of the revolt. Similar intelligence failures were evident with regard to the EPR's first public appearance (Wager and Schulz 1995, 9–17; Turbiville 2000, 47).

Another factor contributing to the development of insurgent groups was the weak legitimacy of the state. In its war declaration, the EZLN called on the congress and the judiciary to restore the "legality and stability of the country" by removing the president from power. This obviously alluded to the dubious PRI victory in the 1988 presidential elections. Moreover, electoral fraud in state and local elections was particularly notorious in those regions. Electoral conflicts were exceptionally bitter in Guerrero after 1988. Before the EZLN uprising, it even happened that the PRI obtained more than 100 percent of the votes cast in some of the municipalities that later became Zapatista bases (Henríquez Arellano 2000, 57–8; Rojas 1995; Bartra 2000a, 139–55; Gutiérrez 1998).

Apart from alienating the people from the government, electoral fraud also buttressed the belief that pacific forms of political participation were useless. To this, one has to add the legitimacy losses resulting from the perception that the government had adopted openly anti-peasant economic policies.

Finally, although the state was weak in the future rebel zones, its presence was often seen as a threat rather than as an asset. Violent clashes were common between peasant organizations and government forces in Chiapas, leaving an impressive number of people dead, prisoners, and injured. Even moderate organizations such as the Union of *Ejidal* and United Peasant Groups (UU) met with violent reactions from the government. Partly, this was due to the alliance between the state government and the local (especially landed) upper class.[38] Partly, repression was also a result of inter-elite conflicts: in many instances, one government faction—seeking to create troubles for a rival elite group—violently attacked an independent organization. The repressive presence of the state was often felt in the zones where the EZLN was developing (Harvey 1994, 160–4).[39]

In Guerrero, and especially in the areas where the EPR later developed, the state was particularly repressive during its anti-guerilla campaigns in the 1960s and 1970s, leaving hundreds of people dead or "disappeared." Although clashes for land possession were rare in these areas, official repression also resulted from the government's attempts to control autonomous economic organizations. Conflicts arising from municipal elections also took on a violent character. Finally, there was "preventive" repression, the most notorious case being the *Aguas Blancas* massacre.[40]

Organizational Factors

Intense independent organizing predated the emergence of the EZLN in Chiapas. This included radical but unarmed peasant groups, such as the *Emiliano Zapata* Peasant Organization (OCEZ) and the Independent Confederation of Agricultural Workers and Peasants (CIOAC), which began work in several parts of the state in the mid 1970s. It also included economically oriented organizations that tried to establish collaborative links with the government, such as the UU, whose main area of influence would later become the main stronghold of the EZLN. Also important was the work of the *San Cristóbal* Diocese of the Catholic Church, heavily influenced by the Liberation Theology, and especially active in the future EZLN zones.[41]

By itself, independent peaceful organizing did not lead to rebellion, but it created a supportive milieu. A group of armed struggle promoters, forming the National Liberation Forces (FLN), took advantage of these opportunities. Created in Monterrey, a prosperous city in Northern Mexico, this group moved to Chiapas in the early 1970s, only to be fatally hit by the federal army shortly afterward. In the early 1980s, surviving and new members of the group came back to Chiapas, this time to successfully build a relatively large insurgent army (Tello Díaz 2000). There is abundant evidence that this group drew on the existing organizational structures (especially those linked to the Catholic Church and the UU), not only to create its political and military underground structure but also to extend its political influence after the uprising.[42]

Similar developments took place in Guerrero, especially in the region where armed rebellion developed. In the early 1990s, economically oriented organizations, many of them participating in the *Ejido* Coalition of the *Costa Grande* (CECG) underwent a profound crisis. In that period, organized sympathizers of the left-wing PRD met with violent reactions from the government. This created opportunities for the development of organizations that, while demanding concrete material benefits, adopted a much more radical stance toward the government. Most of the victims of the 1995 *Aguas Blancas* massacre were members of one of these organizations (the Peasant Organization of the Southern Mountains, or OCSS). Members of these organizations, whose leaders were persecuted by the government in the aftermath of the massacre, welcomed the public appearance of the EPR one year later.[43]

The history of the armed group that took advantage of these organizational structures is less well known than that of the creators of the EZLN. The EPR emerged in a zone of Guerrero that had been the stronghold of the Party of the Poor (PDLP), the main rural guerrilla group of the 1970s. The remnants of this group allied themselves with the Workers' Revolutionary Clandestine Party—Union of the People (PROCUP).[44] In May 1995, the PDLP and the PROCUP joined with twelve other groups to form the EPR (Turbiville 1997; Lemoine 1998).[45]

4. INSURGENCY'S IMPACT ON DEMOCRATIZATION

The coexistence of insurgency and democratic transition at the national level may entail segmentation rather than real combination: some people might participate in elections, while others would support insurgency or directly take part in it. If that were the case, then the connection between democracy and insurgency would be purely external. At the micro-level, coexistence would only amount to juxtaposition of two mutually exclusive forms of political participation performed by different sets of people.

Very careful micro-level analysis is necessary to settle this question. However, available evidence already shows that important numbers of people have not seen radical armed organizing as incompatible with peaceful electoral participation. Insurgent leaders have not usually condemned or openly opposed elections. The EZLN general command has been rather ambivalent in this regard, but the leaders of the EPR and its offshoots have openly proposed to combine elections and rebellion.[46] Evidence also shows that sympathizers and even armed militants of the rebel groups often participate in elections as well.[47] The other side of the coin is the violence that both federal and local authorities have often used against peaceful opponents in areas with real or supposed rebel presence. In these cases, authorities treat members of social organizations or legal political parties as rebels, thereby contributing to blurring the differences between insurgency and peaceful political participation.[48]

Insurgency has had mixed effects on democratic transition. Several authors have affirmed that, however paradoxical it may seem, the EZLN uprising contributed to Mexico's peaceful move toward democracy.[49] Evidently concerned with the potentially disrupting effects of the uprising, all the important presidential candidates signed the "Accord for Peace, Democracy, and Justice" in late January 1994. This document, which called for the peaceful solution of controversies, established the guidelines for a series of electoral reforms that eventually contributed to making the 1994 federal elections cleaner and more legitimate (see Fernández de Cevallos et al. 1995).

From January to the Election Day in August, Mexican political leaders, intellectuals, and common citizens seemed particularly concerned with electoral fairness. Not surprisingly, electoral turnout was notably high (75 percent) and in spite of several minor complaints, opposition candidates recognized the legitimacy of the electoral process.[50] Even the EZLN tacitly promoted electoral participation and eventually recognized the results of the presidential race.[51]

After 1994, the EZLN' actions were not clearly favorable to electoral fairness and electoral pluralization. During the campaign period leading to the October 1995 state-level elections in Chiapas, the EZLN adopted an ambiguous attitude. However, just a few hours before the voting booths opened, it ordered its forces and sympathizers not to vote. This move certainly contributed to the electoral success of the PRI, thus limiting the pluralization of the political institutions in Chiapas. In 1997, the EZLN also had an ambiguous attitude during the campaigns and finally decided to sabotage the federal elections in its strongholds, forcefully preventing people from voting and burning down several voting booths. Afterward, members and sympathizers of the EZLN have simply refrained from voting, without further interfering with the electoral processes.[52]

The attitude of the EPR and its offshoots toward elections has been less problematic: they have declared unilateral cease-fire during federal and state elections and have even encouraged people to vote. There were seemingly well-founded rumors that the ERPI was preparing to trigger an insurrection in the event of an electoral fraud in the federal elections of the year 2000; this might have prompted the government to capture the main leaders of this organization in October 1999 (Turbiville 1997, 2000).

The evolution of electoral turnout after 1994 also shows that the effects of insurgency on electoral democratization have not always been positive. In 1994, voluntary voting participation swelled in the Chiapas and Guerrero areas most affected by insurgency. Nevertheless, afterward it lowered again, revealing, as one observer puts it, "an important limitation" to "political and electoral transition" in those Mexican states (Rubín Bamaca 2000, 209; Gutiérrez 1998).

However, insurgency's most negative consequences for democratization have come through "militarization" and human rights violations. Chapter 5 will present a more systematic analysis of militarization's effects on democratic transition.[53] Here, it suffices to show the facts that have a direct link with insurgency. Among other things, militarization alters the balance between civilian and military authorities, increasing the influence of the latter and weakening civilian control. It also interferes with the day-to-day life of common people, thus limiting the freedom of the "public sphere." By so doing, it tends to undermine both accountability and the democratic rule of law.[54]

The number of soldiers in Chiapas, according to Wager and Schulz (1995, 15, 30), swelled from 2,000 in late 1993 to 20,000 in September 1994. In the subsequent years, official sources have affirmed that the number of troops in Chiapas has oscillated between 15,000 and 25,000, but independent sources have put the figure as high as 80,000 (Castro Soto 2000b, 132).[55]

Figures for Guerrero also vary widely, but they all agree that there has been an increase in the number of troops in that state. Official data reported 4,500 troops there in 1993. In 1997, this figure might have increased to 23,000, although opposition sources put the number at 40,000 (Gutiérrrez 2000).[56]

As part of its counterinsurgent tasks, the army has performed constant patrolling and set up roadblocks in the "risk areas." Equally importantly, the army has covertly taken up basic police functions from the civilian police. Although this has been part of a nationwide trend, especially materialized in the creation of the Preventive Federal Police (PFP), its effects have been stronger in the regions most affected by insurgency.[57]

Except for certain critical periods, militarization has had a predominantly "preemptive" character, seeking to reduce the mobility of insurgents, obstruct their growth, and dissuade them from launching attacks on government personnel or facilities. In this, it has been remarkably successful. However, it has had many other effects. Authors and organizations have documented numerous human rights violations in the context of counterinsurgency. The military campaign against the EZLN in January 1994 resulted in numerous abuses, including illegal imprisonment, extrajudicial executions, torture, and at least fourteen cases of "disappearance." Indeed, human rights organizations have documented a sudden rise in the number of "disappearances" in Mexico after 1994, many of them directly linked with counterinsurgency and taking place in the states and regions most affected by rebellion.[58] Interestingly, the campaign against the EPR and its offshoots has also provoked an unusually high number of "short term disappearances": peasants have been "detained by members of the Mexican army and state policy . . . and held in clandestine detention centres. . . . They were tortured and released free of charge days later, usually following national and international campaigns on their behalf" (AI 1998, 24). The record of politically motivated extrajudicial executions, illegal detention, and torture also increased after the beginning of Mexico's current insurgency and counterinsurgency wave. Members of peasant organizations and indigenous people have been the most common victims of human rights abuses, which contrasts with the more humane treatment that high-level insurgent leaders have received.[59]

Finally, both insurgency and the government's efforts to control it have also severely affected democratic transition by legitimizing anti-system (frequently violent and usually illegal) forms of political action. Levels of violence, both political and "common," considerably increased in Chiapas after the EZLN uprising, and something similar has occurred in Guerrero, which already had a longstanding violent tradition.[60]

In summary, the coexistence of insurgency and democratic transition has put considerable geographical areas, social groups, and dimensions of Mexico's political life beyond the reach of electoral democracy and the rule of law. The analytical import of this is easy to grasp: according to proponents of the "procedural" definition, at the very least, democracy means elected *civilian* rule. The existence of relatively sizable armed groups explicitly opposing the state, the legitimacy of anti-system forms of organization and political action, militarization, and extensive human rights violations contradict even this minimalist definition. By itself, this already shows the descriptive and analytical limitations of the transition literature, which focuses almost exclusively on formal political procedures. Moreover, as the following sections shall demonstrate, not only does democratic transition fail to address the deep roots of insurgency; it also contributes to prolonging it. In this way, procedural democratic change ends up reproducing a form of political action that openly contradicts it.

5. REASONS FOR THE SURVIVAL OF INSURGENCY

Democratic transition did not create the conditions that led to insurgency. However, it has been utterly unable to solve the conflict and has greatly contributed to prolonging it.

There are two basic ways to eliminate insurgency: military annihilation or negotiated disarmament. Mexico's new regime has vacillated between one extreme and the other.[61] Its need to maintain electoral support has prevented it from launching a decisive military offensive against the rebel groups. Its incapacity to introduce basic changes in the socioeconomic structure of the country has prevented it from seriously seeking a negotiated settlement of the conflict.[62] Under these circumstances, the rational answer from government leaders has been to avoid major confrontations with the insurgent groups, circumscribe them to their main regional bases, and pass the problem on to the next administration.[63]

In several specific ways, democratic transition prevents the military annihilation of insurgency. Most insurgents come from desperately poor social sectors; insurgent organizations invariably denounce the gross inequalities of the country. The government itself has recognized the connection between insurgency and deprivation in many occasions.[64] In these circumstances, an all-out military offensive against insurgents would be extremely unpopular and would have high electoral costs for the party that promoted it. The enraged popular reactions to the government military offensives against the EZLN in January 1994 and February 1995 clearly showed these risks.

In principle, the electoral risks of launching a military offensive could be defused if, in spite of its differences in ideology and interests, the political elite presented a united front against "anti-system" challenges and openly rejected armed opposition to the elected authorities. This has not happened in Mexico. Indeed, the analysis of insurgency gives one the opportunity to observe the shallowness of the consensus on the rules and procedures of electoral democracy.

The recent evolution of Mexican politics has shown that virtually every important political leader supports the existence of free and fair elections in the country, with all the basic institutions that this entails. However, political leaders have often taken advantage of insurgency to weaken the incumbent party or at least have refused to form a common front with the government against armed radicals. Factions within the governing elite have also acted in this way. Whether motivated by sincere ideological inclinations or by sheer political ambitions, this attitude shows that the extended democratic consensus is far from deep. Apart from being shallow, the democratic consensus might also be negative: political leaders might support the rules of procedural democracy not so much because they believe in their intrinsic virtues but because they lack any other publicly defendable political project.

Evidence on how the elite's weak commitment to democratic rules has contributed to prolonging the conflict is abundant. As explained above, in the immediate aftermath of the EZLN uprising, virtually all the Mexican political forces condemned violence and quickly expressed their commitment to peaceful electoral competition. This was the only juncture at which a "democratic front" against anti-system actors appeared to exist, probably because the uprising caught politicians by surprise and nobody knew how to take advantage of it.

Nonetheless, reactions toward the Chiapas uprising in 1994 already showed the limits of the elite's democratic commitments. Members of the government elite, even those within President Salinas' intimate circle, took advantage of the rebellion for their internal struggle for power. The best-known case is that of Manuel Camacho, a defeated contender for the PRI presidential nomination, who prevailed on the president to appoint him peace commissioner. Often with contrasting political interests, Camacho and other members of the political elite endeavored to magnify the Chiapas problem seeking to debilitate the official presidential candidate, Luis Donaldo Colosio (who was eventually killed in March 1994). Ostensibly because of the Zapatista uprising but surely motivated by intra-elite fighting over the presidential succession, President Salinas also took advantage of the crisis to reshuffle his cabinet, ridding it of "undesirable elements." Lack of unity in the official political elite surely encouraged the government to stop its military counteroffensive in January 1994 (Castañeda 1999, 277–318, 459–523; Oppenheimer 1998, 111–27).[65]

Government weakness played a contradictory role in the military offensive against the EZLN in February 1995. Overwhelmed by opposition within his own party and by the devastating economic crisis that the country was suffering, President Zedillo wanted to reassert his authority and therefore ordered a military attack that forced the EZLN into its remotest mountain positions. However, conflicts within the official elite (including fights among government agencies and between federal and state authorities) also obstructed efficient military action and made the government afraid of the political consequences of the offensive. That surely contributed to the sudden stop of the military campaign, which failed to reach its declared aims (Wager and Schulz 1995, 34–5; Womack 1999, 295; Oppenheimer 1998, 235–62).[66]

Also relevant to the subject was the attitude of opposition parties. The left-leaning PRD openly condemned the government offensive, and some of its main leaders headed the massive protests against it. The center-right PAN was more sympathetic to military action, but it failed to firmly support the government. Instead of reaching a basic accord against armed insurgency, the main political parties approved the *Law for Dialogue, Conciliation, and Dignified Peace in Chiapas*. In practice, this law prevents the government from unilaterally declaring the negotiations broken and commands it to "guarantee the free transit of the EZLN's leaders and negotiators and make sure that they are not disturbed, in their persons and possessions, by any federal authority."[67]

Finally, the political elite's unwillingness to unequivocally condemn anti-system challenges was also evident in the reactions to President Zedillo's call to use "full force of the state" against the EPR in 1996. The EPR had just launched military attacks that were openly at odds with peaceful forms of political dissent.[68] However, President Zedillo's call met with little enthusiasm from both the opposition and the government elite. More to the point, instead of openly condemning insurgency, Zedillo himself tried to draw the line between the EZLN, a "good" guerrilla group, and the EPR, a "bad" one (*Economist* 1996).

There is an additional reason for the government's reluctance to pay the electoral costs of launching a serious military offensive against insurgents. The next chapter will argue that elected authorities of the new democratic regime are particularly sensitive to the demands of the business elite. In principle, this could encourage the government to annihilate armed leftist opposition. However, top businesses operating in Mexico have no major interests in the areas most affected by insurgency. Among several possible indicators, the evolution of Foreign Direct Investment (FDI) clearly shows this. Official data show that from 1994 to 2000 FDI in Mexico amounted to 75.3 billion dollars. Of that amount, only 8.1 million (0.01 percent) went into Chiapas; 111.6 million (0.15 percent) into Guerrero; and 3.7 million (less than 0.005 percent) into Oaxaca (INEGI 2003b). Another indicator useful on this regard is the degree of "marginality." As table 3.2 shows, Chiapas, Guerrero, and Oaxaca are the three most "marginalized" states in Mexico.[69] They are at the lowest levels in terms of education, income, housing, and economic infrastructure. This obviously makes them scarcely attractive to the economic elite of the country.[70] Although Chiapas has valuable oil fields and quite productive farms, these are all located in the northern and coastal regions of the state, far from the main EZLN strongholds. Similar is the situation in Oaxaca and Guerrero, where the main rebel areas are relatively isolated from the important tourist resorts located in those states.[71]

In several ways, procedural democratic transition has also prevented a negotiated settlement of the conflict. The EPR and its offshoots have not even considered the possibility of starting peace negotiations with the government. Correspondingly, the federal government has shown little interest to negotiate with them. In contrast, negotiations have always occupied a prominent place in the conflict between the government and the EZLN.

The agenda for the first round of negotiations between the government and the Zapatistas (February-June 1994) included thirty-four points, most of them requiring deep political and social changes at the national level. While repeatedly announcing its willingness to negotiate everything, the government only gave precise answers to the most local and limited demands. Larger questions received only declarative answers or were postponed to an imprecise future.[72] This was one of the main reasons with which the EZLN justified its withdrawal from negotiations in June 1994 (EZLN 1994b).

At first sight, the agenda for the second round of negotiations (March 1995-August 1996) seemed more moderate, especially because it only defined four themes (Indian rights, democracy and justice, decent living standards and economic development, and women's rights). However, it is clear that these also require major changes in the Mexican society. It took almost one year for the negotiators to sign the "San Andrés Accords" on Indian Rights. The president failed to ratify the accords and refused to send the proposed Indian Rights Bill to Congress. Negotiation on the other three themes is still pending.

This stalemate should not be surprising. A previous section showed the complexity of factors that provoked insurgency. Removing the ultimate socioeconomic causes of the present wave of insurgency would require abandoning and, in several instances, even reversing the anti-peasant economic policies described above. Purely procedural democratic change seems unable to do so. Despite the many political changes that Mexico underwent in the 1990s, the economic agenda implemented in the country remained fundamentally unchanged throughout that decade; it remains in place even after the electoral defeat of the PRI in 2000. This continuity is not surprising, given the theoretical and practical association between *democratic transition* and the neoliberal agenda.[73]

At the deepest level, removing the ultimate socioeconomic causes of Mexico's insurgency would require a substantial alleviation of poverty and inequality. However, as chapter 4 will show, the operating rules of the newly established democratic regime discourage politicians from implementing even moderate programs of socioeconomic reform that would affect the interests of the business elite. Indeed, as that chapter will show, procedural democratic change might reinforce and legitimate current inequality and poverty patterns. It seems, therefore, that removing the ultimate causes of insurgency would require transcending the "procedural" limits of democratic change.

Decisive military action from the government could force the insurgents to accept a negotiating agenda that does not address the deepest socioeconomic causes of rebellion. However, given the government's evident reluctance to undertake decisive military action against them, they do not feel compelled to do so. Under these circumstances, accepting a diminished negotiating agenda would amount to voluntarily abandoning their status as radical opponents to the political and economic elite of the country. In other words, the logic of procedural democratic transition discourages the government both from addressing the deep causes of insurgency and from imposing a narrow negotiating agenda on its enemies.

A military or a negotiated settlement of the conflict being foreclosed, there is only one option left to the authorities: to keep the problem within reasonable limits and pass it on to the next administration. While avoiding serious military confrontation with the insurgents, the government has deployed enough forces in and around the rebel zones to prevent the conflict from expanding. At the same time, official security forces have performed intelligence work to detect and in some cases dismantle the rebels' underground networks outside their rural bases (Turbiville 2000). It is clear that negotiations have also sought to avoid large-scale confrontations and, if possible, minimize the conflict.

By refusing to make any dramatic decision, authorities have clearly sought to pass the problem on to the next administration. Manuel Camacho, the government chief negotiator in 1994, clearly stated that his main assignment was to keep the conflict within reasonable limits before the elections (González Sandoval and González Graf 1995, 123–8). After the elections, the government made no serious effort to approach the EZLN. Similarly, after 1997, when his presidential term had reached its middle point, President Zedillo made no serious attempt to resume negotiations with the Zapatistas, evidently looking forward to the federal elections scheduled for the year 2000.

After the electoral defeat of the PRI in July 2000, one would have expected decisive changes in the government's approach to insurgency. No one questioned the electoral legitimacy of the new administration. This would have enabled it to seriously seek a negotiated settlement of the conflict. In the event that the insurgents did not show any serious determination to give up armed opposition, then the new regime would have been able to launch a decisive military offensive against them. Years after the opposition victory, nothing like this has happened.[74]

During his presidential campaign, Vicente Fox promised to launch a military offensive against guerrilla groups other than the EZLN, simultaneously seeking a quick peace agreement with the Zapatistas (Aponte 2000). However, the situation evolved in a more ambiguous way. The EZLN reacted to Fox's openings by demanding three pre-conditions, or "signals," before considering entering negotiations: the release of all EZLN members in prison, the dismantling of seven military camps close to the EZLN main strongholds in Chiapas, and the approval of the Indian Rights Bill accorded in 1996.

In response, the government liberated around one hundred prisoners and dismantled several military camps. However, the troops were relocated within the conflict zone, so that no "demilitarization" took place in practice. The most controversial point was the Indian Rights Bill. To promote it, the EZLN general command, including Sub-commander *Marcos*, toured several Mexican states and met with members of the Mexican congress in Mexico City in March 2001. Nevertheless, Congress passed the proposed bill only after several fundamental modifications. The Zapatistas denounced the approved bill and refused to initiate negotiations with the government.[75] In

July 2003, citing the low turnout level in the latest federal elections, the EZLN announced its decision to "totally suspend any contact with the federal government and political parties." In August, it created five regional councils to administer twenty-nine "autonomous municipalities" in Chiapas. This, according to the EZLN, meant the *de facto* implementation of the Indian Rights Bill.[76]

After its inauguration, the Fox administration moderated its bellicose attitude toward the EPR and its offshoots. Years later, it had not undertaken any decisive action against them. The Mexican press has documented occasional violent clashes between these groups and the government forces.[77] Apparently, none of them seems pressed to sign peace agreements with the post-PRI government. The EPR has affirmed that with the year 2000 federal elections, there was a change in the presidency, but not in power, which is still "in the hands of the national oligarchy." It has also denounced the new government's negotiation offers as "instruments of war" and has announced its decision to continue the fight. The other groups have made similar announcements (Olmos 2001; EPR 2000; Irízar 2001).

6. REASONS FOR THE LIMITED CHARACTER OF INSURGENCY

If so many conditions have allowed insurgency to survive for several years, then what has prevented it from posing a greater threat to the Mexican political system? Analyzing this further shows how procedural democracy interacts with insurgency.

Insurgent groups have adapted to the opportunities and limitations created by the country's new political regime. The insurgents have not found convincing arguments for trying to overthrow a democratically elected government. Therefore, they have adopted a wait-and-see attitude, seemingly hoping for a major political crisis that would put them in a more advantageous situation. While the specific nature of this crisis is hard to foresee, they have certainly hoped for a patent electoral fraud that, by removing the electoral foundation of the government, would allow them to attack it frontally, probably provoking a large-scale insurrection (Le Bot 1997, 249–55; Gutiérrez 1998, 301–16). Such a crisis has not happened and is unlikely to happen in the near future. However, the insurgents seem to see that the newly established regime's incapacity to transform the Mexican society will eventually justify their armed rebellion (Olmos 2001).

Although they have often pointed to the "deficiencies" of electoral democracy, Mexico's insurgents have not condemned it. In this, they are different from most of their Marxist predecessors. If they openly rejected elections, they would feel justified to overtly defy the new regime, but at the same time they would legitimize a violent government offensive against them. This explains their seemingly "incongruous" attempts to combine armed struggle with peaceful electoral participation (Bruhn 1999a, 38).

Although they have not given up their goals of seizing power or transforming the foundations of the Mexican society, they have postponed them to an uncertain future. In the meantime, they either engage in prolonged negotiations, or mount "armed information campaigns" combined with limited, "self-defense" military actions.[78]

Despite their usual condemnation of "neo-liberalism," current Mexican insurgents lack a coherent, publicly defendable, alternative socioeconomic model. Many of their concrete proposals and demands deal with socioeconomic matters.[79] What is lacking is an overarching framework that they can oppose to the neoliberal model. This is a major difference between them and many previous insurgent movements in Latin America, which openly claimed to be fighting for socialism. As a result, the rebels have avoided ideological or programmatic definitions, or have resorted to specific causes that have failed to attract large social sectors.

The EZLN quickly dropped its initial references to socialism. Apart from presenting its lack of definition as a virtue (Le Bot 1997, 260), the Zapatista leadership has tried two basic substitutes: "civil society" and Indian rights. By embracing civil society, the EZLN has tried to position itself as an alternative to the government and political parties. By doing so, it has also sought to develop a new model of democracy "from below" based on networks of autonomous organizations. The EZLN's efforts to build permanent organizational structures with civil society have included: the National Democratic Convention (1994), the Movement for National Liberation (1995), the Zapatista Front of National Liberation (1996), and the Continental Encounter for Humanity and Against Neo-liberalism (1996). These attempts have attracted considerable numbers of people, bolstered the public image of the EZLN, and contributed to the creation of international networks of sympathizers. However, they have utterly failed to materialize in permanent organizations (Womack 1999, 327–32).

The eleven demands put forward by the EZLN's war declaration were all of a national character, having to do with general socioeconomic problems or with broad political causes. Later, however, the EZLN concentrated on Indian demands. This change provided it with a very important political shield: the socioeconomic situation of Mexico's indigenous population being so desperate, no armed initiative against an Indian organization would obtain widespread support from the Mexican population. By embracing this cause, the Zapatistas have established firm links with numerous indigenous organizations in Mexico, and made a decisive contribution to attracting public attention to the subject. However, this has not materialized in basic institutional changes (especially because the San Andrés Accords on Indian rights have not been converted into law) and has not led to any substantial improvement in the economic situation of the indigenous population.[80] Moreover, attempts to define the EZLN as an Indian organization have set limits to its efforts to represent Mexico's entire society—which is mostly mixed, both culturally and racially.[81]

The EPR and its offshoots have made more frequent mentions to socialism, but they have denied that it is their main goal. However, even when avoiding broad ideological definitions, they have retained many traits of the traditional Marxist discourse (Bruhn 1999a, 36–40). Nevertheless, they have partially made up for this lack of flexibility by explicitly tolerating electoral participation. The EPR has called for the overthrow of the current regime and the establishment of a "revolutionary government." However, it has refused to declare war on the present regime.[82] Rather than defining a new socioeconomic model, the ERPI has proposed its notion of "popular power," according to which the "people" itself will determine the new organization of the country.[83]

The broad political initiatives presented by these groups have been much less fortunate than those of the EZLN. As mentioned above, they have a close relationship with organizations working in several regions in Guerrero. However, none of their nationwide political initiatives has come to fruition. In February 1997, they proposed the creation of a "Truth Commission" that would investigate the legal situation of the country. One year later, they proposed the framing of a "new constitution" for the country. These calls received only marginal attention from the public.[84]

Some authors have argued that the capacity to build an "anti-regime coalition" is a basic condition for successful insurgency. This coalition must include a variety of domestic actors (including members of the elite and the middle class) as well as "key international actors that serve as sources of refuge, training, and material and diplomatic support" (Dix 1984, 435; Ryan 1994). Current Mexican insurgents have been clearly unable to build such a coalition.

However thin it might be, the consensus on electoral democracy prevents members of the elite from actively supporting insurgency. Opposition parties and other members of the political elite may take advantage of insurgency to undermine the legitimacy of their rivals, but they are not willing to actively support it. The electoral costs of openly defying the democratic rules of the game can be prohibitive.[85]

Moreover, as mentioned above, top economic actors have no major interests in the rebel zones and have had no major conflict with the new democratic regime. Therefore, they deny any political and economic support to the insurgents.

Unlike most of their predecessors in Latin America, current Mexican insurgents do not have access to any decisive source of international support for armed struggle. As mentioned before, EZLN sympathizers have set up international networks. These networks have provided the Zapatistas with political support that has been functional in preventing government military attacks and have given the EZLN access to important international circles. However, they have not provided practical assistance—in the form of weapons, military training, financing, ideological encouragement, or political backing—for armed insurrection.[86]

Incapable of building a domestic "winning coalition" and deprived of international support, the insurgents can only count on their own resources. However, as has been explained above, their main areas of influence and nearly all their militants and sympathizers are utterly poor. Therefore, the resources that they can command are plainly insufficient to sustain a powerful offensive against the government forces.[87] In this way, the same reason that ultimately explains the emergence of insurgency also contributes to its incapacity to expand (Wager and Schulz 1995, 11, 30–1).

7. FROM INSURGENCY TO LOCAL "CIVIL WAR"

Apart from making the problem chronic, the tacit agreement between the government and the insurgents to prolong the conflict has led to bitter local confrontations. In a sense, the situation has evolved from insurgency to limited civil war: the confrontation between rebels and the government has been replaced by a conflict among impoverished social groups. To a considerable extent, this is a further consequence of the coexistence of democratic transition and insurgency.

Except for an encounter between two government columns (with military and police elements) and Zapatista militiamen that left ten people dead in June 1998, there has been no military engagement between the government and the EZLN since February 1995. However, throughout this period, an intermittent, limited "war" has been going on in the Northern and Central Highlands Regions of Chiapas, where the EZLN has numerous sympathizers but a weak military structure. Although no source gives the exact number of casualties caused by this conflict, it surely includes some hundreds of people killed, a larger number of injured, and probably as many as twenty-one thousand people forcibly displaced from their hamlets (Hidalgo

Domínguez 2000, 154).[88] The protagonists of this conflict have been, on the one hand, EZLN sympathizers, supporters of the PRD, and people who collaborate with the *San Cristóbal* Diocese; and, on the other hand, local supporters of the PRI, tolerated and sometimes actively encouraged and supported by government authorities. Many of the latter are organized into more or less structured groups, usually referred to as "paramilitary." Most of the people participating in either side are extremely poor members of the Ch'ol and Tzotzil ethnic groups.[89]

Although there are no precise calculations on this respect, sources agree that the opponents of the "paramilitary" forces have taken larger casualties. Government officials have acknowledged that some local authorities and some ex-members of the security forces have given assistance to the "paramilitary" groups. However, they deny that the government has systematically supported these groups. Authorities have recognized that there are political motivations behind this conflict. Yet, they have insisted that it derives mainly from intra- and inter-community disagreements (PGR 1998). In contrast, independent and opposition analysts have affirmed that paramilitary groups are a central part of the government counterinsurgent strategy (Hidalgo Domínguez 2000).

"White guards"—armed men hired by local strongmen, especially ranchers and landowners—have existed in Chiapas for many decades. However, so-called paramilitary groups are a recent phenomenon. One text defines them as "groups of civilians united in above-ground, peasant-based organizations that employ violence to retain or win political or economic power" (Solomon and Brett 1997, 3). The first of these groups (named "Peace and Justice") appeared in 1995 in Northern Chiapas. Often with support from state-level authorities, it carried out attacks against PRI opponents, who many times hit back violently. Soon, new "paramilitary" groups arose in the same zone and, as the number of casualties grew, the conflict extended to the Central Highlands Region.[90] It was in this region that the *Acteal* massacre, the bloodiest event of this conflict, took place: In December 1997, around sixty armed members of the PRI killed forty-five unarmed sympathizers of the EZLN, most of them women and children.

After the *Acteal* massacre, the number of army and police members in the region increased. These forces did not disarm the "paramilitaries" and were much more efficient in attacking opposition sympathizers. However, no large massacre has taken place afterward, and the number of casualties has decreased. In April 2000, Mexico's Attorney General Office (PGR) created a special office to prosecute "probable armed groups." In November 2000, personnel of this special office captured the main leaders of the "Peace and Justice" group, who were liberated four months later. After the year 2000, when the PRI lost both the presidency of Mexico and the governorship of Chiapas, the press and human rights organizations have continued to report intermittent armed clashes between "paramilitary" groups and EZLN sympathizers.[91]

Some sources affirm that paramilitary forces have performed counterinsurgency tasks in the state of Guerrero as well (Gutiérrez 1998, 187–203). Insurgents operating in that state have also denounced the presence of paramilitary groups (Olmos 2001, 13). There is evidence that the army has certainly used unofficial armed groups in its campaign against insurgents (Castellanos 1998; Díaz 2000). However, a careful review of the sources shows that "paramilitary" groups in Guerrero look more like traditional armed bands controlled by local or state-level *caciques,* who have often used them to eliminate opponents of the state government.

Several authors have questioned the official view, according to which "paramilitary" action is solely the result of local conflicts.[92] These critics affirm that the paramilitary forces are not a number of autonomous groups with purely local objectives, but rather a central component of the government's counterinsurgency structure. Indeed, they see a division of labor between military and paramilitary forces: Military and police units are stationed around the main insurgent areas, avoiding direct engagement with the Zapatistas and maintaining the cease-fire. Subordinated to the army, paramilitary groups undermine the social bases of the EZLN by launching violent attacks against Zapatista sympathizers and dividing the Indian communities. Under the army direction, paramilitary groups perform the "dirty work" (which often leads to gross human rights abuses), thus protecting the image of the army.

In this view, paramilitary groups are mainly an army or government creation. Their internal structure responds to the government counterinsurgent plan, and all the groups act under army or government coordination. In organizing them, the government has drawn on typical counterinsurgent methods developed after the Vietnam War and widely applied in Latin America. In short, according to these critics, paramilitary actions are part of a well-structured "low-intensity warfare" strategy.[93] In support of this view, authors often quote a military document known as "Plan Chiapas," that proposed an integral counterinsurgent strategy in which paramilitary groups had a crucial role to play (Castro Soto 2000b). They also cite well-known cases in which, ostensibly to finance productive projects, the government has subsidized groups that engage in paramilitary actions.[94] These critics also cite well-founded evidence that the authorities have harshly punished the real or feigned crimes committed by opposition groups, which contrasts with their lenient attitude toward the "paramilitary" organizations (Solomon and Brett 1997). Finally, critics also refer to evidence proving that government authorities tolerated or actively supported the perpetrators of the *Acteal* massacre (PGR 1998; SIPAZ 1998).

To be sure, there has been government complicity with the "paramilitary" groups. Moreover, even if it were not actively involved, the government (both federal and statewide) is ultimately responsible for failing to prosecute and disarm those groups. And it is true that the government has used those groups in its fight against the EZLN.

However, depicting the conflict in the Central Highlands and Northern Chiapas as the result of a well-structured counterinsurgent plan of the government has several drawbacks. To start with, this view fails to grasp the socioeconomic basis of the "paramilitary" groups, and therefore does not realize that, to a considerable extent, these groups are self-generated. Competition for extremely scarce resources has been at the basis of the animosity between impoverished people sympathizing either with the government or with the opposition (EZLN, PRD and the Catholic Church).[95] People who have joined the government (or PRI) side have been motivated by sheer necessity, hoping for whatever aid they can get from the authorities. Ridiculous as it may sound, a major controversial point that led to the *Acteal* massacre was the possession of a sand-and-gravel pit (Womack 1999, 342). Local bosses traditionally allied to the PRI and the government have capitalized on that animosity to defend their chiefdoms against the advancement of the opposition, already important before 1994 but bolstered by the EZLN uprising.

The critical view presented above also overestimates the coherence of the government strategy. So-called paramilitary groups lack centralized command and do not seem to act in a coordinated way. Indeed, the government has not had a coherent and stable counterinsurgent strategy, with well-integrated political and social components. Rather than adopting a proactive approach, the government has only sought to limit the conflict and postpone any decisive action against it. While doing this, it has certainly capitalized on local conflicts, supporting the groups that are willing to collaborate with it. These groups have indeed served to isolate and undermine the EZLN. However, much of what has happened in the Chiapas "paramilitary war" has been the result of government indifference. Provided that "peace" with the EZLN is maintained (and unless there is a notoriously violent clash), top political leaders do not care to intervene in local conflicts that have no direct bearing on national politics and do not endanger central economic interests.

Finally, affirming that this local conflict is the result of a coherent counterinsurgency plan implemented by the government also fails to see the way in which the EZLN strategy has contributed to it. Trying to avoid frontal confrontation with the government, the EZLN has concentrated its efforts in the "internal" front, targeting local chiefdoms, destabilizing traditional power structures, and seeking to consolidate its political control of the zones adjacent to its main military strongholds. This was especially true of the EZLN's decision to set up "autonomous municipalities," which coexisted with official municipal authorities and became a major controversial point between EZLN and government sympathizers. Most of these parallel councils were established in early 1996 and several were dismantled two years later, when the government launched a violent offensive against them. This offensive suddenly stopped after government forces and EZLN militiamen clashed on June 10, 1998 (Castro Soto 2000b; Womack 1999, 57).

In this way, while avoiding direct military engagement, the EZLN and the government have contributed to igniting local conflicts in the areas surrounding the main rebel strongholds. Thus, the fight between insurgents and the government degenerated into a "civil war" between their equally impoverished sympathizers. In a sense, the "paramilitary" conflict is the cost that many communities in Chiapas have had to pay for the enduring cease-fire between the EZLN and the government. This is perhaps the main contribution that those poverty-stricken communities have made to Mexico's "peaceful" transition to democracy.[96]

CONCLUSION

In terms of size and casualties, recent insurgency in Mexico is not comparable to major conflicts that took place in other Latin American countries—such as Nicaragua, El Salvador, Guatemala, and Colombia—during the 1980s. Nor has it been as profound as the civil wars that erupted in other regions of the world after the end of the Cold War. Nevertheless, it has been an important component of Mexico's process of political change.

This wave of insurgency might come to an end. People might get tired of supporting a limited rebellion that seems to be going nowhere, and the rebel groups might slowly fade away. Internal divisions might eventually break up the groups and make them plainly insignificant. An unlikely government action could succeed in capturing or killing all the main insurgent leaders, thus eliminating the conflict without excessive bloodshed. In any case, the seeds for new rebellions in the near future would remain and the current wave would have succeeded in showing the capacity of insurgency to coexist with democratic transition and even with procedural democracy.

Furthermore, the fact that so far Mexican insurgency has taken place in impoverished rural areas does not rule out the possibility of much larger insurgent movements in the future, with a firmer footing in the urban zones or in richer, but highly unequal rural areas. Latin America's large cities (some of which rank among the world's most populated) are characterized by "marked economic and social polarization and intense spatial segregation," and there is "great potential for translating urban misery into violent political action" (Demarest 1995, 44, 46).

What does the preceding analysis reveal about the descriptive and analytical capacity of the mainstream transition literature? Contradicting the expectations of this literature, Mexico's current wave of insurgency started exactly when democratic transition took its most decisive steps. In Mexico's overall process of political change, insurgency is not a marginal phenomenon. As the previous analysis showed, democratic transition and insurgency are fundamentally linked. Insurgency and counterinsurgency affect democratic transition in several important ways. Militarization, anti-system action, and extensive human rights violations severely undermine the alleged democratic nature of the new regime. Therefore, the real basic rules of the political game in Mexico are far less democratic and institutionalized than the transition literature would suggest.

Even more revealing are the different ways in which democratic transition affects insurgency. Contradicting the expectations of the transition literature, the above analysis showed that, rather than eliminating it, democratic transition tends to make insurgency chronic. Thus, paradoxically, democratic transition contributes to reproducing a form of political action that openly contradicts it. Purely procedural democratic change does not address the deep socioeconomic roots of insurgency. Its electoral legitimacy and its military superiority allow the government to forestall frontal military offensives from the insurgents. The gross social inequalities of the country bolster the legitimacy of insurgency. This legitimacy and the peculiar weakness of the democratic consensus deter the government from undertaking decisive military action against the insurgents. In sum, democratic transition discourages both the authorities and the insurgents from earnestly seeking a negotiated settlement of the conflict and from launching decisive military attacks on each other.

Therefore, for the incumbent authorities, the best option is to keep the conflict within reasonable limits, avoid a major military confrontation, and pass the problem on to the next administration. For the insurgents, the most attractive option is to keep themselves alive and wait for a serious crisis of the regime and the government. As the above analysis showed, this tacit agreement between both enemies easily degenerates into a "proxy" war be-tween their impoverished sympathizers.

In most general terms, what does the above analysis tell about the "moderating" effect of democratic transition? The conventional view has been that, in many Latin American countries, democratic transition made a determinant contribution to eliminating insurgency (Ryan 1994). The analysis of the Mexican case suggests that this moderating effect has been overvalued. As long as gross socioeconomic inequalities persist or worsen, relatively large parts of the population might find armed political action legitimate and desirable. As long as the democratic consensus remains superficial and the state remains weak, determined promoters of armed struggle might find ways to translate those structural opportunities into actual rebellion.[97]

Chapter Four
Authoritarian Structures and Practices

At least in principle, insurgency seems openly at odds with the image of moderate and peaceful change depicted in most texts on democratization. There is, however, a less spectacular and yet greatly consequential trend that silently corrodes democratic transition in Mexico: the survival of authoritarian practices, such as *clientelism,* authoritarian corporatism, *patrimonialism,* populism, and vote manipulation. These practices, which enjoy considerable legitimacy and affect particularly the poorest social sectors, have shown their capacity to colonize formal democratic procedures and coexist with pluralized state institutions. Rather than fading away as democratic transition advances, they are apparently becoming functional in competitive politics.

Why have authoritarian practices and institutions been able to outlive the authoritarian regime in which they seemed functional? Why do former opposition parties reproduce these authoritarian practices? What are the effects of competitive elections upon these practices? What consequences does the survival of these practices and structures have for the nature of Mexico's political regime? Answering these questions is crucial for the analysis of political change in Mexico and for the comparative study of democratization.

Because of its overriding concern with formal political procedures, the mainstream literature on democratic transition rarely focuses on these informal but potentially influential authoritarian practices. When it does, it views them as the effect of "inappropriate" political institutions, fragile political parties, deficient democratic governance, an undemocratic political culture, or insufficient democratic "consolidation."

In the transition literature, formal political institutions like electoral systems, the presidency, and congresses have been held responsible for the weakness of democratic structures and the consequent persistence of authoritarian practices.[1] However, what one needs to explain is why formal political institutions that work reasonably well in established democracies perform so poorly in the newly established "democracies." To understand this one has to shift the focus away from formal political institutions and toward socioeconomic structures and historical patterns (Power and Gasiorowski 1997).

The explanation in terms of the fragility of political party systems seems equally frail. If weak party systems explain the poor quality of democracy, then what accounts for the former? Moreover, as the analysis presented below shows, what needs to be explained is why decisive segments of the "democratic" elite (from virtually any important political party) implicitly agree to perpetuate authoritarian practices precisely when elections become more competitive.

As for cultural explanations, they are clearly insufficient and might even be misleading when applied to the study of political change.[2] How can one explain that countries sharing the same historical and cultural background have different democratic records? How can a country have different political regimes over a relatively short period, considering that its cultural basis remains essentially the same? In any case, as section 4 below suggests, the effects of political culture can be better understood after the consequences of poverty and inequality are properly assessed.

The explanation in terms of democratic governance can also be misleading: what is under analysis is not so much the incapacity of a weak but democratic government to impose its rule on the population, but rather the fact that authoritarian practices distort or impede the functioning of democratic procedures. Vote manipulation, clientelism, and authoritarian corporatism can significantly alter the nature of seemingly clean and fair elections. Therefore, what these practices affect is not the "output" of the democratic regime, but the quality of political participation and thereby the very nature of the political regime. Indeed, by distorting voting practices, the survival of "authoritarian" forms of political participation affects the core component of procedural democracy.

Finally, putting the problem in terms of democratic "consolidation" might also be misleading. Within the transition literature, the concept of *consolidation* has often served to analyze away all that is undesirable, paradoxical, or "structural" in the process of democratic change.[3] However, as the foregoing analysis shall show, the corruption of formal democratic procedures might be an enduring phenomenon, capable of persisting at all stages of apparently democratic change.

The central argument of this chapter is that widespread poverty and extreme socioeconomic inequality are the main causes of the survival of authoritarian practices. Poverty and, especially, inequality are distinctive characteristics of Latin America and Mexico. While, as discussed below, specific estimations vary greatly, probably more than half of the Mexican population lived in poverty or extreme poverty during the 1990s; this remained basically unchanged in the early years of the following decade. Moreover, although they disagree on the exact figures, all the analyses show that (like most of Latin America) Mexico has particularly high inequality levels, aggravated by huge regional, sectoral, and ethnic disparities.

In this context, the survival of authoritarian practices that corrupt formally democratic procedures should not be seen as an aberration. Clientelism, authoritarian corporatism, and the like, are rational responses of political actors in procedurally democratic but extremely unequal societies. These practices do not necessarily result from a vertical imposition: they may also arise from a voluntary, if unequal and usually tacit, pact. They enjoy legitimacy, even if they do entail violent imposition. These practices seem aberrant only because of the inadequacies of the model used to explain political change. In any case, the basic aberration lies on the unequal socioeconomic structure, not on its political consequences.

In principle, the incompatibility between democracy, on the one hand, and extreme inequality and widespread poverty, on the other, can express itself in different ways. In the current international political and ideological context, it does not usually take the form of outright democratic breakdown. It rather tends to provoke the corruption of formal democratic rules and practices, often combined with political instability and perhaps even the "temporary suspension" of democracy. Fujimori, rather than Pinochet, is the prototypical political leader ruling over today's distributional conflicts in Latin America. Purely procedural democratic change may help legitimate and perpetuate this situation.

1. AUTHORITARIAN PRACTICES IN THE POST-REVOLUTIONARY REGIME

Authoritarian corporatism, clientelism, *caciquismo,* patrimonialism, populism, and vote manipulation performed crucial functions in Mexico's post-revolutionary regime. They enabled the regime to include, mobilize, and control large groups of the population, without widespread use of violence and maintaining some trappings of democracy. In spite of their many differences, these practices share some basic characteristics. They all violate or distort the basic democratic principle of one person, one vote, or encroach upon the autonomy of citizens. In principle, they all can be legitimate, although they always entail some degree of coercion. Their main social targets are the lower sectors. A brief look into the post-revolutionary regime may help understand their ability to survive in a more competitive environment.

Perhaps the most visible and institutionalized of these practices was corporatism. The particular type prevalent in Mexico has been usually defined as *state corporatism*. As opposed to pluralism, corporatism has "constituent unities" that are arranged into "compulsory, noncompetitive, hierarchically ordered and functionally differentiated categories." As opposed to "societal" corporatism, state corporatism has noncompetitive relationships created or imposed by the state, rather than by the social groups involved.[4] This distinction, however, might be misleading. Rather than solely an authoritarian creation of the state, Mexican corporatism in the post-revolutionary period was the result of an unequal pact between the government and some important labor groups (Middlebrook 1995). To some extent, it was social but *authoritarian* corporatism, rooted in, and legitimized by, an unequal and authoritarian social structure.[5]

In the post-revolutionary system, authoritarian corporatism—actively supported by the state—flourished in the labor sector. The corporatist "pact" proved extremely resilient, surviving even as the state implemented openly anti-labor measures during the successive rounds of economic crisis and adjustment initiated in the early 1980s. With far less success, the PRI regime also tried to create large corporatist organizations in two other social sectors—peasantry and the "popular" sector.

Clientelism[6] was another basic institution of Mexico's post-revolutionary system. The president acted as the supreme patron, presiding over an "extremely unstable and fluid" patron-client infrastructure. This flexible structure delivered goods and services to the lower classes on a particularistic basis in exchange for political acquiescence and often for active political support (Purcell 1981, 200–11). Clientelistic networks were able to penetrate the formal administrative system, thereby introducing a particularistic approach to public administration and to the delivery of public goods (Roniger 1990, 57–92). Clientelism flourished even in intergovernmental relations, with the federal government acting as the patron of state and municipal authorities.[7]

A *cacique*, according to a widely accepted definition, is a "strong and autocratic leader in local and regional polities whose characteristically informal, personalistic, and often arbitrary rule is buttressed by a core of relatives, 'fighters,' and dependents, and is marked by the diagnostic threat and practice of violence" (Friedrich 1977, 266).[8] Perhaps its most distinctive characteristic is its local or regional nature: at its core, it consists of "strong local power organized pyramid-fashion so that the 'boss' systems or 'chief-doms' interlock with one another" (Kern and Dolkart 1973, 2). In Mexico's post-revolutionary system, *caciquismo* tended to form a nationwide structure at whose apex stood the president (L. Meyer 2000; Knight 2000). Historically, it was especially prominent in the backward areas of the country; yet, it also proved capable of developing in modern settings (see Cornelius 1973).[9]

In Mexico's post revolutionary regime, the president's "personal style of governing" was decisive; state functionaries were personally subject to him, and public resources were often seen as the rulers' personal property (Cosío Villegas 1976). This was the patrimonialistic dimension of the regime. According to Weber's original formulation, in "traditional domination," of which patrimonialism is a subtype, "the person exercising authority is not a 'superior' but a personal master, his administrative staff does not consist mainly of officials but of personal retainers, and the ruled are not 'members' of an association but are either his traditional 'comrades' or his 'subjects'" (1978, 227).[10]

Populism is perhaps the most diffuse and theoretically imprecise of the categories analyzed here. Especially lately, several authors have defined it in purely economic terms, as a form of economic management particularly averse to fiscal discipline and with a rhetorical commitment to redistributive policies.[11] However, populism is above all a *political* phenomenon.[12] In Mexico and other Latin American countries, populist leaders traditionally have adopted an "eclectic and flexible" program, staying away from any specific doctrine, which has enabled them to reach broad social sectors. Their vague promises of economic development, combined with "a variety of mechanisms to distribute favors," have made them particularly appealing to the lower sectors (Conniff 1999, 5, 10). In post-revolutionary Mexico, presidents Cárdenas (1936–40) and Echeverría (1970–76) have been usually described as populist. However, other political leaders who, on the whole, cannot be described as populist also established populist relations with the lowest and least organized social sectors (Basurto 1999).

A final method of controlled political participation in the post-revolutionary system was "vote manipulation." This usually included a variety of practices, short of outright electoral fraud, such as violations to the secrecy of voting, putting illegal pressure on voters, and the illegally conditioned delivery of social benefits.

2. AUTHORITARIAN PRACTICES IN MEXICO'S DEMOCRATIC TRANSITION

The federal elections of 1997, 2000, and 2003 were the cleanest in Mexican history. That of the year 2000, when the PRI lost the most important position in the political regime, was particularly important; it was the culminating step in a long process of democratic transition. The analysis of these elections shows how procedural cleanliness can interact with authoritarian practices and institutions.

Evaluating the year 2000 presidential election, electoral observers and journalists registered important irregularities, most of them affecting the poorest social sectors. Several NGOs observed that, while it was a "great democratic advancement for Mexico," this race also showed the deficiencies and "unfinished tasks" of Mexico's electoral system. "Old electoral practices, like putting illegal pressure on voters, conditioned delivery of social welfare benefits, threatening, and *acarreo*[13] have not yet been overcome. Southern and Central states were most affected by these practices. In urban sectors, irregularities had a notorious incidence in the state of Mexico, as well as in marginalized zones of the Federal District (Mexico City)."[14]

The conclusions of the Mexico Working Group (a coalition of Canadian organizations) were similar: the year 2000 contest demonstrated that Mexico "has made remarkable progress in its federal election system, particularly since 1996 and notably in regard to the election machinery." However, there was also "widespread misuse of public resources to influence or coerce voters, particularly through social programs" (Mexico Working Group 2000, 4–5).

According to the National Democratic Institute's (NDI) observing mission, the 2000 federal election "marked the beginning of a new era in Mexico's history" (NDI 2000b). However, as the NDI had previously recognized, "the closeness of the election has led to certain practices, particularly by the ruling party, that are reminiscent of past elections. . . . Federal assistance programs . . . are being used to illegally influence voters" (NDI 2000a).

A survey conducted by *Alianza Cívica*,[15] less than two months before the presidential election, showed that 40 percent of the population thought that PROGRESA (the Education, Health and Nutrition Program—the main antipoverty program implemented by the federal government since 1997) and other social welfare programs belonged to the PRI. Eleven percent of the people interviewed thought that getting benefits from the government's social programs bound them to vote for a specific candidate or party, but this figure grew up to 14 percent in rural areas and 18 percent among poor and marginal sectors. Eleven percent of the overall population thought that the vote was not secret in reality or believed that there would be retaliations for voting for certain candidates or parties. This figure grew up to 24 percent among poor and marginalized sectors.[16]

The combination of the above perceptions explains why electoral support for the PRI was higher among beneficiaries of social programs, especially in the poorest sectors. According to the same survey, 33 percent of the polled population intended to vote for the PRI, but among recipients of social welfare this percentage increased to 46. This difference was still bigger in the case of PROGRESA: 65 percent of its beneficiaries intended to vote for the PRI.[17]

Illustrative evidence also comes from newspapers. Writing for the *Washington Post*, Anderson and Moore (2000) described how "Two Mexicos Go to the Polls." Based on pre-electoral surveys, they portrayed the election as a "battle" between "two starkly different countries:" "rural, poor and less-educated voters . . . who favor Mexico's ruling Institutional Revolutionary Party, against urban, middle-class and educated Mexicans, who . . . tend to favor the opposition."

Another journalist described the voting procedures in a small village, which he saw as illustrative of "what Mexico's fairest election in history looked like" in the impoverished rural areas. In such areas, "generations of poor peasants . . . have become accustomed to thinking of basic government services—paved roads, electricity, water—as political gifts." This perhaps accounts for the passive acceptance of the gross violations to the secrecy of the vote that he described: "Voters took their ballots and stepped to a table where an observer from the ruling . . . PRI watched them mark their choices. The voters handed their ballots to the official, who checked off their names in his notebook, folded their ballots and dropped them into the ballot box. Perhaps one or two voters out of a hundred used the curtained-off voting booth—stamped in bold letter, 'The vote is free and secret'" (Sullivan 2000).[18]

Although significant by themselves, denunciations of irregularities, especially on the Election Day, are only the most visible manifestation of the problem.[19] Indeed, that some government and party leaders had to openly pressure voters at the voting booth only illustrates the failure of other forms of political control. The legitimacy that authoritarian practices still enjoy is more evident when one observes the results of basically free and fair electoral processes.

In his analysis of the presidential election of 2000, Klesner insinuates a paradox—even if he does not try to explain it: the PRI enjoys most support in the most impoverished areas of the country, precisely where it has most often resorted to authoritarian practices (2001, 108–9). Voting behavior clearly warrants this judgment, as the following analysis (based on official data on socioeconomic "marginality"[20] and electoral results) demonstrates.[21]

As table 4.1 shows, the opposition candidate that defeated the PRI in July 2000 won in the thirteen states classified as least marginal (with "low" and "very low" marginality levels). In contrast, the PRI candidate won in the three most marginal states. Indeed, the PRI won in eleven of the nineteen states with "very high," "high," and "medium" marginality levels.[22] As table 4.2 shows, the PRI's share of the vote grew as the degree of marginality increased, ranging from 30 percent in the group of least marginal states to 40 percent in the poorest states.

It is also interesting to observe that the poorest states had a higher proportion of invalid votes. As table 4.2 shows, the percentage of annulled votes in the most marginal states was almost twice as high as in the least marginalized states. The difference is consistent across marginality levels: the higher the degree of marginality, the larger the share of void votes.[23] A void vote might result from ignorance about the voting procedures or might voice an anonymous protest against the electoral or the party systems. What is certain is that it often indicates a non-compulsory rejection of the right to vote.

Many authors have suggested that, in the 1990s, the idea of "change" played a prominent role in the definition of electoral preferences among Mexican voters. According to this view, the most basic decision a citizen had to make was whether to support the PRI or not—which amounted to backing or opposing the authoritarian regime.[24] What is revealing in this context is that when people in the poorest regions voted for change, they often chose the candidate of the left-leaning PRD, precisely the opposition party that has been most often accused of reproducing the clientelistic and populist practices of the PRI. The PRD candidate's share of the vote in the two highest categories of marginality was sensibly larger than in any of the other levels. As table 4.3 shows, the combined vote for the PRI and the PRD—the parties that have resorted to authoritarian forms of political participation most often—consistently declined as the marginality level decreased.[25]

Data on the 1997 federal elections confirms the above analysis. These elections were also highly competitive, yielding the most plural legislature that post-revolutionary Mexico had ever had. As in 2000, in 1997 the PRI was the most voted party in the most marginal areas of the country.[26] It won in the eleven states with highest degree of marginality. Competition was concentrated in the states classified as having "medium," "low," or "very low" marginality levels. However, in 1997 the PRI did manage to win some of the states belonging to the "low" or "very low" marginality categories. Thus, between 1997 and the year 2000, the PRI lost control of the least poor Mexican states (see table 4.5).

Data on the 1997 federal elections allow one to make comparisons at the municipality level, which is the smallest governmental unit in the country. The trends identified above are much stronger in the nation's 100 poorest municipalities. The majority of electors in those municipalities voted against change, giving the PRI 58 percent of the vote, 20 points above its national score. Candidates of the PAN, which three years later would dislodge the PRI from the presidency, obtained only 6 percent of the vote in those municipalities. Equally significantly, the proportion of invalid votes in those municipalities was four times as high as that of the whole country (see table 4.6).

Several authors have argued that regional differences account for diverging electoral choices in Mexico better than socioeconomic cleavages do.[27] In this view, irrespective of their socioeconomic status, people in the modern northern part of the country, strongly influenced by the United States, would be much less tolerant of authoritarian practices than voters from the "backward" south. Data from the nation's 100 most marginal municipalities cannot contradict this view, because most of those municipalities belong to some of the country's most marginal states, most of them located in the south. However, there is strong evidence that the incidence of poverty and inequality, rather than regional differences, largely explains people's support or tolerance for Mexico's traditionally authoritarian party.

To see this, one can compare the electoral results from the poorest municipality in each state with those of its least marginal counterpart. Aggregating data from the thirty-two Mexican states,[28] one finds that the PRI's share of the vote in the set of most marginal municipalities was more than 15 percentage points higher than in the set of least marginal ones. This difference is consistent across states. Only in three of the thirty-two states did the PRI get less support in the poorest municipality than in the least marginal one. This means that, regardless of region, the legitimacy of the PRI regime tended to be stronger in the most marginal settings of the country. Not surprisingly, the percentage of annulled votes was also higher in the set of thirty-two poorest municipalities than it was in their least marginal counterpart (see table 4.7).

Analysts of Mexico's democratic transition have also argued that the urban/rural divide is a crucial determinant of support for the PRI. It is difficult to establish how much of the rural population's support for the PRI comes from its rural character rather than from poverty, since poverty is particularly high in the countryside.[29] Moreover, as some authors have demonstrated, the marginality index used above tends to underestimate urban poverty (Rubalcava and Ordaz 1999). The subject needs extensive research, but available evidence does suggest that the urban poor have also expressed support or tolerance for authoritarian practices in Mexico.[30] Indeed, the analysis of public surveys shows that, in 2000, "most of the voters artificially mobilized came from urban areas" (Cornelius 2002, 20).

The electoral results analyzed above show a relation—at the aggregate level—between poverty and support for the party that best represents authoritarian practices in Mexico. However, post-electoral surveys provide more accurate descriptions of individual voting behavior. An exit poll conducted in 2000 provides a "voter profile" that largely sustains the analysis presented above.[31] Variations in age and gender (two variables not considered in the above analysis) are evidently linked with support for the PRI. The PRI's share of the vote in the presidential election was higher among women than among men; younger electors voted for change more often than their older counterparts.[32] Beyond that, the socioeconomic factors reported by the survey point into the same direction as the foregoing analysis.

For example, support for the PRI candidate consistently decreased among the better educated. People with least formal education (with no schooling, or with primary school only) gave 46 percent of their votes to the PRI, a proportion twice as high as that of the PRI supporters among the better educated. The education variable is particularly important in this context. Available data does not allow for a temporal analysis of voter's preferences that includes all major components of socioeconomic inequality and poverty. However, as Székely has argued, at least in the Mexican case education might function as a "screening device" for the study of poverty and income distribution: the better educated are consistently better off in terms of income and economic well-being (1998, 77–82, 108). Based on several electoral polls, table 4.8 shows that, between 1988 and the year 2000, increased electoral competition did not affect all educational levels equally. Although support for the PRI decreased in all the categories, the decrease in the lowest educational levels was moderate (from 63 percent in 1988 to 46 percent in the year 2000). Among the best educated, the change was dramatic, falling from 51 percent to 22 percent during the same period. With important casualties, the PRI was able to keep its electoral strength among people with least education, but lost the support of the better educated.

The 2000 exit poll referred to above also reports differences across five employment categories (public sector, private sector, self-employed, student, and housewife). In all but one of these categories, it is impossible to make any inference regarding income differences. Each category necessarily includes people with very different socioeconomic levels. The only exception is the "student" group: one can reasonably infer that few persons from the lowest sectors would be included in it. Interestingly, support for the PRI was lowest in this category of voters (19 percent); in the other four categories, that percentage ranged from 31 to 43, not far away from the PRI's proportion of votes at the national level (36 percent).[33]

In short, data from electoral polls uphold the hypothesis that poverty and socioeconomic inequality are major determinants of active or passive support for Mexico's traditionally authoritarian party.[34]

The first "post-transition" federal elections were held in July 2003. The analysis of this contest confirms, in its basic shape, the pattern identified above. As table 4.9 shows, the PRI was dominant in the most impoverished parts of the country, winning in all five states with "very high" marginality. Indeed, the PRI won in fourteen of the twenty states with "very high," "high," and "medium" marginality levels. In contrast, it only obtained 28 percent of votes in the group of states with "very low" marginality. These results are all the more significant because, as analyzed below, in the post-transition years, the PRI has preserved—and in some cases even strengthened—the authoritarian structures it traditionally used for mobilizing the lower sectors.

A distinctive feature of the 2003 elections was the very low turnout level: only 41.7 percent of potential voters took part in the contest. Voter participation was particularly low in the category of most marginal states, where it amounted to only 38.1 percent (compared to 42.8 percent in the group of least marginal states). A poll conducted among those who did not vote revealed extremely interesting data. For instance, 49 percent of nonvoters agreed with the statement "all political parties are the same." Only 52 percent believed that votes are respected in Mexico; 37 percent believed that they are not respected. Exactly half of them did not agree with the statement "I have complete trust in elections"; only 39 percent agreed with it. Sizable majorities of them considered that "politics is disappointing" (66 percent) and "there are too many political parties" (79 percent).[35]

3. THE PLURALIZATION OF AUTHORITARIAN PRACTICES

Increased electoral competition has not rendered the PRI's authoritarian structures and practices useless. Not only have those authoritarian components proved difficult to eliminate; they have also demonstrated their efficacy in times of tight electoral competition. They have shown their capacity to partially "colonize" formally clean electoral procedures and become functional in competitive politics.

The traditional organizations created by the PRI in the 1930s survived in the 1980s and 1990s, even in the face of a general offensive against some of their foundations (Basurto 1999, 81–91). Since the mid-1980s, the federal government started to dismantle the economic and political structure that underpinned its traditionally unequal alliance with the lower sectors. The reduction of the state's role in the economy severely shrank the basis for the clientelistic or patrimonialistic delivery of goods and services to the poor.[36] The "reform of the state" implemented during the Salinas presidency (1988–94) further weakened the political structure that connected the official political elite with the lower sectors.[37]

After its deficient electoral performance in 1988, the PRI started a process of reform whose fate reveals the resilience of authoritarian structures. Although divisions within the governing elite were the most visible cause of the PRI's poor electoral performance in 1988, the incoming president put most of the blame on the traditional corporatist organizations of the party. The argument was that the corporatist structure was unable to win the support of Mexican "citizens," especially from the middle class and the urban poor. Consequently, the president promoted what purported to be a wide-ranging reform of the official party. The main component of the reform was the "territorialization" of the party, aimed at replacing the traditional corporatist structure (organized by social sectors) with a new, geographically-based network directly appealing to citizens. In 1990, the PRI's XIV National Assembly approved the reform project. Accordingly, the assembly reformed the party's National Executive Committee, excluding the corporations from it and giving additional power to the president of the party. Another crucial decision was that, except in special circumstances, the party would select its candidates at the local level. This intended to reduce the power of state governors, corporatist leaders, and the national party elite itself.[38]

It is difficult to evaluate the electoral impact of these changes. The 1991-midterm elections showed an extraordinary recovery of the PRI. However, there is no evidence that the party reform played any role in this recovery. As discussed below, the president's direct appeal to the people, and the social program he promoted, seemed to have been much more important. Besides, the reform program was never implemented in its entirety. The PRI national leadership, under President Salinas' control, did not give up its traditional prerogative in the selection of candidates.[39] In so far as it was implemented, the reform project took power from the corporatist organizations and state governors and put it in the hands of the president, rather than in those of common citizens. Moreover, with the 1994 presidential elections approaching, the XVI National Assembly of the party restored the corporatist organizations' positions in the National Executive Committee. For all practical purposes, by late 1993 the PRI reform project was abandoned.

To compensate, at least partially, for the weakening of the traditional structure of the PRI, the government created new forms of political control based on the exchange of material benefits for political support. It did so for reasons of political and, especially, electoral convenience. The best-known case is the National Solidarity Program (PRONASOL), created in 1989. The program had three stated objectives: "to improve the living conditions of the marginalized poor, promote balanced regional development, and promote and strengthen the participation of social organizations and of local authorities" (Rodríguez 1997, 76). Its budget rapidly grew from $680 million in 1989 to 1.7 billion in 1991, to 2.2 billion in 1993.[40] After the midterm 1991 elections, Salinas upgraded PRONASOL to cabinet level by creating the Ministry for Social Development (SEDESOL).

Several analyses have demonstrated that PRONASOL did not try to fully achieve its stated objectives. Its limitation as an anti-poverty program will be discussed below. What is relevant in this context is its political dimension. Dresser (1991) described it as a set of "neopopulist solutions" to the political problems created by neoliberal economic policies. While bypassing traditional corporatist and bureaucratic structures, PRONASOL created a new network of clientelistic and populist relations under the personal control of the president.[41]

Based on a careful analysis of the Mexican budget, Rodríguez (1997, 88–114) demonstrated that the allocation of PRONASOL resources did not follow impartial criteria; its discretionary nature is better explained by political reasons. Indeed, several authors have demonstrated that President Salinas used PRONASOL's budget and structure to undermine the power of his rivals within the PRI and the opposition parties, especially the PRD.[42]

PRONASOL paid off in electoral terms. The 1991 electoral "resurrection" of the PRI, was largely due to a very favorable public opinion about Salinas' performance. PRONASOL was determinant in this regard. Part of the strategy of the program was to create a large number of grassroots committees that in practice bolstered the president's image throughout the country.[43] Mexicans rated PRONASOL and the promotion of free trade as President Salinas' two main achievements. However, this perception was not homogenously distributed. People from the lower social sectors viewed PRONASOL as the president's most valuable achievement, while people from the upper and middle sectors clearly preferred the promotion of free trade. Especially among the lower sectors, PRONASOL was a major determinant of electoral support for the PRI (Domínguez and McCan 1996, 134–5, 249–50).

In the first post-Salinas years, because of a combination of adverse economic and political factors, there were no centralized clientelistic policies. The 1995 economic crisis further shrank the state's resources for patronage politics. Several measures taken to control the crisis (like the increase in the Value Added Tax, or VAT) were so utterly unpopular that it was extremely difficult for the federal government to wrap them up into populist rhetoric. Moreover, the "social" team of the Zedillo administration was deeply divided, with people from the Finance Ministry opposing SEDESOL. President Zedillo was unable (and ostensibly unwilling) to take control of the whole structure of informal and formal power developed by the post-revolutionary system. The consequence was that traditional actors staged a partial comeback and local and regional leaders regained control of their areas of influence.[44]

After the 1997 elections, however, the presidency tried to put together a timid clientelistic network, especially with the creation of PROGRESA, an anti-poverty program that despite its tight "targeting" mechanisms was often associated with the PRI.[45] During the year 2000 presidential campaign, opposition parties often denounced the "electoralist" bias of the program. So did a special multi-party commission set up by the Chamber of Deputies to oversee the use of public resources during the electoral process.[46] Despite its vacillating character and narrow reach, the program managed to influence the electoral preferences of its recipients. The best proof is that, according to a survey quoted above, beneficiaries of PROGRESA tended to associate this program with the PRI and felt obligated to vote for this party in the presidential election (Alianza Cívica 2000).

Other PRI-related clientelistic networks remained in place in many regions of the country, and became especially active in election times.[47] However, for the most part they lacked national coordination, and many times conflicted with the only political actor that could have coordinated them—the president.

The PRI internal election held in 2002 showed, in a particularly notorious way, the capacity of authoritarian practices to thrive in a formally competitive environment.[48] Both groups bidding for the PRI leadership bitterly accused each other of perpetrating the same fraudulent practices that the party had used against its enemies in the previous decades. The commission overseeing the election even recognized *acarreo*[49] as a legitimate practice. The worst violations to the integrity of the vote took place in impoverished areas of the country, especially in the South East and the countryside. Coincidently, as explained above, in the federal elections held one year later the PRI performed particularly well in many of those areas.[50]

A brief look at the fate of corporatist labor organizations traditionally allied to the PRI is also illuminating. Organized labor affiliated with the PRI was among the fiercest defendants of the "authoritarian" post-revolutionary regime.[51] In the last decades of the twentieth century, Mexican unions became more independent from the state. However, undemocratic labor corporatism has shown an astonishing capacity to survive. Contradicting early predictions, the end of the PRI regime did not provoke the fall of the unions that the government had previously sponsored and controlled.[52]

Traditionally, Mexican labor coalesced around two unequal blocs: a number of very large organizations subordinated to the state, and a relatively short number of small independent unions. Throughout the 1990s, the entire labor sector underwent several organizational changes.[53] However, after a decade of transformations its general structure remains essentially unchanged.[54] At the beginning of the twenty-first century, the formerly "official" corporatist bloc remains largely predominant, showing no intention to democratize its internal structure, maintaining its alliance with the PRI, and commanding the unofficial recognition of the non-PRI federal government. The "non-official" or independent sector grew modestly and seems more stable. However, many of these organizations (integrated into the National Union of Workers—UNT) are not notable for their internal democracy. The "independent" organizations outside the UNT are still few and relatively small.

In summary, despite the partial deterioration they underwent during the 1990s, the authoritarian structures and practices of the PRI largely retained their electoral efficacy. This explains the paradox, shown by the electoral statistics presented above, that the PRI was most successful in maintaining the support or acquiescence of the sectors and regions where it most often resorted to those authoritarian practices and structures.

Whether the PRI will retain the considerable support it still enjoys among the most impoverished social sectors is an open question. State and municipal elections held in 2001 and 2002 showed its capacity to thrive in a highly competitive environment.[55] The federal elections of 2003, when the PRI emerged as the largest party, confirmed this trend.[56] However, for the purposes of this analysis, the important point is the persistent legitimacy of authoritarian forms of political mobilization. That the PRI has traditionally used them does not mean that it has a monopoly on them. Indeed, authoritarian practices may become one of the foundations of competitive party politics. As parties other than the PRI come to control public resources that can be exchanged for political support, and as they come to government positions where they have to deal with the lower sectors on a regular basis, they have both the need and the opportunity to resort to authoritarian forms of political control.[57]

There is abundant evidence that the PRD has widely used authoritarian forms of political mobilization. Cuauhtémoc Cárdenas, its main founder and leader, has been often defined as a populist figure and even as a traditional *cacique*. Prominent PRD leaders, including Cárdenas himself, have recognized that the party "reproduces clientelistic practices and incurs the same vices" as the PRI. They have also admitted that, "in many cases," the PRD has allocated "party positions, candidacies, and jobs in the public administration" following patrimonialistic criteria (Cárdenas et al. 2000).

Evidence on this respect is particularly notorious in the relation between the PRD and grassroots organizations.[58] Since its inception, the PRD conceived itself as a party closely linked to independent social movements. This link, however, have been highly problematic. Apart from their political aspirations, grassroots organizations seek material benefits. Initially, their alliance with this party increases their bargaining leverage with non-PRD authorities, but afterward it invites government hostility or indifference and therefore becomes an obstacle to the satisfaction of their economic demands. Eventually, amid mutual accusations, the alliance is broken or strained. Facing these problems, many PRD leaders often try to control popular organizations through corporatist or clientelistic mechanisms. When the party refuses to establish authoritarian forms of political control, its relation with popular organizations becomes even weaker (Bruhn 1997b).

This intense but problematic relation with social organizations also affects the internal life of the party. Each important party leader controls a number of popular organizations and uses them to undermine rival party leaderships. Therefore, the opportunities for internal "anti-system" behavior are numerous.[59] The capacity of authoritarian practices to penetrate the party and impede the functioning of internal democratic procedures was particularly evident in the 1999 internal election. The accumulation of partial electoral frauds (committed by virtually all candidates to the party presidency) was so large that it was impossible to tally the votes. Therefore, a new internal election had to be held, with the only aim of legitimizing the "result" previously arranged through an intra-elite pact.[60] The internal election held three years later was again plagued by notorious irregularities.[61]

Authoritarian practices have also affected the PRD governing style.[62] Internal divisions, *personalism*, and low party institutionalization have influenced the way the PRD governs. Perhaps more than is the case in other political parties, many PRD supporters expect to share in the material resources, job opportunities, and power resources attached to public offices that the party wins. When their patrimonialistic or clientelistic expectations are not met, they usually denounce the newly elected officials as "authoritarian" (Bruhn 1995, 126–7; 1999b, 36–7). This might account for the often inefficient and conflict-ridden character of several PRD municipal administrations. Reports on the PRD government in Mexico City also point into this direction.[63]

It is also interesting to observe how the PRD has provided recycling opportunities for discontented PRI leaders. At the end of 2000, the PRD had won six of Mexico's thirty-two governorships.[64] The successful candidates were very recent acquisitions.[65] Five of them came to the PRD after they failed to obtain the PRI nomination. None of them was known for his previous sympathies with the PRD program, and some were outspoken enemies of this party.[66] All of them had had strong links with the authoritarian structures of the PRI. The fact that only through PRI deserters has the PRD been able to win statewide elections testifies to the enduring legitimacy of authoritarian structures and practices.[67] It also shows how those structures and practices can, paradoxically, bolster electoral competition, and promote the formal pluralization of public authority.

The leaders of the PAN usually portray it as the most enduringly prodemocratic party in Mexico. Part of the PAN's identity has been grounded on its denouncement of the PRI use of undemocratic forms of political control.[68] Yet, this image of unyielding democratic commitment has some important drawbacks. In the 1990s, the PAN willingly participated in actions of doubtful democratic character. Prominent among these were the behind-the-scenes deals between President Salinas and the party leadership, which helped the PAN win several state governorships in exchange for supporting the president's economic agenda (Domínguez and McCann 1996, 119). Moreover, the selection of the PAN candidate to the presidential election of the year 2000 had a typically populist flavor: "the self-nomination of Vicente Fox with total disregard for party procedures . . . indicated the potential vulnerability of party structures to the weight of charismatic figures" (Serrano 1998, 5).

For the purposes of this work, most important is the evaluation of the PAN governing style. Because of the social origin of its leaders and its ideology, the PAN has found it difficult to obtain the support of the poor and marginal. In the 1990s, in terms of social background, there seemed to be little difference between the leadership of the PAN and that of the PRI

(Camp 1995b, 77). Nevertheless, there was a crucial difference: the PRI had a number of top and middle-level leaders specialized in dealing with the lower sectors through corporatist and clientelistic networks;[69] the PAN lacked such a network, as its organizational links have been traditionally focused on the business community and the middle sectors.[70]

The PAN can win elections relying almost exclusively on its middle and upper class supporters and capitalizing on strong anti-PRI feelings.[71] However, the task of governing forces it to deal with people from the lower sectors that expect material benefits from the newly established government. Although the PAN's victories have taken place in some of the most "developed" parts of the country, even the richest Mexican cities have large numbers of people living in poverty or extreme poverty. Several times, PAN administrations have lacked the resources, the administrative machinery,[72] and even the will to deal with those sectors in an efficient way—which often requires establishing undemocratic forms of political control.[73] This has been the source of many troubles for PAN governments and has set the basis for the return of the PRI. This happened, for example, in the city of Puebla (Vanderbush 1999). The PAN candidate won the city government in 1995, when anti-PRI reactions pervaded the country. However, the PAN governing team, drawn mainly from the local business community, was unable to cope with confrontational grassroots organizations that existed in the city, some of them linked to the PRI. For the most part, the PAN administration sincerely refused to strike particularistic deals with those organizations. Doing so, however, worsened the conflicts instead of ameliorating them. This seems to have been a central cause of the PAN electoral defeat in 1998.[74]

Some PAN administrations have been more pragmatic, using undemocratic forms of political control when dealing with the mobilized poor. Mizrahi (1998) has referred to this as the "costs of electoral success." Facing the demands of "material incentives and private benefits" from their electors (and "without an alternative to political clientelism as a form of social mobilization") PAN governments have adopted the old rules of the game (Mizrahi 1998, 108). A case in point was the PAN state government in Baja California: it implemented a program modeled on President Salinas' PRONASOL, which helped the party retain the state government in the 1995 election. Shortly later, the PAN government of Chihuahua followed this example, seeking to recover from its notably deficient electoral performance in the midterm state elections held in 1995.[75] The Fox administration—the first post-PRI federal government—has had a vacillating attitude, sometimes refusing to strike particularistic deals with the leaders of authoritarian social organizations; sometimes openly adapting itself to the "old" rules.

4. EXPLAINING THE LEGITIMACY OF AUTHORITARIAN PRACTICES

The above analysis has shown the link between the survival of authoritarian practices and high poverty and inequality levels. Indeed, the incompatibility of high economic inequality and democracy is an old subject, even if the main contributors to the transition literature tend to neglect it. Long ago, Aristotle affirmed that, "Where one set of people possesses a great deal and the other nothing, the result is either extreme democracy or unmixed oligarchy, or a tyranny due to the excesses of either" (1981, 268).

The conclusion of the philosopher seems to have retained its validity throughout the centuries. However, it is also necessary to investigate the specific mechanisms through which poverty and inequality distort formally clean democratic procedures: What explains the authoritarian practices' resilience, their electoral functionality, and their capacity to "colonize" formally clean democratic procedures? The analysis presented above allows for some observations on this regard.

One can mention several mechanisms through which poverty and inequality corrupt formal democratic procedures. Poverty might destroy the sense of dignity that is necessary for a person to participate in orderly and moderate political processes. Poverty might also instill in the people the seemingly conflicting attitudes of submissiveness and unruliness, each equally incompatible with the self-restraint necessary for the appropriate working of democratic procedures. High socioeconomic inequality might also eliminate the sense of political equality implied by the one-person-one-vote principle, encouraging the members of the elite to manipulate their hypothetically equal fellow citizens from the lower sectors.

Without dismissing all these explanations, it is important to notice the rational and realistic, if usually implicit, pact that leads to the corruption of seemingly democratic procedures in highly unequal societies with extensive poverty. From this standpoint, the survival of authoritarian practices is not necessarily an aberration (provoked by inappropriate institutional design or by "undemocratic" cultural inclinations) but rather a rational response to prevailing circumstances.

An influential author has argued that democracy becomes self-sustainable because it offers a lengthened time-horizon to political actors. Defeated actors accept the results of electoral competition because they know that the democratic method will give them opportunities to win in the future (Przeworski 1991, 19). Dahl argued that although democracy does not have a directly distributive socioeconomic component, the functioning of the democratic method encourages the political elite to pay attention to the demands of the poor. Some members of the elite will eventually become the "representatives" of those groups and, while seeking their votes and support, will—perhaps unwittingly—promote their interests. In this way, democratic procedures indirectly empower the weak (Dahl 1971, 23–5).

Mexico's democratic transition shows that the adoption of democratic procedures does not necessarily lead to such desirable goals. Rather than broadening it, poverty (and especially extreme poverty) narrows the time-horizon of the poor. The poor need immediate, tangible goods to satisfy their equally immediate and tangible needs. Given their paucity of resources, they can use their vote as yet another tool for survival. They can hardly use this resource for a long-term investment, even if this possibility would look more advantageous in the long term. Thus, the poor might willingly exchange their votes or their political allegiance for immediate means of survival or for credible promises of them, even if this means reproducing traditional authoritarian practices and structures.[76] This does not mean that the poor are necessarily supportive of authoritarianism per se. It only signals the powerful, even if indirect, effects that distributional factors can have on the practice of formal political rights.

The distinction between public and private goods is also relevant in this context. A decent and efficient government might seem a highly desirable public good, but the poor can hardly afford to sacrifice the satisfaction of their private needs, especially if every one else seems to be acting in the same way. Therefore, they might be ready to trade their publicly recognized right to vote for material benefits (coming from the public budget but delivered on a particularistic basis).[77]

The difference between political and material benefits is also useful in understanding the motivations behind the survival of authoritarian practices. These two kinds of interests might conflict with each other. In her analysis of Mexico's social movements, Hellman (1994) discovered that this contradiction is especially pressing for grassroots organizations. Preserving autonomy is a valuable political goal for the leaders and rank-and-file members of those organizations. However, their need for material benefits is even more pressing. Therefore, they willingly forsake their political independence if doing so helps them achieve their material demands.[78] If this is true for members of independent social organizations, it is all the more valid for organizations traditionally subordinated to the state machinery through officially recognized corporatist or clientelistic networks.[79]

While not necessarily irrelevant, the effects of political culture are "bracketed" under highly unequal social conditions. The amount of political virtue that would guarantee that a middle-class citizen performs his or her democratic duties would be clearly insufficient for a citizen on either extreme of the socioeconomic and political structure. It would take an unlikely high level of civic virtue for a citizen in extreme poverty to disregard the immediate, individual, and material rewards that can be obtained in exchange for supporting certain leaders or candidates. It would also take a rare level of civic virtue for a political entrepreneur to disregard the opportunities for undemocratic mobilization that poverty and inequality create.

To accurately understand the motivations behind the survival of authoritarian practices, one must also consider the costs of organizing. In a democratic context, the poor and marginal could benefit most from collective action. This does not mean, however, that they are the most likely to organize in an independent way. Indeed, they seem to be the least self-organized sectors. Collective action has costs: it needs time, experience, work, money, loyalty, and so forth. Coping with urgent survival needs often leaves little time for independent organizing. The potential costs of confrontation (losing job, facing government repression, and so on) are high. Under these circumstances, members of independent grassroots organizations face strong incentives to betray or defect. Therefore, rather than forming broad and independent coalitions, individuals and organizations from the lowest sectors tend to compete among themselves for material benefits that can be obtained through political means.[80] Obviously, this increases the opportunities for undemocratic political mobilization.

The case of labor corporatism is significant in this respect. As said above, large and undemocratic corporatist organizations remain dominant in the Mexican labor sector. This is even more remarkable because the two most visible legal foundations of PRI corporatism—collective affiliation to political parties and compulsory affiliation to one union—were removed or weakened in the 1990s.[81] The survival of labor authoritarian corporatism cannot be understood without looking at the structural situation that underpins it. The labor sector is in a paradoxical situation: it occupies a subordinated position in the Mexican social and political structure, but it is a privileged sector within the underprivileged part of society.[82] In the late twentieth century, labor largely lost the protection of the state. At the same time, neoliberal reforms made employers more independent and powerful. The threat from below (from non-unionized workers, from workers outside the formal sector, and from the unemployed) also increased with the economic crises that haunted the country in the 1980s and 1990s. Facing all these risks, organized labor has strong motivations to maintain internal discipline and unity. Individual workers have many reasons to support or tolerate their traditional leaders in exchange for job stability and for preserving some of their privileges. This structural situation is a powerful force against labor democratization; it largely explains the survival of authoritarian labor corporatism in the context of procedural democratic change in Mexico.[83] Moreover, as corporatist organizations become independent from the state, they might also become "plural," capable of negotiating and setting alliances with different political parties.[84]

In sum, in the context of widespread poverty and high inequality,[85] it is not surprising that the members of the elite fail to act according to Dahl's predictions. The acceptance of authoritarian forms of political control among the lower sectors creates a unique opportunity for "rent-seeking" politicians who, instead of becoming "representatives" of those sectors, become their patrons in clientelistic or patrimonialistic relations.[86]

Once the basic opportunity structure for patronage politics is in place, some other obvious conditions should obtain. First, a party or leader must have economic resources that can be exchanged for political support. Usually, these are public resources that become available to a party that reaches government positions. Second, there must be an organizational structure linking political leaders and the lower sectors. This structure can be either governmental or partisan, or a combination of both.

To some extent, the organizational structure can make up for the lack of economic resources, especially when a party is capable of providing the mobilized poor with an institutional network that helps them put pressure on government officials. This is what the PRD did for many years with several social organizations. Organizational structure can also make people believe that a party is capable of taking power, thus making its promises of future material rewards credible.

Two other basic points deserve consideration. First, contrary to a widely shared belief, parties and political regimes that engage in patronage politics do not lack institutionalization. It takes a very complex organizational network to connect people from the lower sectors with the political elite. This also requires established rules that allow for predictability and mutual trust. Even populism needs a great number of intermediate cadres that convey the personal image of the top leader to his or her followers. Those institutions are also necessary to ensure the opportune delivery of goods.

The second point is that, to a considerable extent, patronage politics is ideology-neutral. Politicians and organizations of any ideological inclination can resort to it if the opportunity structure exists and they have the necessary organizational and economic resources to take advantage of it. Left-leaning populists or traditional nationalists do not have a monopoly on authoritarian practices. Nor are these practices confined to regimes that promote state economic interventionism or protectionist models of development. "Neoliberal" politicians have also proved skillful in this respect.[87]

5. EVOLUTION OF POVERTY AND INEQUALITY

The previous analysis shows that to understand the survival of "undesirable" political practices it is necessary to analyze the "opportunity structure" that makes them possible. As long as the socioeconomic structure that explains the survival of authoritarian practices and institutions remains in place, electoral reform—even as intense as it has been in Mexico—may be unable to eliminate them.

Members of the political elite, especially from the "democratic opposition," may accept the traditional rules of the game for reasons of political expedience. Once in power, they might try to transform them. After many years of political change in Mexico, it is possible to ask whether democratic transition has built the socioeconomic basis for enduring and stable democracy in the country.

Estimations of the incidence of poverty in Mexico vary widely. Table 4.10 shows that, by different calculations, between 31 percent and 79 percent of the population lived in poverty during the 1990s. Between 15 percent and 29 percent of all Mexicans lived in extreme poverty.[88] The difference between these estimates is huge, but even if one takes the most conservative ones, the proportion of people living in poverty is remarkably high.

Equally impressive are estimations of income inequality. According to a rather conservative calculation, the richest 10 percent of the Mexican population earns 57.5 times as much as the poorest 10 percent (Lustig 1998, 203). Data quoted by Aguilar Gutiérrez (2000, 96) shows that, in 1996, Mexico's richest 1 percent earned 3.3 times as much as the poorest 40 percent.

In reality, these general data conceal huge sub-national disparities which, when included, yield a bleaker image of the "social question" in Mexico. By a rather cautious estimation, "Rural poverty is between seven and ten times higher than urban poverty." Moreover, poverty in the southeastern part of the country (which includes the states of Guerrero, Oaxaca, and Chiapas) is "close to forty times higher than in the Federal District" (Lustig 1998, 202–3).[89]

Differences among economic sectors are also important. For example, in 1996, the average person working in the services sector earned virtually twice as much as a person working in the agricultural sector. A person in the industrial sector had an income 84 percent higher than his or her counterpart in the primary sector (Aguilar Gutierrez 2000, 123).

Ethnic disparities are also relevant. Official data for 1990 shows that "living in a 50 percent indigenous *municipio* increases the probability of a household head being poor by a substantial 24.5 percent." Similarly, "*municipios* of increasing indigenous concentration experience higher percentages of . . . extreme poverty" (Panagides 1994, 133, 136). Indeed, "the indigenous population density in a *municipio* strongly correlates with the incidence of poverty. In *municipios* where less than 10 percent of the population is indigenous, the poverty headcount is 18 percent." In municipalities with more than 70 percent of indigenous inhabitants "over 80 percent of the population is poor." Something similar happens with extreme poverty (Psacharopoulos and Patrinos 1994, xviii).

According to virtually any source that deals with the subject, poverty and inequality worsened with the several episodes of economic crisis and market-oriented reform that took place in the 1980s and 1990s. This situation did not improve with the advancement of democratic transition in the country. Table 4.10 presents four different estimations; although they use different poverty lines, they are all based on data collected by the same official institution.[90] Allowing for their differences, they all show that there was no important improvement (and perhaps no improvement at all) in Mexico's social situation during the 1990s.[91]

It may be argued that political factors have no responsibility in the increase of poverty and inequality during the 1980s and 1990s. However, even authors who believe that "sound" economic growth, under a "market-oriented" model, is the best way to alleviate poverty and inequality recognize that policy decisions are important in determining the distribution of costs and benefits (Morley 1995). Market-oriented reforms reward those agents that from the outset were endowed with the best income-earning assets, but tend to punish the initially deprived sectors. Therefore, an explicitly distributive policy package is indispensable to undo the disparities introduced or accentuated by the model (Székely 1998, 147–50, 242–50).

During the 1990s, distributive policies in Mexico consisted mainly of two anti-poverty programs (PRONASOL and PROGRESA). If one considers the overall evolution of poverty and inequality in the country, it seems that these programs had no remarkable positive effect. Of course, the obvious objection to this view would be that, without those programs, economic deprivation and income inequality would have increased even more. Székely made a more precise analysis of PRONASOL's impact and found that this was almost negligible. One obvious reason for this would be that, as discussed above, the government often used PRONASOL as a political tool, partially disregarding its effects on poverty alleviation. However, even using the program's stated criteria, Székely's econometric analysis reaches the "unexpected conclusion that there is not much difference between providing universal benefits in Mexico, and distributing the resources with the criteria adopted by PRONASOL."[92]

However, even more stringent targeting criteria have not yielded significantly better results, as the case of PROGRESA shows.[93] Established in 1997, PROGRESA (2000, 4) had the double objective of "combating current poverty" and "reducing future poverty levels by investing in education, health and food." By the end of 1999, it supported 2.6 million families (about 13 million people). PROGRESA delivers its benefits to those families through monetary and non-monetary transfers.

In a sense, PROGRESA can be accused of "over-targeting." Through a three-step process, it managed to exclude more than half of the population living in extreme poverty. The program supports only the extremely poor families that live in extremely poor localities, all of them rural. This means that all the urban poor are excluded; yet, according to virtually any source, although it is more widespread and intense in rural areas, poverty is predominantly an urban phenomenon in Mexico.[94] The poor who do not live in regular family units are also excluded, which is likely to affect part of the migrant poor. Obviously, the same happens with extremely poor people who do not live in extremely poor localities.

An evaluation requested by PROGRESA itself estimated that the program might have eliminated 8 percent of poverty incidence in the localities where it is applied. It also anticipated that the program would increase the average years of schooling of the benefited children in about seven months (PROGRESA 2000, 16, 21). These results, which look rather meager in isolation, are dismaying if one recalls that the program has left aside more than half of the population in extreme poverty. Indeed, the same evaluation found that the "over-targeting" of PROGRESA resources was scarcely beneficial even for the selected poor: its poverty-reducing effects were "only 3.05 percent better than they would have been if every household in the localities where PROGRESA is being applied had been included" (PROGRESA 2000, 15).

These observations lead us to the central limitation of these programs: their extremely small budgets. Dresser (1991, 11) divides PRONASOL's 1990 budget ($950 million) by the estimated number of people living in extreme poverty (seventeen million).[95] The result is that, should the resources been exclusively targeted on them, the extreme poor would have received a daily allocation of $0.15 each. In 1993, the program's budget reached $2.2 billion. Performing the same calculation, one finds that, during that year, each individual in extreme poverty would have received $0.35 a day.[96]

Similar calculations can be performed with PROGRESA's data. Monetary transfers account for most of the benefits of PROGRESA (1999, 25–9). According to PROGRESA itself, between November 1998 and October 1999, those monetary transfers amounted to about $0.84 per family a day (about $0.17 per person).[97] This figure refers only to the extreme poor benefited by the program. If one includes the more than 50 percent of people in extreme poverty that the program leaves aside, the figures are even more dismaying. In 1999, total funding for PROGRESA reached almost 730 million.[98] Dividing this amount by the estimated twenty-nine million people living in extreme poverty in 1998 (see table 4.10), it turns out that PROGRESA could have delivered a daily allotment of $0.07 to each individual in that condition.

The mismatch between stated goals and resources is amazing. With such a limited funding, not even a perfectly targeted program could significantly eliminate poverty in the country.[99]

6. THE FISCAL SITUATION

The scarcity of resources for social programs is not surprising if one observes the fiscal situation of Mexico. Among members of the Organization for Economic Cooperation and Development (OECD 1999b, 64), at the end of the twentieth century Mexico had by far the lowest level of total tax revenue as a proportion of GDP (16.9 percent). By way of comparison, one can mention the cases of Sweden (51.9 percent), France (45.1 percent), Canada (36.8 percent), the United States (29.7 percent), and Turkey (27.9 percent).

However, the figure for Mexico quoted above is misleading, since it includes income from the state oil company and other non-tax sources. Deducting these, the Mexican tax burden was less than 11 percent of GDP. This figure can be compared with those of countries at roughly similar economic levels (in terms of GDP per capita). The tax burden amounted to 30.4 percent of GDP in Poland, 28.2 percent in the Czech Republic, and 17.7 percent in Chile. The Mexican tax burden was low even by Latin American standards. In a list of twenty Latin American countries published by ECLAC, Mexico's figure was only superior to those of Ecuador, Guatemala, and Haiti—all with much lower GDP per capita. For Latin America as a whole, the tax burden was 14.5 percent of GDP.[100]

During the 1980s and 1990s, the government preferred to correct its fiscal balance mainly by cutting expenditure, rather than by increasing revenue. This method contrasts with the experience of other Latin American countries, like Colombia and Costa Rica, which, coincidently, managed to distribute the costs of the crisis more evenly (Morley 1995). Apart from that, the government has relied heavily on revenue sources that are not likely to generate any distributional conflict, notably from the state oil monopoly: between 30 percent and 40 percent of total government revenues in Mexico come from oil-related sources (OECD 1999a, 70).

Once the regime becomes plural, one might reasonably expect a change in the fiscal situation of the country. Given the current tax structure in Mexico, increasing the tax burden is far from being an extremist measure. The Mexican Constitution gives the legislative full authority to determine the federal budget: both the Senate and the Chamber of Deputies must approve the income side of the annual budget (Federal Income Law), while the spending side (Federal Expenditure Budget) is under the exclusive authority of the Chamber of Deputies. The Mexican Congress has had a truly plural composition since 1997.[101] After the year 2000, no party holds the majority of seats in either chamber. Therefore, since 1997 opposition parties could have modified the Mexican tax system and increased the resources for social policies.

However, the evolution of Mexico's tax burden since 1990 shows no connection with the progress of democratic transition (see table 4.11). It largely followed—to borrow the terminology of economics—a pro-cyclical pattern, rising or falling as the economy grew or shrank. It fluctuated between 8.9 percent and 11.6 percent of GDP, reaching its highest point in 2002 and its lowest in 1996.

A rapid glance at the congressional debate on the budget for the year 2000 and for 2001 (passed in December 1999, and December 2000, respectively) is illustrative. According to press reports, the debate was strong, especially in December 1999, when the Chamber of Deputies had to hold two extraordinary sessions to get the budget approved.[102] However, specific proposals from all the important political parties and the government were astonishingly similar.[103] In the first of the two years analyzed here, the opposition strove to make some marginal changes to the budget proposed by the president, seeking additional resources for state and municipal governments and some extremely small increases in social security.[104] Something similar happened in the legislative debate held in December 2000.[105]

More interestingly, no increase in the tax burden was even discussed. Additional revenue for the budget of 2000 came mainly from a change in the expected price of oil exports. In the 2001 budget, the legislative increased resources by augmenting the expected public deficit (from 0.5 percent to 0.65 percent of GDP) and by slightly increasing the expected revenues from VAT and Income Tax (IT). These small increases in tax revenue would come from diminishing tax evasion, rather than from any increase in tax rates.

Even before its inauguration, the first post-PRI federal government announced its intention to promote an "integral" fiscal reform. After many delays, the government presented its proposal to the Mexican Congress in April 2001. Analyzing the characteristics and evolution of this proposal gives one a unique opportunity for understanding the interaction between procedural democratic transition and distributive issues in a country like Mexico.

With the reform, the government expected to increase Mexico's tax burden by between 1.5 percent and 3 percent of GDP. Most of this increase (around 1.5 percent of GDP) would have come from changes in VAT: the reform purported to set a single 15 percent rate of VAT, applicable to all products in the market, eliminating exemptions (food and medicines) and the special 10 percent rate for border zones. The reform also expected to collect between 0.13 percent and 0.19 percent of GDP by eliminating the "special regimes" that provide for IT exceptions in agriculture, fisheries, and land transportation. Moreover, the reform purported to extend the tax system into the informal sector of the economy. Finally, it sought to *decrease* IT rates for people at the highest income levels, lowering the top rate from 40 percent to 32 percent.

The potential consequences of these proposed changes are easily evident. As mentioned, most of the expected revenue increase would come from changes in VAT, which is the most regressive part of the Mexican tax system (GFB 1999, 8, 15).[106] Apart from being openly regressive, lowering the top IT rate would *decrease* tax revenues—unless a surge in investment counteracts this reduction by widening the "tax base." Even proponents of the reform recognized that the expected gains from a partial elimination of the "special regimes" would add less than 0.2 percent of GDP, which is very small.[107] Apart from being difficult, including the informal sector into the tax system "may not have a large direct impact on tax revenues as the larger part of it seems to be related to micro-business and low-skilled/low-income employment" (OECD 1999a, 89).

In summary, this reform sought only a modest increase in Mexico's tax burden and had strongly regressive components. While recognizing the need to increase state revenues, opposition parties (PRI and PRD) quickly voiced their hostility to the proposal (Ramos 2000; Rosas 2000a, 2000b). Eventually, the Mexican Congress rejected it in December 2001. However, although they denounced the regressive effects of the Fox initiative, opposition parties never made any serious proposal for a progressive overhaul of the fiscal system.

In late 2003, the government presented a new fiscal reform proposal, this time advocating a single 10 percent VAT rate, applicable to all products, including food and medicines. The proposal triggered a heated confrontation and was twice rejected in December.

The overall evolution of these proposals shows that, when approaching the fiscal situation, the Mexican party system is pulled by strong and contradictory forces. Political parties obviously recognize the fiscal weakness of the Mexican state. They all seem unwilling to incur the electoral costs of supporting an openly regressive reform. At the same time, they are evidently afraid of alienating the economic elite by sincerely promoting a progressive reform. Under these circumstances, the competitive electoral system strongly encourages political parties to preserve the current fiscal situation. This, among other things, keeps the government incapable of implementing decisive social programs, and thereby contributes to preserving the "opportunity structure" for authoritarian forms of political mobilization.

CONCLUSION

A conspiracy theory is not necessary to understand why elected politicians are so reluctant to undertake serious redistributive measures. Due to their crucial economic functions, their privileged access to politicians, and their role as "political investors," top businessmen are able to remove some basic issues from public contest in all capitalist democracies (Lindblom 1977; Ferguson 1995). In a country like Mexico, this situation seems compounded. Politicians are more dependent upon the acceptance and support of the business elite, who control a disproportionate share of politically influential economic power. Besides, as chapters 3 and 5 analyze, in Mexico the new political regime and the state are peculiarly weak; aware of this weakness, "reasonable" politicians prefer to avoid highly sensitive distributional issues. The country's position in the international economic structure and particularly the need to attract and retain foreign investors, further reinforces this reluctance.

In principle, the large numbers of people living in poverty and extreme poverty could greatly benefit from collective action in a competitive political system. Still, the high costs of independent organizing and their pressing economic needs strongly encourage them to trade their political support for immediate means of survival, even if this means reproducing traditional authoritarian practices and structures.

This context creates a common ground, where the interests of the economic elite, the political leaders, and the large number of impoverished citizens may meet. In this context, political competition does not affect the fundamental distribution of economic power, and traditional forms of political mobilization remain functional. Thus, democratic change stays within purely procedural limits, and formal democratic procedures coexist with deeply undemocratic practices.

Procedural democratic change does have important effects upon authoritarian forms of political mobilization. It does not eliminate them, but it makes them less dependent upon legal or semi-legal compulsion. It makes them more spontaneous or "natural," determined by the free play of social and economic impulses. It also permits the pluralization of those practices, as former opposition parties have both the need and the opportunity to reproduce them.

This analysis shows that the concentration of economic assets might become self-sustainable under competitive politics. It also shows that procedural democratic change may legitimate economic inequality and authoritarian forms of political mobilization. It shows, moreover, that in a country with massive poverty and huge economic disparities, purely procedural democratic transition may make democratic "consolidation" unachievable.

Chapter Five

Transition and Illegal Drugs

At least since the mid 1970s, the illegal drug business has been a major phenomenon in Mexico. In the 1990s, the country consolidated its position as a producer of cannabis and heroin, substantially increased its participation in global cocaine trafficking, and seized new opportunities created by the emerging "synthetic drug" market, becoming a major methamphetamine producer.

Not only has democratic transition failed to eliminate this illegal trade; during the 1990s, when the crucial steps toward political liberalization and pluralization took place, the political, economic, and social influence of drug trafficking groups became even more evident than under the previous "authoritarian" governments. The arrival of the first non-PRI administration did not change this situation.

Throughout these years, serious cases of drug-related corruption became visible. However, as this chapter shall show, government corruption is not the only—and not even the most important—political consequence of the drug business.

To a certain extent, the drug business follows a purely economic logic and affects many countries regardless of their political characteristics. Seen in this way, current criminality is a transnational economic phenomenon aptly described as the "dark side" of globalization. Yet, the following analysis shall show that political factors can make crucial differences. Not all political regimes give the illegal drug market the same opportunities to develop and they are not equally vulnerable to the corrupting influence of this business.

Abundant evidence shows that countries with "transitional" economies and political regimes are more vulnerable. Nevertheless, the most famous texts on democratic transition say virtually nothing about this subject. Larry Diamond, himself a major contributor to the transition literature, proposes an explanation for this neglect. "Democratic theorists," he contends, disregard crime "perhaps because it seems so mundane or so inviting of illiberal response" (1999, 90). Diamond does recognize that crime may threaten democracy. However, he views it only as a problem of "political performance" in "post-transition countries," where it can become an obstacle to the "consolidation of democracy." Yet, evidence strongly suggests that large-scale criminality influences not only the performance of a government; it may also affect the very nature of the regime. Moreover, by defining crime as a post-transition problem, one may overlook the way in which regime *transition* and crime influence each other, modifying the entire process of political change.

Guillermo O'Donnell (1999), another major contributor to the transition literature, has lately referred to the political consequences of large-scale crime. In his view, widespread criminality can affect the rule of law, which is a crucial component of "fuller democracy." This is why some countries that recently underwent regime transition are democratic only in a strictly political ("regime-centered") sense. Nonetheless, he claims that the adoption of a limited "democratic regime" is a crucial stage in the path to full democracy. What O'Donnell neglects is the logical possibility that the combination of crime *and* democratic transition might make democracy in its fuller sense unachievable. The analysis of the Mexican case shall show some of the circumstances in which this logical possibility can materialize.

The fact that the transition to democracy literature neglects or underestimates the political consequences of crime is not incidental. An analytical framework that concentrates on elite relations, party competition, and formal institutions, leaves little room for studying the interaction between legal and illegal forces. Therefore, this view tends to overvalue the law-enforcement effects of electoral transformations, underestimate the political consequences of illegal drugs, and ignore the drug problem's capacity to coexist with changes in the formal rules of the "political game." Even more importantly, this view fails to see how crucial components of the transition process can exacerbate drug-related crime and its political effects.

Assessments of the illegal drug business often overstate, undervalue, or otherwise distort the characteristics of the problem. In part, this is due to the illegal nature of the market; but, as shall be elaborated upon below, information on the drug business is particularly vulnerable to political manipulation. Seeking to escape from this problem, the first two sections of this chapter present some essential data on the global drug business and analyze the social and economic consequences of Mexico's drug trade. Afterward, the chapter focuses on the political consequences of illegal drugs and subsequently considers how democratic transition has affected the problem.

Finally, it analyzes how the relationship between democratic transition and illegal drugs evolved after the "culminating elections" of the year 2000.

The main argument of the chapter consists of the following propositions. The illegal drug trade does not only affect the law-enforcement capacities of the state and the political regime. By undermining the rule of law and democratic accountability, fostering "militarization," and provoking human rights violations, this business challenges the alleged democratic nature of recent political change in Mexico. Conversely, by weakening the state and the regime, dispersing law-enforcement responsibilities, and increasing the need for campaign funding, democratic transition creates new opportunities for illegal drug entrepreneurs. Rather than being separate phenomena, democratic transition and drug-related political corruption are interconnected parts of the overall process of political change in Mexico. Simply referring to this whole process as a *democratic transition* would neglect or underestimate those basic connections.

1. THE GLOBAL DRUG MARKET

Contributors to the transition literature have hailed the dual movement toward "free markets" and procedural democracy in many parts of the world. While doing so, they usually neglect or underestimate an accompanying transformation: increased global criminality, of which the illegal drug trade is a major component. Available evidence shows that there are fundamental links among these three processes. It is impossible to fully understand the Mexican case without glancing at this global situation.

The world's illegal drug trade has an annual value of at least $100 billion and probably as much as $600 billion.[1] The lower figure is higher than most countries' GDP. The higher figure puts this trade only below the global arms trade. A middle value of $350 billion would amount to about one-third of the world's $1 trillion organized crime business (Tullis 1995, 2). Indeed, some authors have considered the illegal drug trade as the "king of the criminal world" (Smale 2001).[2] Its middle value of $350 billion would put this trade above the global petroleum industry. Moreover, illegal drugs are certainly "one of the world's largest—and perhaps the most lucrative—commodities" (Flynn 2000, 45). This large trade serves an estimated market of 200 million drug users.

Cocaine, opiates (opium, heroin, and morphine), cannabis (marijuana, ganja, and hashish), and a number of "synthetic drugs" (especially methamphetamine) are the main commodities in the illegal drug trade—with cocaine, heroin, and methamphetamine being most important. Opium poppy cultivation is concentrated in two regions: the "Golden Crescent" (Afghanistan,

Pakistan, and Iran) and the "Golden Triangle" (Myanmar/Burma, Laos, and Thailand). Latin America (Mexico and Colombia) produces only a small share of the world's total heroin output, but supplies a large part of the U.S. demand (BINLEA 2001).[3] The Andean countries monopolize cocaine production, with Colombia, Peru, and Bolivia, accounting for 98 percent of the world's total production, most of which is exported to the United States and Europe.[4] Mexican organizations are probably the world's most important methamphetamine producers.[5] The United States is a leading marijuana producer, supplying most of its own demand and probably exporting some of its production (Tullis 1995, 35–6).[6]

The illegal drug trade is truly transnational. Countries taking part in it specialize in production, trafficking, or consuming.[7] Another important component of the business is money "laundering," which conceals the illegal nature of the proceeds and eventually integrates them into the legal economy, thus fulfilling the profit expectations that keep the entire market in motion.[8] Most drug cultivation takes place in the "Third World"; rich nations are leading producers of synthetic drugs; demand is still largely located on the richer countries. Most of the value of illegal drugs is added—and probably kept—in the consumer countries. Data on the North-South drug trade cited by the United Nations Drug Control Program (UNDCP) upholds this claim: distributors in consumer countries keep 54 percent of the profits, international traffickers get 26 percent, "processors and national middlemen" in the producing countries obtain 15 percent, and direct producers get only between 2 percent and 5 percent (*Sources* 1999, 6).

In several senses, the global drug market closely resembles the image proposed by the "dependency theory." Third World countries produce the raw materials and manufacture them, normally using precursor chemicals brought from developed nations.[9] During the 1980s and 1990s, the "terms of trade" deteriorated: product quality (purity) improved but final prices declined because of increased supply.

According to some authors, transnational organized crime[10] became the new global "evil threat" in the late twentieth century. Claire Sterling was the most famous proponent of this view, affirming that the demise of the Soviet Union left a "planet-wide criminal consortium" that endangers the integrity and survival of democratic governments everywhere (1994, 13–4). The U.S. State Department has affirmed that large illegal drug organizations pose a "greater threat to democratic government than most insurgent movements" (BINLEA 1998).[11]

Other authors see the above as an overstatement. They contend that the apparent growth of the illegal drug business might partly reflect better monitoring, rather than any objective change. They also affirm that "transnational organized crime" is not so organized, ubiquitous, and powerful as the more alarmist authors believe.[12] However, even the more cautious authors recognize that transnational organized crime (including illegal drug production and trafficking) has grown since the late 1970s.

Economic globalization has contributed to the growth of the international drug trade. This connection is not accidental: worldwide economic transformations have fundamentally affected the four main activities of the drug business. Freer and more intense international trade creates new opportunities for the circulation of illegal products.[13] Financial liberalization (including "offshore banking") and the new information technology facilitate money laundering.[14] By more easily connecting potential producers and consumers, increased global trade also stimulates drug production. Global food liberalization punishes backward agricultural areas, thus pushing peasants into new activities, among which illicit drug cultivation is an attractive option.[15]

Legal and illegal markets create analogous "governance" problems. The illegal drug business has become global but the main law enforcement institutions are still bound by national borders.[16] In principle, international anti-crime treaties could overcome this problem; in practice, supranational law enforcement remains weak and inconsistent.[17] In this context, transnational enforcement is *de facto* monopolized by the more powerful nations, notably the United States.

In several senses, increased drug trafficking can be seen as "the dark side" of democratization. From a global standpoint, there seem to be important connections between these two sides. The demise of communism was a major factor in the "third wave" of democratization. However, in several countries (notably Russia) the fall of communism created unprecedented opportunities for organized criminals. Illegal and legal money became easily confused in the context of disorderly and corrupt privatization; a weak state—unable to regulate economic life—left wide room for drug entrepreneurs, often acting in alliance with government officials (Scott 2003, 65, 68; Stiglitz 2002, 133–65). Outside the communist world, there is no evidence that the demise of dictatorial regimes contributed to reducing global criminality. The "struggle for freedom and prosperity," which according to Przeworski (1991) motivated the dual transition to "democracy and the market," often also weakened the state's law enforcement capacity and provoked economic disruptions that made criminal activities more attractive.[18]

Throughout the twentieth century, the United States played a determinant role in the evolution of the global drug business. This country was the main promoter of the drug "prohibition regime" and remains its chief supporter (Nademan 1999). U.S. anti-drug policies have largely shaped the illicit drug market, especially since the early 1970s. Obviously, the U.S. influence has been particularly strong in Latin America and Mexico.[19]

In 1969, the Nixon administration launched a "war on drugs," which waned in the late 1970s but resuscitated in the 1980s, with the Reagan administration. The Reagan approach to the problem has persisted until today. This approach gives priority to repressive measures, aimed at reducing drug supply; it seeks to "get at the source," targeting producing and transit countries; it pays less attention to demand reduction and prevention. It advocates increasing the role of the military in the United States and especially abroad.[20] It has an international reach, of which "certification" is an important component since 1986.[21] In contrast with its tough approach to drug users and international traffickers, the U.S. government adopts a more cautious stand toward domestic traffickers and their potential collaborators in the legal business community.[22]

The avowed rationale for the U.S. war on drugs is simple: reducing drug availability in the United States would drive final prices up, thereby making drugs unaffordable to many users. This goal has proven unachievable. Since the early 1980s, the U.S. anti-drug budget has been on the rise, drugs seizures have increased, eradication has scored impressive victories,[23] but worldwide drug supply has increased, final drug prices have decreased, and drug purity has improved.[24]

Despite its failure to increase prices, supply suppression has remained "the principal global strategy to control drugs" (Tullis 1995, 90).[25] The implicit justification is that, "in an ideal world," eliminating drug supply would eliminate the entire drug problem (BINLEA 2001). In the real world, however, evidence overwhelmingly demonstrates that demand control is more cost-effective than any other policy option (Reuter 1998; Bertram et al. 1996). Moreover, the fact that drugs get most of their value in the consumer countries suggests that anti-drug efforts are more cost-effective when applied in these countries or in those closest to them (Kennedy, Reuter, and Riley 1994). However, targeting the illegal drug chain as close to its source as possible has remained the dominant policy option (BINLEA 2001).

Several factors account for the failure of the current approach. One of them is the balloon-like nature of the problem: success in one geographical area or against a particular drug organization creates opportunities for new groups operating in different areas. This has also been called the "hydra nature" of the illicit drug business. For example, the destruction of the so-called Medellin Cartel in the early 1990s empowered its Cali rival.[26] The subsequent destruction of the latter led to the development of new organizations. The break of the "French connection" in the mid 1970s increased the demand for Mexican heroin. Successful law-enforcement along the Caribbean route in the mid 1980s made the Mexican route more attractive.[27]

To some extent, anti-drug policies have failed because of the way they are implemented. Virtually all governments that participate in the drug war wage it in a very selective way. Governments in the producer and trafficking countries often support some groups at the expense of others. Governments in the developed world are evidently softer on their own traffickers than on foreign participants in the drug business. Powerful governments also allow political considerations to override anti-drug international efforts. To a large extent, this selective attitude betrays a dilemma that haunts all governments: legal and political reasons encourage them to appear "tough on drugs," but they also realize that illicit drugs are so intermixed with the legal economy that it would be too costly, in economic and political terms, to uproot them. This selective approach clearly shows the extent to which the drug issue can function as a political tool, for both foreign and domestic purposes.[28]

Official anti-drug rhetoric, as well as several academic analyses, has grossly misrepresented the nature of drug organizations, depicting them as large, centralized, and hierarchical corporations, often controlling the entire productive and distribution chain. If this image were accurate, the problem would be much easier to eliminate. In reality, although there exist some powerful organizations, most participants in the drug market operate in small and often informal groups, usually united in extended networks and very often competing with each other. This makes the criminal drug world more fluid and resilient.[29]

In a more fundamental sense, the current "war on drugs" has failed because of its ultimately self-defeating nature. If successful, current anti-drug policies would drive prices up (thereby, presumably, reducing the number of users), but by doing so they would increase the potential profits from drug sales. This would surely stimulate the beginning of a new "business cycle."

2. ECONOMIC AND SOCIAL DIMENSIONS

In the mid 1990s, the Drug Enforcement Administration (DEA) affirmed that Mexican drug producers and traffickers earned more than $7 billion a year. While it is impossible to make precise calculations on the size of Mexico's illegal drug business, this seems a reasonable estimate.

Using data from the late 1980s, Reuter and Ronfeldt (1992, 95–7) estimated that Mexico's drug export revenues ranged from $2.8 billion to $7.4

billion.[30] This meant between 1.6 percent and 4.3 percent of Mexico's GDP and between 7.4 percent and 19.5 percent of the country's legal exports.

During the 1990s, Mexico expanded its participation in the international drug business. Data from the U.S. State Department (BINLEA 2001) shows that in that decade yearly opium production in the country averaged 50.8 metric tons, similar to the 1988 figure used by Reuter and Ronfeldt. Marijuana output reached a yearly average of 9.5 thousand metric tons, nearly doubling the figure used by Reuter and Ronfeldt (between 4.7 and 5.7 thousand tons). Assuming price stability for Mexico's two drug crops,[31] this increase in marijuana production would add between $1.4 billion and $3.8 billion. After including this, yearly income from Mexico's drug cultivation would total between $4.2 billion and $11.2 billion.

However, Mexico's expanded position in the drug business during the 1990s did not result so much from cultivation as from cocaine trafficking. Revenues from this activity are extremely hard to calculate. Reuter and Ronfeldt's estimation included $600 million from cocaine trafficking (1992, 143). This "highly speculative calculation" assumed that Mexico transshipped one-third of the 450 metric tons of cocaine that entered the United States in 1988, and that Mexican traffickers got a "transshipment margin" of $4,000 per each kilo they handled. During the 1990s, Mexican traffickers handled between 50 percent and 70 percent of cocaine coming into the United States. According to the U.S. State Department (BINLEA 2001) Mexican traffickers transshipped 55 percent of the 300 cocaine tons that came into the United States in the year 2000. Moreover, authors agree that in the 1990s Mexican dealers became the dominant players in cocaine trafficking, overpowering their Colombian counterparts.[32] To take account of these changes, one could assume that Mexican traffickers increased their "transshipment margin" to $6,500 per kilo.[33] Under this conservative assumption, in the year 2000 Mexican cocaine traffickers would have gotten nearly $1.1 billion, that is to say, almost $500 million more than the Reuter and Ronfeldt estimate for 1988.[34] Adding this amount, Mexico's drug revenues would total between $4.7 and $11.7 billion.

As mentioned before, Mexican organizations might have become the world's leading methamphetamine producers and traffickers in the 1990s (BINLEA 2001; Boyer 2001), but no reliable calculation of Mexico's income from this source is available. The United States has also insisted that Mexico was a major money-laundering center in the 1990s and continued to be so after the year 2000.[35] No precise estimations on the income generated by this activity are available either. Conservatively, it may be assumed that methamphetamine and money-laundering activities add just $300 million a year.[36] Thus, it seems reasonable to conclude that, by a definitely cautious estimation, Mexico's yearly drug income totals between $5 billion and $12 billion.[37]

When compared with the entire legal economy, estimated drug income is not impressive. This income would represent at least 1.1 percent and at most 2.6 percent of the country's GDP in the late 1990s.[38] It would amount to between 4.9 percent and 11.8 percent of total legal exports in the decade.[39] However, when considering these figures one should bear in mind that, in the mid 1990s, the Mexican legal economy underwent a severe crisis, which apparently did not affect the illegal drug industry.

Other comparisons suggest that the drug business might be more important than the above figures indicate. From 1994 to 2000, Foreign Direct Investment (FDI) in Mexico averaged $10.75 billion a year (INEGI 2003b). Estimated drug income would represent between 47 percent and 112 percent of that amount. Even the lower drug estimate would favorably compare to total Mexican agricultural exports in the year 2000 ($4.1 billion).[40] Mexican oil export revenues were particularly high in the year 2000—$16.3 billion, up from $9.9 billion in 1999 (World Bank 2001a). The higher drug income estimate would be roughly comparable to these figures.

To varying extents, the illegal drug business is present everywhere in Mexico. The state of Guerrero, in the south of the country, has a long tradition of drug cultivation. Western states such as Jalisco and Michoacán have also been important participants in the drug business. Southeastern states (such as Chiapas, Tabasco, and Quintana Roo) have played an increasingly important role in cocaine trafficking.

Nonetheless, the influence of the illegal drug trade and its organizations has been particularly strong in northern Mexico, especially the zones that border on the United States.[41] Some of these zones rank among the country's most economically developed areas. Some of them were also pioneers of Mexico's democratic transition. Indeed, until 1997, opposition state governments were all located in the northern half of the country and a similar trend was evident at the municipality level.

Traditionally, Mexican drug cultivation has been heavily concentrated in the northern "Golden Triangle," which includes the states of Sinaloa, Durango, and Chihuahua.[42] Mexico's opium cultivation began in that region, probably promoted by Chinese immigrants in the early twentieth century and then encouraged by the United States during World War II.[43] In the 1980s, groups operating around the "Golden Triangle" evolved into powerful "poly-drug" organizations tapping on the cocaine flow from South America (Smith 1999, 95).[44]

Nearly all of Mexico's large drug organizations have developed in the North. In the late 1990s, the DEA identified five such organizations: the "Tijuana cartel," the "Juarez cartel," the "Caro Quintero clan," the "Gulf cartel," and the "Amezcua cartel" (Boyer 2001, 97–104). Four of these groups had their headquarters in Mexican states that border on the United States. The only exception was the Amezcua organization, specialized in methamphetamines. This group initially developed in western Mexico (Jalisco and Colima), but afterward extended to other parts of Mexico and into the United States (especially in the West). In the structure of Mexico's drug business, three northern border cities—Tijuana, Juárez, and Matamoros—occupy commanding positions.[45]

It is hard to find precise data on the number of people taking part in Mexico's illegal drug business. Toro (1995, 52, 83) estimates that about 200,000 people live off marijuana and opium cultivation.[46] An official Mexican source that she quotes affirms that this figure might be as high as 300,000.[47] This, of course, does not include all the direct and indirect jobs created by the drug business in packing, transportation, security, money-laundering, communications, trading, and the like. As Andreas (1998b, 160) affirms, these jobs might number in the thousands, especially if one takes into account Mexico's growing importance as a transit country.

A systematic assessment of the size of Mexico's drug business and its workforce is still pending.[48] However, apart from knowing the absolute amounts of people and money, it is also indispensable to understand the different opportunities that this trade offers to different social sectors. The complex "opportunity structure" that the drug business creates largely accounts for its capacity to persist under changing political conditions.

Assessments of the drug problem usually highlight the large profits it generates. Disclosures of large money-laundering operations, corruption scandals, and aggregate figures on the drug market apparently uphold this view, as does the "cartel" imagery discussed below. Indeed, apart from offering huge profits, the illegal drug business also satisfies basic survival needs. Most participants in the drug business get only a small share of its revenues, with "some sectors within the industry making a loss" (Kennedy, Reuter, and Riley 1994, 58). While this is true of most drug cultivators, it also applies to large numbers of people working at any stage of the business. Reuter and Ronfeldt (1992, 95–6) show that "farm revenues" (the amount that drug farmers presumably received) represented only 26 percent of the "export revenues" (the amount paid to the Mexican exporter at the U.S. border).[49] Moreover, as suggested above, these export prices are much lower than retail prices in the United States. This, incidentally, confirms the assertion that illegal drugs get most of their value within the consumer countries.[50]

Low as they might be, drug revenues have not failed to attract large numbers of people. This is explainable if one considers the limited opportunities generated by the legal economy.[51] The previous chapters already presented data on deprivation in the countryside, increased by changes in agricultural policy avowedly aimed at augmenting productivity. There are some obvious connections between drug cultivation and market-oriented rural reforms. "Liberalization of agriculture and the cutting of state subsidies in rural areas increase the incentives for peasant farmers to produce illegal crops" (Andreas 1998a, 211). These reforms intensified "social disruption and economic pressure" in the countryside, thus "fueling the tendency to grow illicit crops as a household survival strategy" (Browne and Sims 1994, 59). Under these circumstances, Tullis' assertion that marijuana is "the most important cash crop in Mexico" seems warranted (1995, 74).

Similar survival needs have pushed people into drug trafficking. A large proportion of the people arrested on illegal drug charges in Mexico are carriers or minor traffickers, aptly referred to as "mules." Journalistic reports have showed that large numbers of impoverished Indians in southern Mexico have gotten involved in drug trafficking. Indeed, analysis made by Mexico's National Institute for Indigenous People (INI) shows that the geographical distribution of illegal drug cultivation, drug trafficking, socioeconomic "marginality," and Indian communities greatly coincides (González and Turati 2001; Henríquez and Pría 2000, 70).[52]

The complexity of the drug "opportunity structure" clearly suggests that, unless the government is willing to pay an extremely high social cost, a purely law-enforcement strategy would not eliminate the illegal drug business. Similarly, a purely "socially-based" strategy would be equally insufficient; indeed, by relaxing law-enforcement pressure on the business, it would likely increase the profit expectations of drug entrepreneurs. "Crop substitution" has been a preferred complement of law-enforcement in producer countries. Such a program would not suffice as a solution to the social dimension of Mexico's drug problem. In the first place, it would only address drug cultivation, but not drug trafficking and methamphetamine production. In the second place, it would be difficult to find crops that offer competitive prices to peasants, especially if the anti-peasant bias of Mexico's current economic policy is not fundamentally changed. Finally, given that illegal drugs get most of their value within the consumer countries, drug traffickers can easily absorb increases in production prices, thus beating virtually any crop substitution option.[53]

Given the complex implications of the illegal drug business, a sophisticated, innovative, and presumably more efficient approach would be advisable. Such an approach should combine both punitive and socially sensitive policies. At first sight, democratic transition would appear to provide the opportunity for such a change.

3. POLITICAL EFFECTS

Before analyzing the expected and actual effects of democratic transition on the illegal drug business, it is necessary to observe how the drug problem affects the political regime. As mentioned above, the transition literature says little about the relationship between illegal activities and the nature of newly established "democratic regimes." Due to its overriding concern with formal rules and electoral competition, it underestimates the potential political consequences of large-scale criminal activities.

The political consequences of illegal drugs can be separated into two categories: those that affect only the *quality* of democratic policies and democratic rule; and those that modify the very *nature* of the process of political change, undermining its democratic character. To a certain extent, this is only a matter of degree. When the former effects surpass a certain level, they might begin corrupting the fundamentals of the regime.

Effects on the Quality of the Government

The most notorious political effect of illegal drugs is corruption. In this, Mexico is not alone: the illegal drug trade has provoked some level of government corruption in all nations involved (Boyer 2001).[54] In Mexico, drug-related corruption has been particularly evident in the drug enforcement apparatus, from police agents to high-ranking officials in the police, the army, and the Attorney General Office (PGR). The case of the Federal Judicial Police (PJF) has been particularly notorious, leading to numerous reforms and frequent shifts of personnel.[55] Indeed, "pervasive corruption" in the Mexican law-enforcement apparatus is "the greatest challenge to the country's anti-drug efforts" (BINLEA 2001).[56]

Drug-related corruption has gone beyond the law-enforcement apparatus, reaching many members of Mexico's political elite. The cases are so numerous that it is impossible to mention each of them. Drug corruption has affected public officials and politicians at different government levels and from different political parties (OGD 2000, 136). The most notorious cases have included governors, heads of federal ministries, and even close presidential collaborators.[57] It has been argued that drug corruption involved even the PRI candidate for the presidential election of the year 2000 (Waller 1999; Olmos 2000).[58]

Andreas claims that drug corruption functions as a *de facto* tax. According to a study he cites, drug organizations "invest" as much as $500 million a year in political corruption (1998b, 162). He also claims that the structure of drug corruption somehow resembles the "structure and character of the Mexican state. . . . Payoffs are made at each level of enforcement—the higher the position, the higher the payoff" (163).[59]

Political corruption has a market counterpart. Available evidence suggests that several important firms and informal business groups have come to share in illegal drug revenues. Allegations of involvement in the drug business have been particularly frequent in the case of the banking system, especially after the devastating 1995 crisis (OGD 2000, 139–42; U.S. House 1996).

All together, evidence upholds the view that, in the Mexican case, corruption has been a "systemic" component of the drug problem (Lupsha 1995, 85). Paradoxically, as shall be discussed below, it has contributed to reducing the level of violence associated to the problem.

The illegal drug trade has also had notorious effects on public safety, undermining the law-enforcement capacity of the state. Opinion surveys show that crime ranks among the top public concerns in Mexico (Fernández Menéndez 2001, 21–2). Illegal drugs have contributed in many ways to making this problem worse. Drug organizations engage in other criminal activities or associate with other criminals; car theft, arms trafficking, and kidnapping are among the criminal activities that have benefited from this association. Authorities that protect illegal drug activities usually cover up other crimes as well. The recent evolution of criminality also gives evidence of this association: official and academic analyses show that crimes have become more frequent since the mid 1980s, thus coinciding with the growth of Mexico's drug industry. This, incidentally, has also coincided with the evolution of democratic transition in the country. It is also revealing that cities that function as drug trafficking headquarters have some of the worst criminal records in Mexico. This is the case of Tijuana, Juarez, and Matamoros, which along with Mexico City have the worst criminal records in the country (Bailey and Godson 2000, 28).[60]

As will be discussed below, some of those "associated crimes" are necessary consequences of the illegal drug business. Violent clashes between trafficking organizations, often with "collateral" casualties, belong in this category. Traffickers, "law enforcement personnel, government officials, and innocent bystanders" have been the usual victims (BINLEA 2001). Less conspicuous have been the "unintended victims"—rural dwellers who "happen to live" in areas controlled by violent drug organizations (Toro 1995, 58).

Even more telling is the paradoxical fact that anti-drug policies themselves have contributed to mounting criminality. Mexico's law-enforcement agencies have increasingly specialized in anti-drug policies, to the point that the PGR "has basically become an antidrug law enforcement agency" (Toro 1995, 58). Indeed, more than half of the PGR budget and one-third of the defense budget have been spent on anti-drug activities (Toro 1998, 139). This has put an excessive burden on Mexico's justice system, which already suffered from insufficient resources. Thus constrained, the law-enforcement apparatus tends to pay little attention to non-drug crimes. This surely contributes to explaining that, according to official data, in 1996 the Mexican justice system processed only 2.46 percent of the reported crimes.[61]

The illegal drug problem has also undermined the sovereignty of Mexico. Compared to other countries, Mexico has received a rather benevolent treatment from the United States. In spite of its notable anti-drug efforts in the late 1990s, Colombia was "decertified" because of evidence that the election of President Samper was contaminated with drug money. In contrast, allegations of drug-related corruption have never provoked the "decertification" of Mexico.

The fact that Mexico and the United States have a close relationship in important economic, political, and security matters largely accounts for the U.S. policy of "calculated avoidance" toward Mexico. U.S. authorities have worried that a tougher attitude toward drug-related corruption might foster large-scale instability in Mexico, which could have unpredictable consequences for the United States itself (Lupsha 1995, 98–100; *Economist* 1999, 34). During the 1980s, U.S. tolerance might have also been motivated by strictly "strategic" reasons. Mexican drug organizations cooperated with U.S. counterinsurgent efforts in Central America, providing training camps and financial resources for the Nicaraguan "Contras" (Scott and Marshall 1998, 41).

NAFTA deepened the special relation between Mexico and the United States. NAFTA negotiations apparently forced U.S. government officials to publicly understate Mexico's drug problem. After NAFTA went into effect, the United States is evidently more concerned with economic and political stability in Mexico. Moreover, if law enforcement along the border becomes too strict, the intense flow of legal goods between the two countries will inevitably be affected.

It is worth noticing that, to a large extent, illegal drug activities by themselves do not endanger Mexico's national integrity. The greatest national security challenge for Mexico comes from the fact that its powerful neighbor has declared "war" on drugs.[62] The U.S. attitude toward the problem has pushed Mexico into an appalling dilemma: either to maintain a war on drugs that it is unable to win, or face the consequences of U.S. hostility.

The drug issue has provoked some of the bitterest confrontations between the two countries. Bilateral cooperation has coexisted with U.S. complaints of Mexican corruption or inefficiency and Mexican protests against U.S. unilateral or arbitrary actions. In the process, the United States has progressively increased its *de facto* role in the design and implementation of Mexico's law enforcement policies. This is not a minor point: even from a strictly procedural definition, national sovereignty is a precondition for democracy and democratic change (see, for example, Rustow 1970). At its very least, the *de facto* role played by the United States in the design and implementation of Mexico's law enforcement policies interferes with democratic accountability in a crucial dimension of Mexican politics.

Undermining Democracy

Jordan (1999) has presented the "narco-democracy" argument in its most ambitious way. In his view, large-scale criminality can have fatal consequences for some political regimes (especially those undergoing democratic transition). To grasp this, he proposes a new regime typology with three categories: autocracy, democracy, and "anocracy"—an "intermediate" regime "where elites maintain themselves in power despite the existence of democratic procedures." "Narcostatization"—the "criminalization of the state"—is a major path to "anocracy" (pp. 21–2).

Some authors have depicted Mexico as a "narco-democracy," claiming that drug corruption is so deep that it has modified the entire basis of the political regime (Lupsha 1995, 93–4; Paternostro 1995; Valle 1995). Although accurately stressing the risks of drug-related corruption, this view runs the risk of overstating the problem. Apart from relying too much on anecdotal evidence, it does not seem to acknowledge that the illegal drug organizations' overriding goal is to accumulate money rather than seize political power.[63]

The fact that illegal drug organizations are unable and unwilling to seize political power does not entail that their political influence is negligible. In Mexico, the illegal drug problem has undermined the rule of law, weakened democratic accountability, fostered "militarization," and provoked human rights violations. By so doing, it has fundamentally challenged the presumed democratic (or democratizing) nature of the Mexican regime. Both illegal drug activities and official anti-drug policies have contributed to this result.

The illegal drug business has fundamental consequences for the rule of law and democratic accountability, which are basic components of democracy and democratic transition. The illegal world is a complex one, related in multiple and contradictory ways with its legal counterpart. If criminal activities are large and numerous, the relation between the two worlds necessarily provokes some level of illegal violence and corruption. The political significance of these consequences varies in accordance with the characteristics of the underworld and the relative strength of the state and the political regime. In the Mexican case, the coexistence of the two worlds has undermined the rule of law and reduced democratic accountability, which are basic components of democracy and democratic transition.

The political threat posed by the criminal world is a function not only of its size but also of its internal structure. When concentrated in a few groups, illegal drug revenues can subsidize powerfully armed opposition to the state, which is not so likely to happen when drug money goes to large numbers of impoverished farmers.[64] This makes it necessary to briefly investigate the distribution of power within Mexico's criminal world.[65]

Several authors have affirmed that powerful "cartels" rule Mexico's drug business (Lupsha 1995; BINLEA 2001; Horn 1997). The DEA has gone so far as to affirm that Mexico's top drug organizations have coalesced into a criminal "Mexican Federation" (Constantine 1996). This image distorts the nature of the drug problem. Properly understood, a cartel is an organization capable of controlling the market and regulating final prices. Mexican drug organizations are clearly unable to do this, partly because their share of the market is not large enough. Moreover, as Smith (1999, 199) has argued, "relations between [drug organizations] are more competitive than cooperative" and have often resulted in violent confrontations.

The inaccuracy of the "cartel" imagery does not mean that powerful criminal organizations do not exist in Mexico. Indeed, official anti-drug campaigns have dealt fatal blows to groups with scarce economic resources and poor political connections, but have been less damaging to large and powerful organizations. Perhaps unwittingly, these campaigns have contributed to the concentration of power within the drug business (Andreas 1998a, 162; Smith 1999, 195).

Mexico's drug industry is best described as having a "semiorganized" structure, which has remained unchanged for several years despite intense turbulence and personnel turnover (Smith 1999, 199–201). This structure seems made up of three levels: a top section of "three to five organizations" with "fully integrated operations" and solid international contacts; a set of six to twenty middle-level organizations, which usually cooperate with the large ones but many times operate by themselves; and a large number of small groups, perhaps specialized in different parts of the business. This semi-organized structure poses a more complex challenge to law-enforcement than a "cartel" system does (Williams 1998a).[66]

In the absence of an overarching cartel structure, violence is a *necessary* component of the illegal drug world. This is relatively easy to grasp. Much as in its legal counterpart, contract compliance in the illegal economy depends on informal mechanisms, such as mutual trust, profit expectations from continued exchange, ethnic ties, and so on. Yet, in both the legal and the illegal market, force is the ultimate guarantor. Because of their illegal nature, participants in the drug business cannot rely on the state to monitor their contracts and enforce compliance. This explains the drug dealers' inescapable need to create their own "law-enforcement" apparatuses, which in the absence of an overseeing entity are prone to collide with each other.[67] As the illegal drug world becomes larger and more complex, these illegal apparatuses are also likely to grow in size and number, multiplying the risk of violent clashes. In this context, government intervention (whether it targets all drug organizations at once or confronts them selectively) can have paradoxical consequences: successful government campaigns might impede the consolidation of an overseeing structure within the criminal world, thereby preserving the need for "particularistic enforcement."

One might think that the security forces of the drug organizations would inevitably clash with those of the government. Indeed, there are two other possibilities: that the government passively tolerates illegal drug activity or that it actively participates in it. Like ordinary businessmen, illegal drug entrepreneurs usually prefer a stable and safe business environment.[68] In this search for stability, both drug lords and government officials might find firm ground for peaceful coexistence.[69] In principle, violent struggle, corruption, and passive government toleration might be exclusive of each other; in reality, a combination of all three is more likely to exist.

Numerous specific combinations can result from the "structural" characteristics outlined above, and many of them have materialized in Mexico. The government has launched serious campaigns against too aggressive drug organizations. With the exception of the "Condor Operation,"[70] numerous anti-drug campaigns have failed to reduce Mexico's drug business but they have destroyed many small groups and partially dispersed or kept in check large-scale criminal organizations. Clashes among drug organizations have been frequent, as the one that "accidentally" killed a catholic Cardinal in 1993. Some government officials have overseen the illegal drug business, alternatively punishing and supporting some organizations (Astorga 2000, 107–10).[71] Some drug organizations have helped the government enforce anti-drug legislation against rival organizations, as the "Juarez cartel" did when it helped Mexico's "anti-drug czar" attack its rivals from Tijuana (Pimentel 2000, 67). Intra-drug and intra-government conflicts have penetrated each other, so that different government factions have allied with different drug groups to fight their common rivals in the political and the illegal drug world (Oppenheimer 1998; OGD 2000, 140–1).[72]

Whatever the specific combination among criminals and the government, the interaction between legal and criminal forces severely challenges the rule of law. Illegal violence, the existence of armed apparatuses outside the control of the state, corruption, and "cooperation" between drug traffickers and law-enforcement officials create an important economic and political area that is beyond democratic control. Its consequences for democratic accountability are also evident: due to the corrupting influence of drugs, some parts of the state become accountable to drug trafficking organizations rather than to the citizenry. Obviously, this problem is still more serious when it concerns government officials who, at least partially, relied on illicit drug money to win competitive electoral processes. In this case, the link between politicians and criminals might become more properly political.[73]

The illegal drug business has also affected the basic nature of political change in Mexico by fostering militarization and human rights violations. Military participation in Mexico's anti-drug efforts started as early as 1938, becoming permanent after 1948 (Toro 1995, 13). However, the military did not become central to Mexico's anti-drug efforts until the "Condor Operation" in the second half of the 1970s, in which 15,000 soldiers, 1,225 officers, and 20 generals participated (Camp 1992, 59).

The militarization of the war on drugs received new impulse in the mid 1980s, when President De la Madrid for the first time defined illegal drugs as a national security issue. In 1985, "20 generals, 120 high-ranking officers, and 25,000 soldiers—18 percent of the active duty army—were engaged in antidrug work" (Camp 1992, 91). In the late 1980s, President Salinas reinforced the official view of drugs as a national security problem.

This trend continued throughout the 1990s. Between 1990 and 2002, the armed forces remained the main drug eradication agent, contributing between 61 percent and 82 percent of total marijuana and opium eradication in the country. Their share of all cocaine interdiction steadily grew from 4.7 percent in 1990 to 69.6 percent in 2002. Their contribution to marijuana interdiction increased from 26.9 percent to 78.5 percent during the same period (Mexican Government 2003, 478). Meanwhile, in 1996, a new trend seems to have begun. Starting with the northern state of Chihuahua, military men were put in charge of state police agencies. Army elements quickly got control of the National Institute for Drug Control (INCD), the Civilian Anti-Drug Intelligence Center (CENDRO), "23 of the 35 national airports, and every PGR state office along the northern border" (Astorga 2001, 7–9). In July 1999, the government transferred 5,000 members of the army into the recently created Federal Preventive Police (PFP), "Mexico's multidimensional force for internal security" (Turbiville 2000).[74] The defeat of the PRI in the presidential election did not stop this trend.[75]

Partly due to its growing anti-drug role, the armed forces have increased their ranks and their budget, even as government finances have shrank. Between 1990 and 1995, the armed forces budget consistently grew, moving from 0.48 percent to 0.57 percent of GDP (Benítez Manaut 2000, 222–5). Between 1990 and 2002, their troops grew 23 percent.[76]

One powerful rationale for military involvement in anti-drug affairs was the belief that it would improve efficiency and reduce corruption (Camp 1992, 58). As data shown below will suggest, efficiency gains are questionable. More importantly, there is abundant evidence of drug-related corruption in the military. In November 1991, army members attacked federal police agents who tried to seize a plane loaded with cocaine, killing seven of them. In February 1997, Gen. Gutiérrez Rebollo, recently appointed head of the INCD, was arrested on illegal drug charges. In 1998, civilian authorities detected at least fifteen high-ranking army elements who where collaborating with drug organizations. Only four of them were arrested in August 2000 (Boyer 2001, 358).[77]

Militarization has had important consequences for Mexico's political regime. It has put key civilian functions into the hands of the military and has reduced civilian control over the armed forces. By doing so, it has inevitably undercut democratic accountability. Even more importantly, due to its anti-drug role, the military has often interfered with local civilian life to the point of becoming "the supreme authority, or in some cases, the only authority in parts of such states as Oaxaca, Sinaloa, Jalisco, and Guerrero" (Camp 1992, 92).[78]

Army participation in drug combat has also led to notorious human rights abuses. The "Condor Operation," for instance, left "large numbers of peasants arrested and tortured" (Craig 1980). In this, the army has not been alone, since both civilian and military forces have abused human rights as part of their anti-drug efforts. Indeed, as human rights analysts and watchers have observed, "human rights violations and drug trafficking are linked, and each exacerbates the other" (Cassel 1999, 4).[79]

Specific data are hard to find but available evidence show that grave human rights violations (including "extrajudicial executions, forced "disappearance," and torture) increased in the late 1990s.[80] Counterinsurgency, anti-drug campaigns, and actions against common crime are the three main factors behind this increase (Reina 1999, 120). Not surprisingly, drug-related human rights abuses have mainly affected impoverished peasants and small traffickers, which contrasts with the more benevolent treatment accorded to high-level drug criminals (AI 1998; Nelleman and Goulka 1999).

Human rights observers have cautioned that anti-crime legal changes approved in the late 1990s, such as the "Federal Law against Organized Crime" (enacted in 1996) might lead to further deterioration of Mexico's human rights situation. Among other things, the 1996 law gave the police additional powers to detain suspects and intercept telephone calls. In a country with an already poor human rights record, tougher anti-crime law might give free reign to violators (AI 1998, 17–8).[81]

The political significance of these developments is hard to exaggerate. Even proponents of a minimalist definition of democracy would admit that increased human rights violations and progressive militarization fundamentally challenge the declared democratic nature of Mexico's new regime.

The effects analyzed above—undermining the rule of law, weakening democratic accountability, fostering "militarization," and provoking human rights violations—are felt in virtually every country involved in the illegal drug trade. However, they are not equally distributed among nations. Strong and complex regimes, with diversified economies and strong civil societies are less vulnerable (Lupsha 1996, 25). This is the case of most drug-consuming countries, such as the United States and the members of the European Union. In contrast, the political effects of illegal drugs are strongest in the "dark corners of the international system where traditional sovereign controls are weak or nonexistent" (Flynn 2000, 45).[82]

It is worth stressing that in order to be relatively impermeable to the corrupting influence of organized crime, a state does not have to be democratic. Strong "totalitarian" or "authoritarian" regimes, with relatively strong economies and cohesive societies, have managed to keep organized crime at bay. The important point is not only that strong regimes are better able to prevent crime from extending excessively: similar levels of criminality can have very different political consequences, depending on the relative strength of the affected regimes and governments. The corrupting influence of crime depends not only on the structure of the criminal world but also on how corruptible the regime is.

Weak regimes might become more vulnerable to criminal threats in several specific ways. The Colombian case demonstrates that illegal drug cultivation flourishes in "remote areas, where the state's presence is weak, and where the presence of the cartels overshadows the presence of the state" (Cepeda Ulloa 1998, 10). This has also happened in Mexico, where drug cultivation has successfully taken advantage of relatively isolated areas where state's oversight is poor. In regions like these, drug criminals are not only predatory agents. They sometimes take over typical state functions, delivering social services, building some public infrastructure, and acting as "law enforcers" (Piñeyro 1998, 102). Indeed, in some Mexican regions, drug strongmen are above local elected officials (Loret de Mola 2001, 114–21).[83]

As has been argued above, through violence and corruption, the illegal drug business necessarily threatens the rule of law and democratic accountability. However, a strong political regime can mitigate these threats. The risk of confronting a strong state would deter criminals from being conspicuous, encouraging them to settle their "inter-criminal" conflicts in a quiet way. By paying reasonably competitive wages to law enforcers, such a state would reduce the relative attractiveness of corruption.[84] Strong regimes can afford to passively tolerate discreet drug criminals, thus avoiding the social costs of an internal war. No "decertification" threat would force a strong government to follow an anti-drug approach that often complicates the problem. Such a government would be able to find attractive alternatives for people pushed into the drug business by their survival needs. A strong state would have fewer motivations to resort to illegal expedients in its anti-drug efforts, thus reducing the risks of militarization and human rights violations.[85] Finally but equally importantly, a strong government would be able to shift the blame for illegal drugs away from domestic factors and on to foreign criminals.

4. IMPACT OF DEMOCRATIC TRANSITION ON THE ILLEGAL DRUG TRADE

Contributors to the transition literature often insist that democracy does not necessarily enhance efficiency. However, by holding public officials accountable, democracy might deter them from collaborating with drug criminals. Moreover, its democratic legitimacy might enable the government to launch firmer law-enforcement campaigns. If honest and firm implementation of the usual approach fails to reduce the problem, then democracy's flexibility might enable the state to adopt a new strategy.

During the 1990s and subsequent years, drug combat occupied a prominent place in Mexico's public rhetoric. All political actors systematically voiced their concern with the drug problem and expressed their willingness to combat it. However, a rapid review of basic indicators shows that the objective situation has not improved.[86]

No precise data are available on the evolution of Mexico's anti-drug budget, but existing evidence suggests that it grew during the 1990s.[87] According to Toro (1998, 139), the anti-drug budget at least quadrupled under President Salinas (1988–94). Without providing precise data, Andreas affirms that Mexico "tripled its federal anti-drug budget between 1987 and 1989, and tripled it again in the 1990s" (1998b, 161).

Mexico's anti-drug legislation underwent important changes in the late 1990s. All these reforms sought to reinforce the existing approach rather than substantially modify it. In May 1996, the Mexican Congress reformed the Federal Penal Code to criminalize money laundering and tighten banking regulations (Blum 1999, 81). The "Federal Law against Organized Crime" was approved in November 1996, increasing the competences of the police, penalizing participation in "criminal organizations," and calling for the creation of a "Special Unit against Organized Crime" (UEDO). In 1998, the president announced a "National Crusade against Crime," which apart from tightening anti-crime regulations set the basis for the creation of the Federal Preventive Police (PFP).

Table 5.1 and figures 5.1 through 5.7 present official data on the evolution of the drug business and the results of Mexico's policies during the 1990s. Marijuana eradication significantly improved throughout the decade. Opium eradication slightly improved between 1990 and 1995, but remained unchanged in the second half of the decade. Yet, estimated production of these two drugs does not show any important change. Marijuana production decreased in 1991, but remained stable afterward. Opium production shows no significant change over the decade: the unusually low figures in 1999 and 2000 were largely due to a severe drought (BINLEA 2001).

As for interdiction, the most alarming change is the reported decline in cocaine seizures, which coincided with Mexico's increasing participation in cocaine trafficking. In contrast, cannabis seizures steadily grew during the decade. Opium, heroin, and methamphetamine seizures were highly volatile; overall, only opium interdiction shows significant improvement.

Throughout the decade, drug charges led to 143,000 arrests. In social terms, this is a costly result, especially because the underclass of the illegal drug world—mainly small-scale growers and traffickers—contributes a disproportionate share of this figure. Leaving this aside, the evolution of arrests does not show any significant change in the entire decade. The figures were volatile between 1990 and 1994, but remained stable subsequently.

Overall, Mexico's anti-drug efforts in the 1990s had at best a mixed record, with the best results concentrated in Marijuana and the worst in cocaine. With these results, it is not surprising that Mexico's share of the illegal drug market grew during that decade, largely due to its greater role in cocaine trafficking, methamphetamine production, and money laundering. This is also consistent with the fact that, as shown above, allegations of official corruption persisted—and perhaps increased—throughout the decade. Neither augmented budgets and tougher legislation, nor the advancement of "democratic transition" seems to have alleviated Mexico's problem with illegal drugs.

Not only has regime change failed to substantially reduce Mexico's participation in the drug business. The transition to procedural democracy might have contributed to worsening the drug problem in three basic ways: by weakening the state and the political regime, by dispersing law-enforcement responsibilities, and by increasing the need for illegal campaign financing. Transition has also contributed to preventing any substantial change to the current anti-drug approach.

In the first place, it is noticeable that, in several senses, rather than setting up a new and democratic regime, Mexico's transition has simply debilitated the old "authoritarian" one. By doing so, it has contributed to exacerbating the drug problem, since, as argued above, a weak political regime both provides greater opportunities for illegal entrepreneurs and makes a country more vulnerable to the politically corrupting influence of crime.

Mexican authorities never controlled the drug business in a unified and centralized way; yet, through corruption and selective law-enforcement, state agents were able to keep drug organizations in check.[88] However, the "fragmented and competitive" links between criminals and politicians became even less harmonious in the early 1990s. Criminal organizations became more independent and confrontational. The dismantling of the "authoritarian" political regime, with a relatively more centralized and strong state, certainly contributed to this change (Bailey and Godson 2000, 302–7; Astorga 2000, 107–13).[89]

Political change has eliminated several links between the authorities and important societal groups but has been unable to replace them with new—and presumably more democratic—forms of political intermediation. As the two previous chapters have argued, this has contributed to insurgency and to the survival of authoritarian practices. It could have equally worsened the drug problem in rather obvious ways. The bureaucratic mechanisms for social policy often played a role in restraining and punishing illegal behavior. Hence, peasants affected by the cut of social programs would have been more likely to cultivate illegal drugs (Malkin 2001). The state's capacity to control the economy also declined. The legal and illegal mechanisms through which the government restrained the economic elite either disappeared or deteriorated (Maxfield 1990). This has created greater opportunities for alliances between legal and illegal businessmen outside the control of state agents (Blum 1999, 81; Boyer 2001, 156–9).

Conflicts within the official elite also contributed to weakening the state. Intra-elite fighting was particularly evident in the politically motivated killings of 1994 and the nearly permanent confrontations within the PRI during the Zedillo administration (1994–2000). This surely opened up opportunities for new, and potentially more conflictive, alliances between criminals and politicians (Benítez Manaut 2000, 194).[90]

Regime change has coincided with a decline in the "extractive capacity" of the state. As shown in chapter 4, democratic transition has failed to increase public revenues in Mexico: the tax burden has remained unchanged, while other sources of public revenue (especially those linked to state monopolies) disappeared in the successive crises and economic reforms initiated in the early 1980s (see table 5.2). As argued above, falling state resources tend to make illegal money more attractive.

The weakening of the state is not a peculiarity of Mexico's democratic transition. As Mainwaring (1994, 380–1) has pointed out, most of the elected civilian governments in the Western Hemisphere "face major challenges in simply trying to hold together the coalitions that brought them to office." This can be seen as a "transitional" cost of democratization. The problem is that, after several years of political change, the weakness of the state in many countries that transited to procedural democracy does not seem to be going away.[91]

In the second place, by diversifying the formal power structure of the country, the transition to procedural democracy also dispersed law-enforcement responsibilities, without a corresponding redistribution of capabilities. In this way, it created new opportunities for drug criminals. As shown in chapter 2, growing electoral competitiveness pluralized Mexico's federal structure in the 1990s. Most authors hailed this change as a major step toward democracy. Yet, other analysts have warned that, rather than federalism, a "feudal" order might arise which would create new opportunities for criminals.

The pluralization of the federal structure severed the informal but strong links that in practice subordinated municipal and state authorities to the president. By doing this, pluralization also redistributed formal government responsibilities—including law enforcement—among the three government levels. However, the distribution of public resources has remained highly centralized, in both the income and the expenditure sides. In the 1990s, the central government collected over 80 percent of the country's taxes and spent over 70 percent of total government expenditures. States and municipalities are still highly dependent on federal budget transfers. Moreover, over half of these transfers are made on a discretionary basis, and come earmarked by the federal government. After years of "state reform" and increasing political competition at all government levels, Mexico has the most centralized fiscal structure among large Latin American countries (Garman et al. 2001, 215–20).[92]

The asymmetric distribution of responsibilities and real capacities has created a "gray area" full of opportunities for drug entrepreneurs. In this context, accountability becomes diffuse and coordination among law-enforcement institutions becomes problematic. Since 1994, the federal government promoted the creation of a National System of Public Safety (SNSP), which would coordinate the anti-crime efforts of all three government levels.[93] However, as of 2004, the SNSP continued to depend on federal financing, which accounted for 90 percent of its total budget (Mexican Government 2003, 468). The SNSP's capacity to provide for a clear delimitation of law-enforcement responsibilities and capacities remains to be seen. Meanwhile, state and federal authorities have continued to blame each other for drug problems.[94]

In this context, it is not surprising that state opposition governments (that is, from parties other than the PRI) have been unable to reduce criminality. Indeed, alternation at the state and municipality levels might have worsened the drug problem. According to Astorga (2000, 11), criminal agents showed more independence and belligerence in the states where opposition parties made greater progress, such as Baja California, Chihuahua, and Jalisco. The establishment of a left-leaning local government in Mexico City in 1997 also failed to reduce criminality. In the late 1990s, three of the four states with highest criminality levels had governments from the opposition (Benítez Manaut 2000, 214–5).

To a certain extent, the electoral growth of opposition parties has also resulted in the "pluralization" of complicity. As early as 1992, Reuter and Ronfeldt (p. 103) pointed out that the three main political parties in Mexico had all been accused of having links with the drug trade. An official report included the National Action Party's governor of Baja California in a list of high level politicians actively involved in the drug business (see Boyer 2001,

114).[95] An influential international drug-watcher has also observed criminal links in all political parties (OGD 2000, 136).[96]

Also interesting is the fact that opposition governments have not attempted to modify the prevailing approach to the drug problem. These governments have continued (or intensified) the policies initiated by their PRI predecessors, including the most polemical ones such as the militarization of drug enforcement (Benítez Manaut 2000, 214–5).

A third effect of procedural democratic change upon the illegal drug trade comes through campaign financing. Serious research on the use of illegal drug money in electoral contests is particularly scanty. The transition to competitive electoral systems creates mixed incentives in this regard. On the one hand, increased electoral competitiveness necessarily intensifies the need for campaign funding, potentially from both legal and illegal sources. In a country where the drug business is sizable and where drug organizations "invest" a large share of their profits in corrupting public officials, parties and candidates are likely to find this source attractive. On the other hand, in a competitive system evidence that a party or candidate used "dirty money" can have high political costs. Therefore, participants in a tight electoral race would find it attractive to use drug money as long as it is possible to conceal its illegal origin.

Incentives within the illegal world are less ambiguous: like their legal peers, drug entrepreneurs would like to support certain candidates as a way to secure favors from future government officials. Given their illegal nature, drug businessmen are more dependent on the goodwill of the government, which necessarily increases the expected profits from political "investment."

Many factors can modify the basic incentives identified above, among them the tightness of the electoral race, the campaign strategy of each candidate and party, the costs of campaigning, the opportunities to surreptitiously use drug money, party ideology, and so on. Particularly relevant are the accountability rules established by the electoral legislation. The 1993 reform of the Mexican electoral legislation set limits to private contributions to political parties; the 1996 reform tightened those regulations. Parties are forbidden to take contributions from business firms, foreign sources, religious organizations, and government agencies other than the Federal Electoral Institute (IFE). No single private contribution to any party may be superior to 0.05 percent of total public financing to all political parties; the sum of private contributions to any party may not exceed 10 percent of this total.[97] Finally, articles 49 and 182 of the federal electoral law (COFIPE) mandate the IFE to set campaign spending ceilings that parties and candidates may not surpass.

To compensate for the above restrictions, the 1996 electoral reform generously increased public financing, which grew from $58 million in 1994 to $322 million in 2000—a 455 percent increase in six years.[98] According to official data, private funding decreased to less than $20 million in 1995 (down from around $200 million the previous year); afterward, it started to grow again, totaling almost $50 million in 2000. All together, these figures show that increased electoral competition has been accompanied by a remarkable growth in total party spending, which according to official sources, grew from $260 million in 1994 to nearly $370 million in 2000. Most of this growth reflects the fact that parties and candidates have increasingly resorted to the mass media, especially television, which are highly expensive. In the year 2000, payments to the media accounted for 54 percent of total campaign spending (Lujambio 2001, 10–2; Curzio 2000, 137–8).

In spite of tight regulations, important legal holes exist. To start with, limitations to private funding are very flexible in practice. In 2000, according to the limits set by law, private donations to any single party might have totaled $16.1 million; individual donations might have been as high as $80,500.[99] Moreover, parties may receive contributions from their militants and dividends from party investment in financial instruments. These sources are not subject to the limitations mentioned above.

Electoral authorities have recognized the existence of several deficiencies in the legislation. For all the complicated regulations, as of 2000 the IFE estimated that it was able to oversee only 77 percent of party finances. Compliance with regulations concerning private donations has been particularly hard to oversee. Payments to the media are virtually impossible to verify. Rules concerning bank secrecy further complicate financial overseeing. No regulations apply to intra-party competitions, especially party primaries (Lujambio 2001, 9; Curzio 2000).[100]

The media and some academic analysts have disclosed several cases of probable "dirty" campaign funding. In 1993, daring revenue-raising initiatives on behalf of the PRI revealed the increased financial needs associated with tight electoral competition (Andreas 1998b, 164–5; Oppenheimer 1998). According to apparently well-founded rumors, the Colombian "Cali Cartel" might have contributed as much as $40 million to the PRI campaign in 1994; in any case, real PRI campaign spending surpassed the legal limit by far (Lupsha 1995, 93). Rumors of "dirty" financing—involving high-level businessmen—seemed particularly well founded in the case of the gubernatorial race in the state of Tabasco in 1994. Traces of illegal money were also notorious in the PRI presidential primaries in 1999 (OGD 2000,

140–2). Financial irregularities in the electoral campaign of President Fox proved impossible to clear up, thus evidencing the weakness of official overseeing (Ambriz 2001).[101] Several other cases, relatively less important, have been disclosed.[102]

With these precedents, some general observations can be made. Coming electoral races are most likely to remain highly competitive. Public financing to each of the three main political parties is quickly becoming similar.[103] In these circumstances, the need for private funding intensifies. Prevailing conditions in Mexico (among them the large sums available for corruption, the numerous opportunities for money laundering, and the holes in party financing regulations) suggest that opportunities for intermixing legal and illegal campaign funding remain high.

In this context, the "discreet" use of dirty money by leading candidates, regardless of their party affiliations remains tempting.[104] This will probably combine with occasional excesses, some of which will get media coverage. What is important in this context is that, while it might augment the political costs of using "dirty" money, the transition to competitive electoral systems creates new incentives for illegal campaign funding. By so doing, it contributes to keeping the illegal business in operation and to the survival of drug-related corruption.

Finally, democratic transition may contribute to the persistence of the illegal drug problem by preventing a change in the existing anti-drug approach. As discussed above, surveys have consistently showed that crime and public safety are an extremely important public concern in Mexico. While in campaign, candidates have normally promised to bring on a new and more effective anti-crime strategy. Yet, once in power they adopt an extremely cautious approach to the problem, implementing essentially the same policies, and consistently obtaining the same results as their predecessors.

The nature of the existing democratic consensus might contribute to the continuation of this irresolute attitude. To understand this, one should recall two ideas presented in the preceding chapters: the superficial (and negative) consensus on the rules of procedural democracy, and the short-term view that these rules instill in the political actors. Political leaders are not willing to unite with their rivals in an unambiguous defense of the rule of law; and they want their party to retain power in the next elections. Therefore, incumbent politicians avoid confronting any fundamental problem that can only be solved in the medium term, since such a confrontation might have disruptive short-term consequences on which their adversaries would surely capitalize. Under these circumstances, the most rational option for the incumbent government is to "administer" the problem and pass it on to the next administration. The adoption of an audacious, serious, and innovative approach to illegal drugs belongs to this category of problems. As the two previous chapters argued, this combination of reasons also discourages the political elite from adopting a serious distributive agenda and dissuades it from seeking a definite settlement of insurgency.

Social distrust of the government's anti-crime policies further compounds the problem. As Bailey and Godson (2000, 305) have remarked, "society is not ready to ally with the state to combat crime and corruption." In this way, social distrust and government impotence reinforce each other, guaranteeing the continuation of the problem even as democratic transition advances and "consolidates."

5. AFTER THE PRI

The defeat of the PRI in the presidential election of the year 2000 was the culminating step in Mexico's democratic transition. By observing the first post-PRI administration, one can obtain decisive evidence on the effects of regime transition on large-scale criminality.

Several institutional changes directly linked to anti-drug policies took place at the beginning of the Fox administration. On the date of its inauguration (December 1, 2000), the incoming administration created a new cabinet position—the Ministry for Public Safety and Services to Justice (SSP). This new ministry controls the PFP and heads the SNSP. The new government also created the office of the presidential National Security Adviser, a post that failed to assume an important role vis-à-vis the older law-enforcement institutions. In January 2001, the Mexican Supreme Court authorized the government to extradite Mexican nationals to the United States—something that the United States had demanded for a long time (BINLEA 2001).[105] In October 2001, the government disbanded the notorious PJF and replaced it by a Federal Investigative Agency (AFI).[106] In June 2003, a Special Deputy Attorney General Office Specialized in Organized Crime (SIEDO) was created, the largest institution ever set up within the PGR for prosecuting organized crime and illegal drug activities.[107]

Apart from these, rather modest, institutional changes, the government's relation to illegal drugs has remained essentially unchanged.[108] To start with, this relation has continued to combine limited conflict with strong anti-drug public rhetoric. In January 2001, the government announced a "National Crusade against Drug Trafficking and Organized Crime." In May, police agents arrested the former Quintana Roo governor Mario Villanueva, who was charged with drug crimes. In May, the government captured a leader of the "Methamphetamine Cartel." In June, the police arrested Alcides Magaña, presumably a prominent drug lord in South Eastern Mexico. The army captured the alleged chiefs of three large drug organizations: Benjamin Arellano Felix, of the "Tijuana Cartel," in March 2002; Osiel Cárdenas Guillén, of the "Gulf Cartel," in March 2003; and Armando Valencia Cornelio, of the "Milenio Cartel," in August 2003.

None of the above actions seems to depart from the traditional pattern of selective law-enforcement. Official figures largely confirm this impression. As table 5.1 shows, in terms of eradication, interdiction, production, and arrests there was no significant improvement between 2000 and 2002. Indeed, the overall situation seems to have worsened. In 2002, cocaine seizures dropped to an all-time low of 12.6 metric tons; seizures of cannabis, opium, heroin, and methamphetamine also decreased with respect to 2000. Eradication had a mixed performance, with a slight decrease in cannabis and a considerable improvement in opium. Both cannabis and opium production increased, with the latter almost doubling between 2000 and 2002. Finally, there was a significant decrease in the total number of arrests. In this context, it comes to no surprise that drug flows from Mexico have stabilized or augmented after the electoral defeat of the PRI.[109]

Perhaps the best indicator that the new administration has maintained the traditional rules of the game is an indirect one. One cannot reasonably expect a peaceful reaction from drug organizations if they see that the government is effectively determined to destroy them. Neither the Mexican record with illegal drugs nor that of other countries would justify this expectation. In 2001, drug groups dealt some blows to the government, especially in January when the notorious drug lord Joaquín "El Chapo" Guzmán escaped from a high-security prison and the governor of Chihuahua Patricio Martínez was shot, presumably by people in the drug business. In early 2004, a wave of crimes—evidently linked to drug trafficking—affected several states.[110] The most notorious case took place in Michoacán, where a strongly armed group of around forty people broke into a jail and liberated several prisoners. This and other crimes were allegedly committed by a group known as the "Zetas," formed by individuals who deserted the army's elite forces and joined the "Gulf Cartel" (Gutiérrez 2004). Nonetheless, nothing close to a major war between drug organizations and the government has broken out.

The relatively peaceful coexistence between the government and the illegal drug business has another important implication: the continuation of government corruption. There is no evidence that the Fox administration has made any decisive inroad against drug-related corruption. In March

2002, the U.S. State Department recognized that: "pervasive corruption in Mexican law enforcement institutions continued as the greatest challenge facing the government of Mexico in its efforts to fight drug trafficking and organized crime" (BINLEA 2002). This view changed a year later. According to INCSR 2002, "Mexican leaders worked energetically to detect and punish corruption among law enforcement officials and military personnel" (BINLEA 2003b). Among the most important facts cited to back this appreciation are the disbandment of an army battalion and the subsequent legal prosecution of over forty soldiers, the conviction of two generals, and the arrest of twenty-five mid-level personnel from the PGR, PFP, the military, and other law enforcement entities—all of them on drug-related charges. Nonetheless, as mentioned above, prosecution of security and police elements has been recurrent in Mexico's "war" on drugs—both before and after the electoral defeat of the PRI. Even more important, the facts cited by the U.S. State Department may be interpreted in exactly the opposite sense: as the persistence—and perhaps the intensification—of drug-related corruption in the police and armed forces.

The Fox administration has retained the law-enforcement team of its predecessors, accelerating the trend toward "militarization."[111] Before taking over, Fox and his main collaborators announced that they would redefine drugs as a "public safety" rather than as a national security issue. Among other things, this would entail withdrawing the military from drug combat. Once in office, President Fox substantially enlarged the number of military personnel serving in the country's main law-enforcement agency (PGR). For the first time in Mexico's history, he appointed a serving army general as the chief of the PGR. His choice to head the Defense Ministry was a general identified with the group that controlled the army during the two previous decades. Something similar happened in the Navy. Only lesser law-enforcement agencies escaped from this trend, among them the civilian intelligence agency (CISEN), the SSP, and the National Security Adviser office. Not surprisingly, the new administration has undertaken no major cleaning operation within the law-enforcement apparatus.[112] Indeed, together with the economic policy team, the armed forces are perhaps the part of the state that has been least affected by democratic transition.[113]

Finally, the Fox government has also failed to take a firmer approach toward the United States. Indeed, U.S. pressure was the decisive factor that forced the Fox administration to retain the military as the key anti-drug entity (Fernández Menéndez 2001, 53–9; Astorga 2001, 9). Obviously, the *de facto* role played by the United States in designing and implementing law-enforcement policies in Mexico has been strengthened.[114]

CONCLUSION

The previous analysis shows that democratic transition in Mexico is more superficial and limited than it initially appeared to be. The illegal drug world and regime change are fundamentally intertwined. To a considerable extent, the illegal world has colonized the recently established regime. Moreover, whatever its own importance, the illegal drug trade should be seen as only one instance of politically challenging crime; other forms of large-scale criminality can have similar political effects. But democratic transition has not been a passive victim: in several ways, it has also contributed to exacerbating the drug problem and to increasing its political consequences.

Mexico's situation is not unique. Democratic transition has coincided with growing illegal drug production and trafficking in Latin American countries such as Peru, Bolivia, and the Central American nations. Even a "textbook case" of democratic transition as Chile has been tainted by growing participation in the illegal drug trade—with the associated increase in political corruption and legal business' complicity.[115] As this chapter has shown, to accurately understand this combination of legal and illegal changes, it is necessary to go beyond the analytical framework provided by the mainstream literature on democratic transition.

Although it seems unlikely to disappear, Mexico's illegal drug business might decrease in the near future. This, however, is not likely to result from more efficient implementation of current anti-drug policies. It would rather be the consequence of external changes. On the one hand, the United States might move away from its current approach to the problem, presumably toward a more demand-oriented strategy. Although unlikely, a change like this would substantially modify Mexico's illegal drug situation.

Alternatively, international drug organizations—especially cocaine traffickers—might come back to the Caribbean routes that they partially abandoned in the late 1980 (Andreas 1998a, 165; Smith 1999, 213–4). This might be supplemented by changes in the structure of drug demand. Available evidence shows that consumption of "synthetic drugs," which are comparatively easy to produce domestically, has been rapidly expanding in the United States (ONDCP 2001, 20–4). If continued, this trend would inevitably undermine Mexico's position in the international drug market. Obviously, while they could improve the Mexican situation, changes like these would eliminate neither the global problem nor its politically corrupting consequences for other countries.

Mexicans can do more than wait for external changes. As this chapter endeavors to demonstrate, eliminating Mexico's participation in the global drug business is an unrealistic goal, but downsizing the problem and ameliorating its socially and politically corrupting influence is not. This should prompt Mexico to adopt a new anti-drug strategy, relying more on social consensus and less on repression. Among other things, this would require the government to combine punitive actions seeking to disperse large and centralized drug organizations with the creation of greater opportunities for legal employment. A new strategy would distribute the country's scarce law-enforcement resources in a more comprehensive way, overcoming the current anti-drug bias of the justice system. This would entail placing less emphasis on anti-drug efforts and more on other forms of crime. A reformed anti-drug approach would necessarily put more emphasis on curtailing domestic consumption, instead of focusing almost exclusively on cutting illegal drug exports.[116] It would also imply relieving the military from its current anti-drug responsibilities. Such a strategic reformulation would inevitably face opposition from foreign proponents of the current approach, notably the United States. However, relying on its democratic legitimacy, a strong and determined government would be able to carry out such a change, showing powerful international actors that it is a necessary and advantageous innovation.[117]

This chapter has argued that weak states and political regimes are particularly vulnerable to the corrupting influence of large-scale criminality. Other things being equal, a similar degree of involvement in the illegal drug business has worse consequences for a weak regime than for a strong one. Therefore, apart from adopting a realistic anti-drug agenda, efforts to restrain the corrupting influence of the illegal drug trade should seek to strengthen the political regime. The next chapter will make some suggestions in this regard. As it shall argue, doing this would also entail going beyond the optimistic—and ultimately unrealistic—expectations implicit in the transition to democracy literature.

Chapter Six
Beyond Democratic Transition: Toward a Redistributive Agenda

How should one characterize the general process of political change in Mexico? How can the Mexican political situation be improved? What are the implications of this study for the analysis of democratic change in other countries?

In addressing such questions, this chapter summarizes the preceding analysis, proposes some avenues for future research, outlines an alternative approach to democratic change, and puts forth a series of practical measures necessary for the construction of democracy in a country like Mexico. Given the centrality of distributive issues, emphasis is placed on the need to take into account the non-procedural elements of democratic change and adopt a large-scale redistributive agenda.

1. POLITICAL CHANGE IN MEXICO

This research has showed that what at first sight seemed a problematic democratic transition is in reality a combination of four broad sets of phenomena: the adoption of democratic procedures, a number of apparent "anomalies," a weakened state and political regime, and the persistence of an extremely unequal socioeconomic structure. These elements are closely interrelated and mutually reinforcing, but they also follow different logics. Together, they form a contradictory but potentially enduring whole.

During the late twentieth century, but particularly in the 1990s, the formal political institutions of the country underwent unprecedented changes. Elections became unmistakably competitive. Citizens can now choose among several parties and candidates. Numerous constitutional and legal changes reinforced the separation of powers. Progressively competitive elections in effect pluralized the Mexican state. With the break of the PRI's near-monopoly on elective posts, all branches and levels of government became more independent than ever since the end of the Mexican Revolution. Several legal restrictions on civil and political rights were removed, but with the exception of those directly related to voting such rights remain weak in practice; similarly, despite legal and institutional innovations, Mexico's human rights situation in several respects worsened in the 1990s.

Taken together, these changes convincingly show that, by the standards of the mainstream literature, Mexico has undergone democratic transition.[1] However, the country has also undergone changes and continuities that clearly contradict the idea of democratic transition. "Authoritarian" practices and structures have shown their capacity to interact with, and partially colonize procedurally clean and competitive elections. A new wave of insurgency started in 1994, demonstrating that "anti-system" actors can survive and interact with competitive political parties and plural state institutions. Finally, just as transition accelerated in the 1990s, Mexico expanded its participation in the illegal drug business, showing that politically influential criminal forces can coexist with formally democratic institutions.

Seen from the standpoint of the transition literature, those phenomena might look like "deviations" or "anomalies," occurring at the margins of Mexico's move toward democracy and bound to disappear as democracy becomes "consolidated." The previous chapters have shown the inadequacy of such a view. Growing electoral competitiveness, pluralization, liberalization, surviving authoritarian practices, insurgency, and the illegal drug business—all are components of the general process of political change in Mexico. Nothing but theoretical preconceptions justifies seeing some of them as more fundamental or "normal" than the others. Democratic transition has contributed to either the emergence or survival of the "anomalous" phenomena; the latter have undermined in practice the formally democratic nature of the new regime. Overall, this presents a complex, contradictory, and indeterminate process of change—very different from the peaceful, moderate, and increasingly institutionalized move toward democracy suggested by the idea of democratic transition.

Moreover, in several respects, the newly established democratic regime seems to be a mechanism for not making basic decisions. This is because, in many senses, enhanced pluralism in reality has weakened the state and the political regime.[2] Overwhelmingly concerned with the short-term electoral costs of their decisions, incumbent politicians systematically avoid confronting any fundamental problem that can only be solved in the medium or long term. This helps explain why the new democratic regime has failed to implement a firm anti-poverty and redistributive agenda. It is also a strong reason behind the government's unwillingness to decidedly seek either a military or a negotiated settlement of its latent conflict with insurgent groups. Finally, it has also prevented the authorities from adopting a new and more realistic approach to the illegal drug problem.

Several reasons explain the weakness of the state and the regime. To begin with, transition has been far better at dismantling the old regime than at creating a new and strong one. Transition has eliminated several links between the authorities and important legal and illegal social groups, but has not replaced them with new and more democratic connections. Severing the links between the state and the lower sectors set the scene for the "pluralization" of traditional authoritarian practices: increased competition encouraged parties other than the PRI to use traditional forms of political control and mobilization.[3] The dismantlement of traditional political and bureaucratic links between the state and the countryside contributed to the emergence of insurgent groups and made illegal drug cultivation and traffic more attractive. The balance of power between the state and the business elite changed in favor of the latter, thus undermining the democratic politicians' capacity to make economic policy decisions. Finally, dismantling the "authoritarian" system also eliminated several informal mechanisms through which the political elite maintained illegal drug organizations under relative control.

By pluralizing the formal structure of power, democratic transition decentralized accountability and government responsibility; at the same time, it has preserved an overwhelmingly centralized distribution of public revenues in both their income and expenditure sides. In spite of several changes, federal authorities still collect most public income in Mexico and decide how to spend it. Therefore, there is a remarkable mismatch between the formal competences of state and municipal authorities and their independent financial capabilities. This asymmetry necessarily weakens the capacity of the Mexican state for making binding decisions and preserving the rule of law.

In Mexico, democratic transition has coincided with decreasing state revenues. Throughout the 1990s, Mexico's tax burden remained low even by Latin American standards. Democratic transition did not create this situation, but it has discouraged politicians from solving it. As chapter 4 explained, while political parties are unwilling to incur the electoral costs of promoting regressive changes to the country's tax structure, they are equally afraid of alienating the economic elite by proposing a progressive tax reform. Not surprisingly, the few proposals made in this respect have sought only marginal increases, often through regressive changes. This trend, also evident in the rest of Latin America, sharply contrasts with that of the "exemplary" transitions of Southern Europe, where regime change resulted in higher and more progressive tax burdens (Maravall 1995, 230).

A further source of weakness is the peculiar nature of the democratic consensus. No important political force in Mexico questions the desirability of democracy. However, this extended consensus is mostly superficial and often negative. Politicians voice their support for democracy largely because they lack any publicly defendable alternative, but they are unwilling to unite with their rivals in an unambiguous defense of democratic rules. Rather, as the analysis of insurgency and illegal drugs showed, they take advantage of "anti-system" forces to weaken the incumbent party. Moreover, electoral cycles tend to shorten the time horizon of government and party leaders. Together, this short-term view and the superficial consensus on democratic rules become a powerful force against decisive action. Regardless of ideological inclinations, the most rational option for government leaders is to "administer" the problems of the nation and pass them on to the next administration.

It would be tempting to attribute many actions and omissions of the elected authorities to some complicity between the economic and the political elites of the country. While there are some grounds for such a "conspiracy theory," in many instances the regime has been guilty of weakness and incapacity rather than complicity. The weak and "neutral" state in practice benefits the most powerful private agents, thereby further eroding the basis of political stability and democracy.[4]

Recognizing the above does not amount to a moral justification of the political elite. Nor does it entail a negation of political agency. But it clearly shows the inescapable link between socioeconomic power and the political regime; by so doing, it also suggests some realistic opportunities for improvement.

2. POVERTY, INEQUALITY, AND DEMOCRATIC CHANGE

The transition literature pays little attention to the relationship between democratic change, on the one hand, and poverty and inequality, on the other. This absence is noteworthy, especially because most of the "third wave" of democratization took place in impoverished nations with high levels of inequality. The very few texts that focus on this relationship do so in an obviously ambiguous way. When focusing on poverty, they tend to view it as determined by aggregate economic levels, rather than by the distribution of economic assets. Moreover, while some authors admit that poverty and inequality might be politically significant, they usually affirm that democratic transition is essentially independent from well-being and equality levels.[5]

This view is congruent with a central claim of the mainstream literature—that democratic change is largely free from "substantive" or structural constraints. In a more fundamental sense, such a view is congruent with the procedural definition of democracy, which explicitly seeks to free the "democratic method" from substantive "preconditions" or "contextual factors."

The preceding chapters showed the inaccuracy of such a view. Poverty and, especially, inequality are among the most prominent features of Mexican society—and they are far from irrelevant for democratic change or for the functioning of the democratic "method." Indeed, the association of massive poverty and high inequality with procedurally clean and competitive elections largely accounts for the survival of traditional authoritarian practices and the corruption of formal democratic procedures in the country.

By different estimations, between thirty million and eighty million Mexicans—from 30 to 80 percent of total population—live in poverty or extreme poverty.[6] Even more impressive are the estimations of income inequality, according to which the richest 10 percent of the Mexican population earned 57.5 times as much as the poorest 10 percent, and the richest 1 percent earned 3.3 times as much as the poorest 40 percent. The progress of democratic transition did not improve the distributional situation. Democratically elected politicians have made no systematic effort to seriously reduce poverty, consistently shunning any redistributive program.[7]

Within Latin America—the most unequal region in the world—Mexico occupies an intermediate position. As measured by the Gini coefficient, income inequality in Mexico (0.539) ranked ninth in a list of eighteen Latin American countries elaborated by ECLAC (2002).[8] At the top of the list came Brazil (0.635), Nicaragua (0.583), and Guatemala (0.582). Uruguay and Costa Rica were the least unequal nations in the region (0.454).[9] In terms of people living below the poverty line, Mexico again occupies an intermediate position (46.6 percent). The most impoverished societies were Honduras (79.3 percent), Nicaragua (73.8 percent), and Bolivia (60.6 percent). The countries with least poverty were Chile (26.3 percent) and Costa Rica (23 percent). The overall distributional situation (in terms of inequality and poverty) seems worst in Honduras, Nicaragua, and Bolivia and best in Costa Rica, Uruguay, and Chile.[10]

In Mexico, amidst widespread poverty and extreme inequality, even the cleanest electoral processes have been corrupted. Large-scale electoral irregularities, usually enjoying the support or acquiescence of voters, have taken place precisely in the most "marginal" and impoverished areas of the country. Underlying this is a rational, if unequal and often tacit, agreement. The poor trade their votes or their political allegiance for immediate means of survival or for credible promises of them, even if this means reproducing traditional authoritarian practices. Not only does this tacit agreement corrupt formal democratic procedures; it also renders poverty and inequality functional in competitive elections. In this way, it discourages both democratic political leaders and electors from adopting a far-reaching redistributive agenda.

Apart from distorting the reality of voting, poverty and inequality also affect the practice of other political, civil, and human rights.[11] As chapters three and five showed, human rights violations are particularly hard on the poor. Similarly, although also resulting from institutional and organizational factors, insurgency cannot be understood without referring to the socioeconomic conditions that led large groups of people to see armed rebellion as a valid form of political action. Democratic transition did not create those conditions, but its inability to overcome them contributes to the legitimacy of insurgency. This explains why insurgent groups have been most appealing in the countryside, where poverty is far worse than in the urban areas. The new democratic regime's inability to fundamentally address issues of socioeconomic distribution greatly accounts for the survival of insurgent groups even as elections become apparently cleaner and fairer.

Not surprisingly, poverty and inequality also compound the illegal drug problem, which corroded Mexico's democratic transition during the 1990s. As chapter five showed, apart from generating large profits, the illegal drug trade also meets basic survival needs. Given the paucity of opportunities in the legal economy, drug revenues attract large numbers of people, even though most participants get only a tiny part of them. This combination of huge profit expectations and sheer survival needs greatly increases the complexity of the illegal drug problem and shows the limitations of a purely law-enforcement anti-drug strategy. Because of its inability to address poverty and inequality, democratic transition contributes to perpetuating this problem.

Overall, it is clear that conceptualizing poverty and inequality as purely "contextual" factors is utterly misleading. Contrary to the claims of the mainstream literature, they are central to democratic change and to the workings of democratic procedures. Acute deprivation and competitive elections are a complicated mix. Unless one purposefully goes beyond the limits of procedural democracy, combining them most likely results in the corruption of democracy and the preservation of poverty and inequality.

What does the above analysis suggest for comparative research? Depending on the starting line, purely "procedural" political change that does not modify the distribution of socioeconomic assets might have diverging consequences across countries. Take, for example, the cases of Spain and

Peru, two pioneers of the "third wave" of democratic transition with very different social situations. In the former case, purely procedural democratization would have meant preserving a relatively fair socioeconomic structure;[12] in the latter, it meant maintaining an unjust—and politically disruptive—social situation.

In the late twentieth century, there seemed to be a clear association between successful democratization and relatively just socioeconomic structures. The list of consolidated democracies and "successful" transitions includes the most egalitarian and least impoverished countries that took part in the "third wave."[13] This is most evident in the case of the "exemplary" cases of Southern Europe. At time of transition, economic inequality in Portugal, Spain, and Greece was notably low by "third wave" standards. More importantly, the newly established democratic regimes explicitly sought to reduce inequality through ambitious redistributive measures.[14]

A similar pattern is observable in the former communist bloc of Eastern Europe and the Soviet Union. During the transition to "democracy" and capitalism, economic inequality increased in all these societies, but there were important differences across nations.[15] Sources largely agree that the Czech Republic, Slovenia, Hungary, and Poland had "exemplary" democratic transitions.[16] It is interesting that, except for Poland, by 2000 these were the most egalitarian in this group of nations (World Bank 2002, xiv). By contrast, Armenia, the Kyrgyz Republic, Moldova, and Russia, which are now among the most unequal nations in the world, finished the century with either "concentrated" or "war-torn" political regimes rather than democratic ones (World Bank 2002, 98).[17]

Comparative analyses of Latin America usually see Chile, Uruguay, Costa Rica, and Venezuela as the countries with the best democratic record in the twentieth century.[18] Coincidentally, these were among the nations with lower levels of poverty and inequality in most of the century (Morley 1995). Among countries that took part in the "third wave," Chile and Uruguay are usually depicted as Latin America's exemplary cases. Interestingly, these are the two nations with the lowest percentage of people under the poverty line (ECLAC 2000, 40).[19] According to Freedom House, along with Costa Rica, these were also the countries with the best record on civil and political liberties during the 1990s (Freedom House 2002a). At the other extreme are countries like Haiti and Guatemala, with arguably the worst democratic and social records in the region.

Obviously, numerous factors have affected political change in these countries and regions. Yet, the above remarks suggest that inequality and poverty may have an independent and decisive influence on democratic

change. Otherwise, it would be hard to explain why, among nations participating in the "third wave" of democratization, some ended up with both
the most successful democratic transitions and the most egalitarian social
structures, while others entered the twenty-first century both with impoverished and unequal societies and with "unconsolidated" democracies.

The comparative hypothesis put forward here is not that a given level
of equality and economic abundance is indispensable for a country to em-
bark upon democratic change. Nor is it implied that, because of their levels
of material well-being, some countries are "condemned" to democracy.
What is suggested is that, in societies with widespread poverty and high inequality, successful democratic change necessarily requires substantial improvement of the distributional situation. By itself, procedural democracy is
not conductive to such redistribution. Purposeful political action—beyond
the procedural limits set by the mainstream literature—is necessary to build
the basis for stable democracy.

3. DEMOCRATIC TRANSITION AND "NEOLIBERALISM"

In several respects, democratic transition seems to be the political counterpart of neoliberalism. Historically, they were associated: both neoliberal reform and the "third wave" of democratization took place in roughly the
same period, often affecting the same countries. Analytically, in spite of their
ostensible efforts to liberate political change from socioeconomic transformations, contributors to the mainstream literature agree that there is a basic
affinity between democratic transition and neoliberal economic reform. At
a deeper level, a strictly procedurally democratic regime seems congruent
with the limited state postulated by neoliberalism.

Based on the above, it would be possible to attribute several problems
analyzed in this text to neoliberalism rather than to democratic transition. It
might be argued that the neoliberal program, not procedural democracy, is
the main obstacle to the adoption of a redistributive program. Besides, it
could be claimed that, by cutting state support to the countryside, neoliberal
policies set the scene for the emergence and survival of insurgent organizations. Finally, it might seem that, by simultaneously worsening inequality
and cutting back the state, neoliberal reform was the main cause of the aggravation of the illegal drug problem. Overall, this view would imply that
democratic transition has been the passive victim of an economic program
that has undermined its legitimacy and reduced its effectiveness. Hence, a revision of the economic program would seem advisable, but a new approach
to democratic change would not be necessary.

This text has showed that such a view is misleading. Democratic transition has had an independent and decisive effect on the problems analyzed here. In the first place, the historical association of neoliberal reform and democratic transition is not a necessary one. Neoliberal systems have flourished under openly dictatorial governments, as the classical case of Chile illustrates. In addition, as the Southern European cases show, democratic change does not need to confine itself within purely procedural limits. Moreover, while not devoid of political effects, when implemented in relatively egalitarian and economically complex nations, neoliberal reform does not necessarily provoke the large-scale corruption of democracy.

While the exclusive focus on neoliberalism would perhaps explain the aggravation of socioeconomic inequality and poverty, it could not account for the corruption of formal democratic procedures. For it is the *combination* of neoliberal policies and competitive elections—in the context of widespread poverty and high economic inequality—that explains the survival of "authoritarian" practices. It is also this combination that encourages democratic political leaders and large numbers of citizens to preserve that socioeconomic situation. Therefore, the analysis of neoliberalism would not explain why purely procedural democratic change ends up legitimating practices and policies that preserve poverty and inequality. Even if there were no neoliberal ideology, purely procedural democratic change in highly unequal societies with massive poverty would most likely provoke the corruption of formal democratic rules.

Neoliberalism inspired several socioeconomic changes that led to insurgency. Yet, it is not responsible for the interaction of insurgency and electoral cycles, the government's unwillingness to eliminate insurgency, and the insurgents' incapacity (and unwillingness) to openly challenge the government. Whether or not it was implementing a neoliberal reform, an openly authoritarian regime would not feel compelled to deal mildly with insurgency; insurgents would not fear the political and ideological costs of openly confronting such a regime. Alternatively, a well established democratic government could rely on its democratic legitimacy to either launch a decisive offensive against its armed opponents or seek a negotiated settlement with them. Indeed, under such a regime, the rebels would not enjoy the passive or active support of large sectors of the population and would most likely become mere terrorists. It is the combination of socioeconomic deprivation (independently of whether it was provoked by neoliberal reform) and an indecisive democratic regime that reduces the reach of democracy and tends to make rebellion chronic.

Finally, the focus on neoliberalism would account for several economic changes that push some impoverished sectors into the illegal drug business and undercut the state's capacity to control criminal organizations. However, it could not explain the interaction between democratic transition and the illegal drug trade. Particularly, it would not explain how—by weakening the state and the regime, dispersing law-enforcement responsibilities, and increasing the need for campaign funding—democratic transition tends to worsen the illegal drug problem and deters authorities from adopting an innovative and audacious approach toward illegal drugs.

4. DEMOCRATIC TRANSITION AND LEGITIMACY

As said above, political change in late twentieth-century Mexico is a mix of four interrelated subsets: the adoption of democratic procedures, a number of seemingly "anomalous" changes and continuities, a weakened regime and state, and a persistently unequal distribution of social, economic, and political power. By referring to this entire process as a *democratic transition*, one explicitly or implicitly overestimates its democratic part. Doing so has important ideological consequences: it covers the entire system with the legitimating mantle of democracy, boosts the idea that the system is basically fair, underplays the importance of its non-democratic components, ignores its deep internal contradictions, and deters critics from openly challenging it. Paradoxically, it also contributes to a progressive disenchantment with democracy.[20]

In this, the Mexican case is far from unique. Democracy is an exceptionally potent legitimating tool. In modern times, it has become an intellectual obligation to revere it. As an often-quoted author cogently put it, democracy is "the appraisive political concept *par excellence.*"[21] In the late 1980s, after the bankruptcy of communism, the normative force of democracy became stronger than ever before, to the point that, in most of the world, no important political leader dares to openly oppose it. A consequence of this is that democracy serves to describe and justify different and often contradictory practices.

Obviously, these observations are also valid for the procedural (or "empirical") definition of democracy that underlies the mainstream literature on democratic transition. As will be discussed below, most of the "democratic" regimes established in the late twentieth century fail to meet the standards of the original procedural definition of democracy. By still calling these regimes democratic, the mainstream literature has contributed to legitimating them. The idea of democratic transition has also served to justify processes of economic reform that have worsened living standards in many countries and have increased economic and social inequalities.[22] Moreover, the idealized view of democratic transition as a moderate form of political change has been often used as an ideological weapon against revolutionary change, communism, and anti U.S. nationalism.[23]

In a more basic sense, the procedural definition of democracy that underlies the transition literature may be particularly elastic, leaving wide room for normative and ideological maneuver. It can be used to legitimize existing regimes even though they fall short of the standards of procedural democracy itself. Thus, an authoritarian regime that holds elections might be defined, rather sympathetically, as "illiberal" or "delegative" democracy (Zakaria 1997; O'Donnell 1994). An authoritarian regime that seems willing to "open" itself might be defined as "liberalizing authoritarianism" (O'Donnell and Schmitter 1986, 20–1). A regime whose electoral processes are plagued by fraud might be defined as an "imperfect" democracy or, in the worst case, as a "semidemocracy" (Diamond, Linz, and Lipset 1988/1989, 1:xvii).[24]

5. TWO TRENDS

The preceding chapters have shown that democratic transition in Mexico has coincided with a number of non-democratic changes and continuities. This is not a peculiarity of Mexico. Indeed, what the mainstream literature describes as a single wave of worldwide democratization includes two diverging trends: the establishment of a small number of new democracies and the emergence of many "other than fully" democratic regimes (Huntington 1997, 10).

Among all the "third wave" democracies of Southern Europe and Latin America, Linz and Stepan (1996, 150, 214) identified only four consolidated ones: Greece, Spain, Portugal, and Uruguay. Chile came close to fulfilling the requirements of consolidation, but the persistence of "reserved domains" for the military excluded it from the list. Their analysis of twenty-seven Eastern European cases showed a similar trend: only a few cases (the Czech Republic, Hungary, and "possibly even Lithuania") were close to becoming consolidated democracies (p. 434).[25] Other analyses confirm this view: in the former communist countries of Eastern Europe and the Soviet Union, "a handful of successful transitions and easy consolidations" coexist with "several incomplete transitions, a few transitions followed by reversion to authoritarian politics, and even some transitions that never really began at all" (King 2000, 145–6).[26]

The list of "consolidated democracies" includes all the Southern European cases, which were the initiators of the "third wave." This might suggest that the above difference is only a matter of time. However, according to Linz and Stepan (1996, 108–13), Spain's democracy was consolidated by 1982, that is to say, just seven years after the beginning of transition. Equally revealing, the pioneers of democratic transition in Latin America (the Dominican Republic, Ecuador, and Peru) are far from being consolidated democracies. This point is even clearer in the case of the former communist countries of Europe and the Soviet Union: they started their transition virtually at the same time, but only a few of them have become consolidated democracies.

Putting the difference only in terms of democratic "consolidation" might underestimate it. In reality, "other than fully" democratic regimes have many undemocratic practices, ranging from human rights violations to electoral fraud.[27] Data from Freedom House, a preferred source for contributors to the transition literature, shows that the number of "free countries" (those that respect civil and political rights) has not grown as much as the number of "democracies" (that is, electoral regimes) did. In 1974, the number of "free countries" was greater than that of democracies (44 and 39, respectively). In the year 2000, that relation had been reversed: there were 119 democracies but only 85 "free countries" (Freedom House 2000).[28]

Facing these facts, contributors to the mainstream literature have created an amazing number of "diminished subtypes" of democracy—many of which are evident oxymora—such as "tutelary," "illiberal," "hollow," or "regime-centered" democracy.[29] Whether explicitly or implicitly, the usual contention is that democracy—at its core—means "electoral competition"; and that whether it respects civil liberties, submits the military to civilian control, or makes the rulers accountable affects the "quality" but not the essence of the regime (Diamond 1999, 8–15). Only through this reduction, which shrinks the procedural definition to its minimum, is it possible to affirm that regimes with evident non-democratic characteristics are nonetheless democratic. Similarly, only in this way is it possible to affirm that the process leading to those regimes is a "democratic transition."[30]

6. WEAKNESS OF THE PROCEDURAL VIEW

As mentioned earlier, the mainstream transition literature is based on a greatly influential definition of democracy, according to which democracy is a "procedure" to select and legitimize the governing elite through competitive elections, in a context characterized by respect for civil and political rights (Schumpeter 1947; Dahl 1971).[31] In its original version, this definition resulted from two basic analytical reductions. First, starting from a critique of the "normative" or "classical" democratic theory, this definition created a new, downgraded, ostensibly empirical and realistic but inevitably normative democratic ideal. The second reduction is eminently empirical: it selects a few features of really existing democracies and, putting these features together, erects an empirical notion of "political" democracy. The politically relevant features excluded from this selection are then defined as "contextual" or "background" conditions.

In a basic sense, *democratic transition* can be understood as a systematic and conscious effort to free political change—and the study of political change—from socioeconomic factors. With this aim, the mainstream literature underscores the role of political "crafting," elites, political parties, elections, and pacts. However, for all their efforts on this score, contributors to this literature approach these factors in a complex and ultimately ambiguous way. They all reject the "modernization" view, according to which economic development directly leads to democratic change. Instead, they affirm that purposive action by the political elite (rather than socioeconomic "preconditions") is the key to democratic transition. At the same time, however, they all agree that "markets" and democracy are essentially compatible, and that, in the end, capitalist development is conducive to democratization. As mentioned above, some of them recognize that extreme economic inequality and widespread poverty can have deleterious effects on democratic development. Yet, through different analytical strategies, they systematically deny or underrate the concrete influence of these factors upon democratic transition.

As pointed out above, by the standards of the mainstream transition literature, most democratic transitions in the late twentieth century failed to "consolidate." Nonetheless, the notion of "consolidation" performs an indispensable function within the transition literature. If transition is a quick agreement among members of the elite, then a later process is necessary to solidify the agreement and trickle it down to the general population. "Consolidating" the initially contingent agreement is a lengthy process, in which structural factors play an important role. Therefore, within the transition literature, *consolidation* performs the function of smuggling back the structural factors excluded from the notion of transition.[32]

The preceding study of the Mexican case shows how misleading this procedural view can be. Contradicting the claims of the mainstream literature, this analysis shows the centrality of apparently "contextual" socioeconomic issues. As argued above, poverty and inequality largely explain the coexistence of authoritarian practices and institutions with procedurally clean elections. They also contribute to the emergence and survival of insurgency and increase the complexity of the illegal drug problem. Therefore, in a country like Mexico, with widespread poverty and extremely unequal economic distribution, distributive issues are important not only for democratic "consolidation." They are rather relevant at all stages of democratic change.

7. TOWARD A NEW INTERPRETATION OF POLITICAL CHANGE

Democratic transition is advanced as a description and explanation of macro-political change. However, the preceding analysis has shown that democratic transition, as defined by the mainstream literature, accounts only for part of the process of political change that Mexico—and many other countries—underwent in the late twentieth century.

This shows the need for a more realistic interpretation of democratization. The analysis made in this book suggests some guidelines in this respect. In the first place, it is crucial to bear in mind that democracy has a double nature. Analytically, democracy is simultaneously a descriptive and evaluative concept. As Skinner (1973) argued, applying this concept to any given political system means that such a system has a number of characteristics *and* that it is good and desirable. At the practical level, the double nature of democracy means that it is simultaneously a form of government and a legitimating tool. Therefore, as long as it remains the most desirable political regime, neither in theory nor in practice will there be an undisputed model of democracy.

Among other things, taking account of this dual nature requires one to analyze who benefits from any particular definition of democracy or democratic change. In the case of a regime that claims to be democratic or to be moving toward democracy, it is necessary to analyze the extent to which the democratic ideal materializes, or is embedded in real practices, institutions, and structures. Some gaps between ideals and practices are clearly inevitable, which means that some normative and legitimating claims of any version of democracy are unwarranted in practice. However, that gap varies across countries, ranging from those where democracy is deeply embodied in practices and structures to those where it barely exists beyond public rhetoric. In other words, the distance between democracy as a form of government and democracy as a normative and legitimizing tool is always variable. This holds not only for countries, but also for any political entity that claims to be organized democratically.

In the second place, "anomalous" or politically relevant "contextual" factors like those analyzed in this book should not be excluded from a basic characterization of political change. In principle, they are as important as the changes emphasized by the transition literature. Instead of analyzing them away as marginal or temporary phenomena, a sound model of political change should explicitly seek to include them. Only a careful empirical analysis would show the relative importance of each of those factors.

In the third place, even a procedural definition of democracy should include (in the concept itself and not as adjectives) the rule of law and the respect for civil and political rights. Doing otherwise misleadingly includes in the category of democracies cases that lack one or more central components of that definition. This shows the analytical risks involved in notions like illiberal, unconsolidated, or delegative "democracies" (see Zakaria 1997; Linz and Stepan 1996, 5–7; O'Donnell 1994; Diamond 1999).

Moreover, it is necessary not to overrate the authoritarian/democratic cleavage. Foremost contributors to the transition literature claim that during the transition the most important political contest concerns the definition of the basic rules of the "political game."[33] This would suggest that the authoritarian/democratic cleavage is analytically and practically more important than any other division. However, ideological and programmatic cleavages are, in principle, as important as cleavages over regime matters. So are conflicts motivated by the sheer desire to acquire political power.[34] In several senses, all these struggles concern the definition of basic political rules. Therefore, ideology, factionalism, and power ambitions are crucial topics in the study of political change.

In addition, it is necessary to avoid the bias toward change. Obviously, democratic transition has to do with political change. Yet, at least in principle, continuities and innovations are equally important. In countries like Mexico—with a poor democratic history—overemphasizing changes at the expense of continuities may misleadingly suggest that democratic transition entails a complete negation of the "authoritarian" past. The bias toward change could prevent the analyst from observing how continuities and innovations interact with each other. Of course, avoiding this prejudice would allow one to see continuities not as aberrations but as components of the political regime in their own right.

Furthermore, it is necessary to avoid the bias toward formal political institutions. Like in many other countries, in Mexico there has always been a large gap between the legal and real structure of power. Throughout Mexico's independent life, there has been a strong contradiction between constitutionally established democracy and authoritarian practices, as well as between legally established federalism and real centralism. Indeed, the "authoritarian" post-revolutionary regime was democratic on paper—and to some extent in practice, as well. In a context like this, the relevant question is not how democratic transition changes the formal political rules, but how such a change interacts with the informal but demonstrably enduring rules of the "old" regime.

Finally, and perhaps most importantly, it is vital not to overrate the real impact of elections. In the mainstream literature, elections are seen as the defining attribute of democracy. However, elected officials are only a small, if highly visible, part of the state, sharing power with the military, the bureaucracy, the judiciary, and several other bodies that are not subject to electoral competition and yet perform crucial political functions.[35] This warning is even more important as regards the entire political system. In a country like Mexico—where the economic elite is disproportionately powerful, the lower sectors are largely disorganized, and illegal forces are greatly influential—it is unreasonable to assume that the overall political system will become democratic just because a competitive electoral system has been established. A general view of political change, if it is to be realistic, has to look beyond competition for government and legislative posts and take account of the general distribution of political power and the basic rules governing it.

8. A REDISTRIBUTIVE AGENDA

To a large extent, Mexico's political reformism seems a sustained effort to stimulate and even manufacture pluralism. This process has served to include the opposition in the state structure. As shown above, it has also resulted in the dispersion of state capacity, making coordination more difficult and increasing the opportunities for disloyal competition among members of the political elite. Given that Mexican political parties are already competitive, some consolidation of the state and political regime would seem desirable. One specific measure would be to reduce the size of the legislatures of the country, bringing them back to their mid-1970s levels.[36] While it would be easy to implement, this reform remains unlikely, largely because of the vested interests of all political parties.

Mexico seems to live in permanent elections. This is the result of differences in municipal, statewide, and federal electoral calendars. Hence, politicians are always waiting for the next elections, which further shortens their time horizon and discourages them from making long-term commitments. Therefore, a second institutional innovation—which would only require a relatively simple constitutional reform—might be consolidating the electoral calendars of the nation.[37]

By themselves, changes like these would have no impact on extreme inequality and widespread poverty, which this research has identified as the two most important factors behind the corruption and weakness of formal democratic procedures. In Mexico and Latin America in general, poverty is largely a consequence of the mal-distribution of income and sources of income. Therefore, circumstances strongly call for the adoption of a redistributive agenda. While proposing such an agenda does not amount to putting forward a new model of democracy, it necessarily entails going beyond the procedural limits set by the mainstream transition literature. It also entails recognizing the political centrality of distributive issues.

The apparent socioeconomic "neutrality" of democratic transition is misleading. In contrast to its unambiguous injunctions against attacks on private property, the mainstream literature does not question the basic compatibility between democratic transition and the dismantlement of state or public property. Indeed, it tends to see economic changes like this as necessary for successful democratic transition, even when recognizing some of its negative consequences for social well-being (Linz and Stepan 1996, 438). Moreover, the call for socioeconomic neutrality is usually based on a biased reading of "exemplary" transitions. As the above reference to democratization in Southern Europe and former communist countries showed, successful democratic transitions did undertake far-reaching measures against poverty and inequality.

Implementing a serious redistributive agenda is necessary even for a procedural version of democracy. This shows the ultimately self-contradictory nature of the mainstream literature. This literature purports to be particularly applicable to the "developing" world, which has the worst poverty and inequality levels. However, in the context of widespread poverty and high economic inequality, purely procedural democratic change inevitably results in the corruption of democratic procedures. Therefore, in such a context, successful transition to procedural democracy needs precisely the kind of socioeconomic changes that the transition literature forbids.

Indeed, a redistributive agenda seems relevant to democratic change regardless of the version of democracy that one adopts. Some scholars and some political actors have proposed a social democratic model for Mexico. However, social democracy has thrived in countries where there is a firm alliance between social democratic parties and strong organized labor.[38] Not "class consciousness" but social dissolution and anomic, fierce struggle among the poor is the natural result of widespread poverty and extreme inequality.[39] When organized labor is weak and strongly threatened by large numbers of unemployed or informal-sector workers, unions show little enthusiasm for democracy (Bellin 2000). In the 1990s, Mexican labor closely approached this scenario.[40] Therefore, a realistic social democratic proposal necessarily has to deal with large-scale distributional issues.

A civil society-based model of participatory democracy has also been influential in Mexico and Latin America. However, several studies have recognized the weaknesses of civil society in the region (Borón 1998, 57–60; Hagopian 1998). The analysis made in chapter 4 suggests that distributional issues play a role in such weaknesses: active self-organizing, largely geared at post-material objectives, is hardly an option for people with pressing survival needs. Therefore, if civil society is to be the basis for an alternative model of democracy, distributional issues have to be seriously confronted.[41]

In the 1990s, the Mexican government tried several "targeted" social programs, notably PRONASOL and PROGRESA. Such programs met with rather negligible success, mainly because they were unable to offset the inequality and poverty arising from macro-economic changes. Compared with the problems they ostensibly sought to solve, those programs had extremely low resources. Therefore, they concentrated in poverty alleviation, leaving the issue of inequality aside.

While working out the details of a redistributive agenda is beyond the reach of this research, it seems obvious that such an agenda should have three basic components:

1.   Anti-poverty programs, both universal and targeted. Targeted programs are necessary to address the most pressing cases and should focus on the regions and social sectors most affected by poverty. Universal programs are needed to ensure that every one has access to basic services, such as education and health care. In distinguishing between universal and targeted programs, one has to recall that the latter are not necessarily more cost-effective. The analysis of PRONASOL presented previously upholds this view.[42]

2.   A progressive tax reform. The immediate cause of the government's incapacity to address poverty and inequality has been its lack of resources. The experience of the late 1970s clearly showed the dangers of financing increased government spending through borrowing. Therefore, significantly increased fiscal revenues are necessary if the state is to perform a serious role in poverty and inequality alleviation. As explained in chapter 4, in spite of rhetorical differences, all parties in Mexico have shunned this issue. Given Mexico's current inequalities, substantially increasing tax revenues through a regressive tax reform is unthinkable. Therefore, the only way for the Mexican state to augment its resources, without incurring public deficit and without introducing further inequalities, is to increase the country's fiscal burden in a progressive manner. Apart from progressively taxing domestic economic actors, the necessary reform might include a tax on foreign capi-

tal. While not free of risks, such a tax might help cement an alliance between domestic economic agents and long-term foreign investors against international financial speculators.

3. A progressive economic development program. The linkages between economic and social policy are so strong that no social policy strategy can eliminate the imbalances introduced by a regressive economic model.[43] To substantially reduce poverty and inequality, it is necessary to redistribute not only income but also sources of income. The alleviation of poverty and income inequality can only become self-sustainable when people are given more equitable opportunities for working and investing. This obviously depends on the evolution of the overall economic structure. The main components of such a development program should be:

a. A more balanced urban/rural model. Around 25 percent of Mexico's population still lives in the countryside. The current model has privileged industrial export growth, at the expense of agriculture. Peasant agriculture has been particularly hurt. In Latin America, the experiences of Colombia and especially Costa Rica suggest that the search for economic efficiency is not necessarily incompatible with the promotion of rural growth and equity (Morley 1995).

b. More support for small and medium sized production units is indispensable. This is true for all sectors of the economy. Agricultural policy has favored big business while abandoning smaller farms to their own resources. Something similar has happened in the industrial and service sectors. The overall incentive structure of the economy should change from its current bias toward big business to a more balanced approach. Among other things, this would entail substantial changes to the government's policies on trade, taxation, and investment.

c. Public investment for infrastructure, especially in currently abandoned economic sectors and regions. This is especially urgent for small and medium sized agricultural production units. Only a vigorous infrastructure-building effort (especially in roads, communication, irrigation, drainage, and technical training) will help small and medium sized farms become competitive. The same is true for industrial and service businesses. Moreover, a decisive infrastructure building effort will help marginal regions overcome their status as self-perpetuating poverty pockets.

d. Higher investment in education and research. In many respects, the Mexican education system is far below international standards.

However, human capital is a privileged economic asset, and education greatly contributes to its development. Moreover, education can also have important distributive implications, facilitating social mobility.

e.   A progressive wage policy. Wages in Mexico, as well as in most Latin American countries, have not come back to their pre-crisis levels. Given the weak structural situation of labor in the region, government neutrality—even if it explicitly recognizes the unions' right to fight for better salaries—would be insufficient. Therefore, wage improvement should also be a component of the overall economic development strategy. Productive rather than cheap labor force is the real asset that a country like Mexico could use to become competitive. It would be impossible to improve the productivity of Mexican labor without improving salaries.

Postponing distributional issues to a "post-transition" stage is as misleading as affirming that a country needs to be egalitarian before it begins moving toward democracy. As said earlier, the analysis of the Mexican case shows that distributional issues are relevant at all stages of democratic change. Indeed, the overall evolution of the "third wave" suggests that extreme inequality and purely procedural democratic transition might combine to make democratic "consolidation" unreachable. Recognizing this gives one a more realistic view of the relationship between democratic change and conflict.

Much of the appeal of the transition literature comes from its praise of moderate, peaceful political change. At first sight, this belief seems well-founded: the "third wave" commenced with the Portuguese "Carnation Revolution"—named after the flowers with which the rebel soldiers blocked the barrels of their guns—and reached its peak in 1989, with the "Velvet Revolutions" of Eastern Europe. Moreover, as that literature highlights, democratic transitions encompassed a series of compromises, in which violence played only a secondary role. Compared to previous processes of political change, late-twentieth century democratic transitions seem eminently peaceful.

Such a view, however, is misleading. By emphasizing moderation and compromise, the transition literature often implies that strong conflict is absolutely harmful to democratic change. Nevertheless, as is usually the case in politics, the connection between conflict and democratization is far more ambiguous. In the first place, without the previous defeat of armed insurgency, the political, military, and economic elite of many Latin American countries would never have consented to the establishment of elected civilian governments in the 1980s and 1990s. Similarly, it is impossible to fully understand the fall of Communism without heeding the crucial importance of the "Red Army's" retreat from Eastern Europe. Therefore, it seems that conflicts did play an important role in making the "third wave" of democratization possible.

The experience of now stable democracies confirms this. Democracy may be a regime that processes conflicts in a civilized and inclusive way, but this does not necessarily mean that the path leading toward it is equally mild. The most well-known democratic regimes usually came into existence after the end of long and often violent conflicts. Indeed, the establishment of democracy through peaceful and democratic ways seems a historical rarity.[44]

By recognizing the complex relation between democracy and conflict one can make a more realistic assessment of past democratization processes and realize the potentially constructive role of conflict. In the Mexican case, it seems obvious that implementing an ambitious redistributive agenda will inevitably provoke some level of confrontation. By definition, a progressive tax reform means imposing higher taxes on people with higher income. A negative reaction from the potentially affected sectors is foreseeable. Other components of a progressive economic program might elicit a similar response. In the worst scenario, such a conflict may even result in the temporary violation of some formal democratic procedures. But the alternative seems even bleaker: avoiding such an agenda is most likely to result in the progressive corruption of democratic procedures and the persisting risk of a major violent outbreak.

Recognizing the fact that some level of conflict is inevitable does not amount to adopting a pessimistic view. Indeed, there are many ways to minimize such a conflict. A vacillating attitude by political leaders would encourage the economic elite to try a number of subterfuges to prevent the redistribution process. This would increase the risk that the struggle over distributive issues might escalate into a major civil contest. Paradoxically, taking the possibility of conflict very seriously from the start is the best way of avoiding a major violent confrontation in the future.

A frequent deterrent of innovative political action in the "Third World" has been the risk of capital flight. While this is a serious possibility, it is not as overwhelming as it might seem at first sight. In many instances, the "business community" fails to act as a true community. Its members have diverging interests and react contrastingly to similar policies. Some international investors (notably mutual-fund managers) are overridingly concerned with obtaining high interest rates, but others (especially stockholders and direct investors) are more interested in growth, and may even consent to an "expansionary fiscal policy" (Maxfield 2000, 101–3). It seems that the latter group would be less resistant to an orderly implemented and firmly backed distributive agenda. Similar differences exist among domestic investors. Moreover, a distributive program would transfer domestic resources from non-productive to productive use. This would make the country less dependent upon foreign capital.

By "Third World" standards, Mexico has a sizable economy and occupies an important position in the structure of world trade. Therefore, international investors cannot afford to stay out of the country for a long time; disinvestment by some firms would be countered by investment from others. This can be a highly effective deterrent of capital flight.

Moreover, anti-poverty and distributive measures can have several positive effects for the "business community." In the medium to long term, decisive anti-poverty action will create better conditions for investing. As chapter 5 analyzed, participation in organized crime is motivated both by survival needs and the expectation of huge profits, a combination that substantially complicates law enforcement. Reducing the survival motivation will surely make anti-crime policies more legitimate and effective.[45] Doing this evidently requires that the legal economy give greater opportunities to people now living in poverty. Less criminality will make the country more attractive to legal investment. Moreover, the adoption of a progressive tax system may be combined with decisive anticorruption measures. In practice, this would mean eliminating illegal "taxes" on business. In many other direct and indirect ways, reducing poverty and inequality would reduce social and political instability. This would make for a more predictable environment, which is a precondition for long-term investment.

On balance, however, it seems unlikely that the business elite will endorse a redistributive agenda unless it is firmly backed by well organized forces and determined leaders.[46] It is crucial, therefore, that the promoters of enduring democracy ally themselves with the potential beneficiaries of redistribution. Coupled with the positive arguments mentioned above, the mobilization of these forces can make the economic elite accept the new rules of the game.

Ultimately, whether a far-reaching distributive agenda will be adopted depends on the existence of a "distributive coalition": strong organized groups and determined leaders bent on breaking the inertia introduced by the "blind" operation of formal democratic procedures. This view—with its reliance on political will and positive leadership—might seem too utopian. Yet, it is not more unrealistic than trying to build stable democracy upon persistent inequality and poverty.

The "third wave" of democratization, which affected dozens of countries around the world, is a truly global phenomenon. So is the expansion of weak, unstable, contradictory, and superficial democracy. The end of the Cold War, a process of economic "globalization" that increases the power of transnational economic elites and their allies, the apparent predominance of economic and political liberalism, the discrediting of military dictatorship, the defeat of insurgency in many countries—all combined to create a negative transnational democratic consensus. Dominant political actors loudly voice their democratic commitments—as long as democratic competition does not interfere with the basic transnational distribution of political and economic power.

This makes it clear that the struggle for enduring democracy has an inherent transnational dimension. Removing the domestic obstacles to the adoption of stable democracy in one country necessarily entails confronting the transnational power structure of which they are part. Similarly, a successful struggle in one country would modify this transnational structure and increase the opportunities for making similar changes in other nations. National changes are thus necessary steps in the path leading beyond the global predominance of purely procedural—that is, largely cosmetic—democracy.

Appendix
Tables and Figures

Table 2.1 Votes for the Mexican Presidency, 1976–2000 (Percentage*)

	1976	1982	1988	1994	2000
PAN		16.4	16.9	26.7	43.5
PRI	93.9	71.7	51.0	50.2	36.9
PPS	3.9	1.6	30.7	0.5	
PARM	2.1	1.1		0.6	0.4
PDM		1.9	1.0	0.3	
PCM/PSUM/PMS		3.6			
PST/PFCRN		1.5		0.9	
PRT		1.8	0.4		
PSD		0.2			
PRD				17.1	17.0
PT				2.8	
PVEM				1.0	
PCD					0.6
DS					1.6
Effective Number of Parties**	1.1	1.8	2.6	2.8	2.8

Sources: For 1976–94, Gómez Tagle (1997, 42); for 2000, IFE (2000)
* Null votes and votes for unregistered parties are excluded
** $N = \frac{1}{\sum p_i^2}$ (N is the effective number of parties, and pi is the proportion of votes or seats of the i-th party. See Laakso and Taagepera 1979)

Table 2.2 Distribution of Seats in the Mexican Chamber of Deputies, 1976–2003 (Percentage)

	1976	1979	1982	1985	1988	1991	1994	1997	2000	2003**
PAN	8.44	9.98	12.75	10.25	20.2	17.8	23.8	24.4	41.4	30.6
PRI	81.86	67.52	74.5	72.25	52	64	60.2	47.8	42.2	44.8
PPS	5.07	4.18	2.5	2.75		2.4				
PARM	4.22	4.64	3	2.75		3				
PDM		3.71	3	3						
PCM/PSUM		6.26	4.25	3						
PST/PFCRN		3.71	2.75	3		4.6				
PRT				1.5						
PMT				1.5						
FDN					27.8					
PRD						8.2	14	25	10	19.0
PT							2	1.2	1.4	1.2
PVEM								1.6	3.4	3.4
PCD									0.6	1.0
PSN									0.6	
PAS									0.4	
Effective Number of Parties*	1.5	2.1	1.7	1.9	2.6	2.2	2.3	2.8	2.8	3.0

Source: For 1976–94, Gómez Tagle (1997, 69–72); for 1997, Klesner (1997b, table 2); for 2000, *La Jornada* (August 24, 2000); for 2003, Mexican Government (2003, 452)

* $N = \frac{1}{\sum p_i^2}$ (N is the effective number of parties and p_i is the proportion of votes or seats of the *i-th* party. See Laakso and Taagepera 1979)

** Preliminary figures by July 2003

Table 2.3 Distribution of Seats in the Mexican Senate, 1988–2000 (Percentage)

	1988	1991	1994	1997	2000
PRI	93.8	95.3	74.2	60.2	46.1
PAN		1.6	19.5	25.8	35.2
FDN/PRD	6.3	3.1	6.3	11.7	13.3
PT				0.8	0.8
PVEM				1.6	3.9
PCD					0.8
Total Seats	64	64	128	128	128

Sources: For 1988–97, Mexican Government (2003, 452); for 2000, *El Universal* (August 24, 2000)

Table 3.1 Mexican States with Highest Proportion of Indigenous Population, Year 2000

States	Total Population	Indigenous Population*	Indigenous Population* (%)
Yucatán	1,472,683	549,532	37.3
Oaxaca	3,019,103	1,120,312	37.1
Chiapas	3,288,963	809,592	24.6
Quintana Roo	755,442	173,592	23.0
Hidalgo	1,973,968	339,866	17.2
Campeche	606,699	93,765	15.5
Guerrero	2,646,132	367,110	13.9
Puebla	4,337,362	565,509	13.0
San Luis Potosí	2,010,539	235,253	11.7
Veracruz	6,118,108	633,372	10.4
Nayarit	815,263	37,206	4.6
Tabasco	1,664,366	62,027	3.7
Other	56,085,826	1,057,411	1.9
Total Mexico	84,794,454	6,044,547	7.1

Source: INEGI (2001)
* Number (or percentage) of people five years or older who speak an Indian language

Table 3.2 Mexican States with Highest Marginality Index, 1995

State	Marginality
Chiapas	2.36
Guerrero	1.91
Oaxaca	1.85
Veracruz	1.13
Hidalgo	1.00
Yucatán	0.80
Puebla	0.80
Campeche	0.78
San Luis Potosí	0.76
Tabasco	0.67

Source: Conapo/Progresa (1997)

Table 4.1 Percentage of Votes by Marginality Level and State in the Presidential Election of the Year 2000*

State	Marginality Index	Degree of Marginality	Fox (PAN)	Labastida (PRI)	Cárdenas (PRD)	Void %
Chiapas	2.36	Very High	26.4	43.1	25.0	4.1
Guerrero	1.91	Very High	18.6	42.6	35.2	2.2
Oaxaca	1.85	Very High	26.4	42.7	24.9	3.5
Veracruz	1.13	Very High	39.9	37.7	18.4	2.2
Hidalgo	1.00	High	34.6	43.5	16.7	2.4
Yucatán	0.80	High	47.1	46.1	3.9	1.9
Puebla	0.80	High	42.5	40.6	12.1	2.6
Campeche	0.78	High	40.0	40.8	13.4	3.6
San Luis Potosí	0.76	High	47.5	39.0	8.7	2.7
Tabasco	0.67	High	25.6	39.4	31.3	2.1
Zacatecas	0.60	High	33.5	38.8	23.1	2.4
Michoacán	0.39	High	28.6	30.2	37.1	2.1
Guanajuato	0.13	Medium	60.8	27.9	6.5	2.7
Nayarit	0.05	Medium	30.1	48.7	17.7	2.0
Durango	0.00	Medium	41.9	44.2	10.1	1.8
Querétaro	−0.19	Medium	51.9	34.4	7.1	2.5

(continued)

Table 4.1 Percentage of Votes by Marginality Level and State in the Presidential Election of the Year 2000* *(continued)*

State	Marginality Index	Degree of Marginality	Fox (PAN)	Labastida (PRI)	Cárdenas (PRD)	Void %
Sinaloa	−0.21	Medium	23.8	63.9	9.4	1.6
Quintana Roo	−0.22	Medium	46.2	32.9	17.6	1.8
Tlaxcala	−0.23	Medium	35.4	36.4	23.6	1.9
Morelos	−0.55	Low	45.5	30.3	19.4	1.9
Tamaulipas	−0.58	Low	47.4	40.5	8.3	1.8
Jalisco	−0.60	Low	53.1	35.9	6.2	1.9
Colima	−0.71	Low	48.4	36.9	10.6	2.0
Estado de México	−0.74	Low	43.7	32.0	18.8	1.8
Chihuahua	−0.78	Low	48.7	40.8	6.8	1.9
Baja California Sur	−0.84	Low	36.2	33.5	26.9	1.6
Sonora	−0.85	Low	50.8	33.6	13.0	1.5
Aguascalientes	−1.05	Very Low	53.9	33.9	7.0	1.7
Coahuila	−1.18	Very Low	48.9	38.2	9.5	1.5
Baja California	−1.27	Very Low	49.7	37.0	9.0	1.7
Nuevo León	−1.50	Very Low	49.6	40.2	6.3	1.8
Distrito Federal	−1.74	Very Low	43.6	24.0	25.9	1.7
National			42.5	36.1	16.6	2.1

Source: Conapo/Progresa (1997) and IFE (2000)
* The PAN and the PRD candidates were supported by electoral coalitions that included several small parties

Table 4.2 Percentage of Votes by Marginality Level in the Presidential Election of the Year 2000*

Degree of Marginality	Fox (PAN)	Labastida (PRI)	Cárdenas (PRD)	Void
Very High	31.3	40.5	23.6	2.8
High	37.3	38.9	19.4	2.4
Medium	45.6	39.9	10.2	2.2
Low	47.2	34.6	13.5	1.8
Very Low	46.5	30.4	17.8	1.7
National	42.5	36.1	16.6	2.1

Source: Conapo/Progresa (1997) and IFE (2000)
* The PAN and the PRD candidates were supported by electoral coalitions that included several small parties

Table 4.3 Percentage of Votes for the Winner and for the Candidates of the Two "Most Traditionalist" Parties in the Presidential Election of the Year 2000

Degree of Marginality	Fox (PAN)	Labastida-Cárdenas (PRI-PRD)	Void
Very High	31.3	64.1	2.8
High	37.3	58.3	2.4
Medium	45.6	50.1	2.2
Low	47.2	48.1	1.8
Very Low	46.5	48.2	1.7
National	42.5	52.7	2.1

Source: Conapo/Progresa (1997) and IFE (2000)
* The PAN and the PRD candidates were supported by electoral coalitions that included several small parties

Table 4.4 Correlation between Marginality Index and Percentage of Votes for the Main Presidential Candidates in the Year 2000

	Marginality Index	Significance Level
Fox (PAN)	−0.61	1%
Labastida (PRI)	0.36	5%
Cárdenas (PRD)	0.40	5%
PRI-PRD	0.59	1%
Void	0.76	1%

Source: Table 4.1

Table 4.5 Percentage of Votes by Marginality Level and State in the Legislative Election of 1997*

State	Marginality Index	Degree of Marginality	PAN	PRI	PRD	VOID
Chiapas	2.36	Very High	12.4	48.2	28.1	5.3
Guerrero	1.91	Very High	5.6	44.9	41.3	2.7
Oaxaca	1.85	Very High	12.2	47.9	29.5	4.4
Veracruz	1.13	Very High	20.9	42.3	26.1	3.1
Hidalgo	1.00	High	15.6	48.4	25.8	3.5
Yucatán	0.80	High	37.5	49.7	7.2	2.6
Puebla	0.80	High	24.7	46.9	17.4	3.8
Campeche	0.78	High	7.8	45.8	34.9	3.6

(continued)

Table 4.5 Percentage of Votes by Marginality Level and State in the Legislative Election of 1997* *(continued)*

State	Marginality Index	Degree of Marginality	PAN	PRI	PRD	VOID
San Luis Potosí	0.76	High	36.6	42.1	10.3	4.0
Tabasco	0.67	High	4.5	50.2	39.6	2.9
Zacatecas	0.60	High	25.2	49.1	13.6	2.5
Michoacán	0.39	High	17.5	34.8	39.2	2.7
Guanajuato	0.13	Medium	41.6	33.2	12.6	3.2
Nayarit	0.05	Medium	22.9	49.7	20.3	2.2
Durango	0.00	Medium	23.8	37.3	10.5	2.3
Querétaro	−0.19	Medium	43.9	35.6	9.1	3.1
Sinaloa	−0.21	Medium	29.4	41.8	22.2	2.0
Quintana Roo	−0.22	Medium	22.7	45.6	22.8	2.7
Tlaxcala	−0.23	Medium	19.0	42.0	23.1	3.1
Morelos	−0.55	Low	15.4	35.5	39.1	2.4
Tamaulipas	−0.58	Low	18.2	46.7	26.1	2.6
Jalisco	−0.60	Low	43.6	34.8	11.4	2.6
Colima	−0.71	Low	37.6	36.5	19.3	2.5
Estado de México	−0.74	Low	19.4	34.3	33.3	2.7
Chihuahua	−0.78	Low	40.0	40.9	10.0	2.9
Baja California Sur	−0.84	Low	18.7	48.5	12.1	2.1
Sonora	−0.85	Low	30.5	36.8	26.9	2.2
Aguascalientes	−1.05	Very Low	35.4	41.2	12.7	2.6
Coahuila	−1.18	Very Low	29.8	47.8	13.8	1.7
Baja California	−1.27	Very Low	41.8	34.6	13.1	3.3
Nuevo León	−1.50	Very Low	48.1	39.4	2.9	2.3
Distrito Federal	−1.74	Very Low	17.6	23.1	44.3	2.2
National			25.9	38.0	25.0	2.8

Source: Conapo/Progresa (1997) and IFE (1997)
* Chamber of Deputies (300 single-member districts)

Table 4.6 Percentage of Votes in the Most Marginal Municipalities in the Legislative Election of 1997*

	PAN	PRI	PRD	VOID
100 Most Marginal Municipalities in the Country	6.3	58.2	20.5	8.4
National	25.9	38.0	25.0	2.8

Source: Conapo/Progresa (1997) and IFE (1997)
* Chamber of Deputies (300 single-member districts)

Table 4.7 Percentage of Votes in the Most Marginal and Least Marginal Municipality of Every State in the Legislative Election of 1997*

| | PAN | | PRI | | PRD | | VOID | |
State	MMM**LMM***		MMM	LMM	MMM	LMM	MMM	LMM
Aguascalientes	14.5	37.8	56.1	37.8	20.2	13.1	3.6	2.6
Baja California	38.2	45.1	35.9	32.7	15.2	11.3	3.4	3.2
Baja California Sur	31.3	9.5	41.2	50.9	22.6	11.1	1.8	2.3
Campeche	4.3	15.6	55.3	38.8	26.7	32.5	4.8	3.9
Chiapas	2.0	22.3	54.0	32.6	38.1	33.0	4.6	2.6
Chihuahua	14.2	39.6	62.1	41.8	2.1	10.0	14.2	2.0
Coahuila	8.7	40.1	71.6	38.4	4.7	13.2	1.9	1.5
Colima	32.6	41.6	56.2	31.7	4.4	20.1	3.5	2.7
Distrito Federal	8.1	30.7	25.2	20.9	54.9	34.9	2.9	1.6
Durango	12.2	21.3	56.4	26.0	8.8	6.6	4.5	2.5
Guanajuato	31.8	55.8	50.1	30.6	5.5	5.4	9.0	2.4
Guerrero	1.6	4.4	40.6	38.5	50.0	52.3	6.2	1.6
Hidalgo	22.8	11.1	44.6	34.0	22.1	40.0	8.1	2.4
Jalisco	30.3	48.3	54.6	30.9	4.7	10.5	4.8	2.4
Estado de México	15.9	28.1	69.8	31.9	6.4	26.9	4.6	1.7
Michoacán	0.5	24.5	45.3	29.7	46.5	33.2	1.8	2.5
Morelos	4.6	23.9	34.2	36.6	50.4	30.0	2.2	2.2
Nayarit	3.4	22.4	74.9	43.6	14.2	25.9	3.9	2.2
Nuevo León	7.5	61.6	75.9	32.2	7.7	1.7	4.5	1.2
Oaxaca	6.9	27.7	16.4	34.9	47.7	29.5	10.9	1.7
Puebla	7.7	32.8	78.7	38.4	3.6	16.7	7.1	2.9
Querétaro	10.1	53.3	58.4	27.5	5.7	8.7	4.8	2.4
Quintana Roo	16.1	25.8	60.3	37.2	17.3	29.2	3.1	1.9
San Luis Potosí	1.6	47.7	55.0	36.6	35.0	7.8	7.8	2.3
Sinaloa	9.8	29.3	80.9	30.9	4.3	29.7	3.6	2.2
Sonora	0.6	45.9	53.9	39.4	43.9	9.7	1.0	2.2
Tabasco	10.6	8.4	54.8	50.4	30.3	34.3	3.0	2.4
Tamaulipas	0.2	6.9	95.3	27.0	3.3	60.1	0.5	1.5
Tlaxcala	7.9	21.7	74.7	37.4	5.6	24.9	4.1	2.2
Veracruz	12.4	3.1	52.0	52.6	8.9	39.6	20.6	1.8
Yucatán	18.0	51.2	69.6	34.4	9.5	7.1	2.8	2.9
Zacatecas	17.2	26.5	55.0	44.8	20.3	13.6	4.2	2.0
National	15.1	37.8	49.6	34.2	25.2	16.8	4.1	2.4

Source: Conapo/Progresa (1997) and IFE (1997)
* Chamber of Deputies (300 single-member districts)
** MMM: most marginal municipality
*** LMM: least marginal municipality

Table 4.8 Percentage of Votes for the PRI Presidential
Candidates in Each Educational Category, 1988–2000

Education	1988	1994	2000
None		64	46
Primary	63*	58	46
Secondary	56	49	34
Preparatory	47	40	28
University	51	41	22

Source: For 1988, IMOP S.A. (Gallup), cited in Dominguez
and McCann (1996, 99); for 1994, Mitofsky International,
cited in Dominguez and McCann (1996, 203); for 2000,
Reforma (July 3, 2000)
* Includes voters with no schooling

Table 4.9 Percentage of Votes by Marginality Level and State in the
Legislative Election of 2003*

State	Marginality Index	Degree of Marginality	PAN	PRI**	PRD	VOID
Chiapas	2.2507	Very high	19.0	40.7	21.0	4.0
Guerrero	2.1178	Very high	6.2	42.3	39.4	3.0
Oaxaca	2.0787	Very high	19.3	46.5	18.4	4.3
Veracruz	1.2776	Very high	35.1	37.7	12.4	2.6
Hidalgo	0.8770	Very high	23.4	47.9	17.1	3.3
San Luis Potosí	0.7211	High	44.1	39.9	8.8	4.9
Puebla	0.7205	High	34.6	46.1	7.9	3.9
Campeche	0.7017	High	40.0	42.2	2.5	5.0
Tabasco	0.6554	High	6.4	49.4	37.7	2.5
Michoacán	0.4491	High	20.1	29.9	36.7	4.0
Yucatán	0.3813	High	44.2	46.9	5.4	2.7
Zacatecas	0.2984	High	12.8	29.2	46.8	2.7
Guanajuato	0.0797	High	45.3	32.4	12.7	3.8
Nayarit	0.0581	High	24.6	50.4	10.6	2.4
Sinaloa	−0.0996	Medium	25.7	52.1	12.8	2.3
Querétaro	−0.1073	Medium	44.7	39.0	8.0	3.3
Durango	−0.1139	Medium	28.5	54.9	4.1	3.2
Tlaxcala	−0.1849	Medium	12.6	36.4	33.4	3.5
Morelos	−0.3557	Medium	30.3	28.6	20.7	3.6

(continued)

Table 4.9 Percentage of votes by Marginality Level and State in the
Legislative Election of 2003* *(continued)*

State	Marginality Index	Degree of Marginality	PAN	PRI**	PRD	VOID
Quintana Roo	−0.3592	Medium	23.9	38.9	8.0	3.0
Estado de México	−0.6046	Low	30.6	36.6	24.3	3.6
Colima	−0.6871	Low	40.7	40.3	12.5	2.4
Tamaulipas	−0.6905	Low	31.7	50.1	7.9	3.0
Sonora	−0.7559	Low	40.6	41.0	11.5	2.8
Jalisco	−0.7608	Low	39.7	40.3	6.8	2.3
Chihuahua	−0.7801	Low	39.1	49.3	6.5	4.0
Baja California Sur	−0.8017	Low	14.9	30.2	45.0	3.9
Aguascalientes	−0.9734	Low	44.0	40.2	7.1	3.5
Coahuila	−1.2020	Very low	33.6	47.3	6.5	2.8
Baja California	−1.2685	Very low	43.8	33.5	6.6	4.2
Nuevo León	−1.3926	Very low	36.9	52.2	2.2	3.3
Distrito Federal	−1.5294	Very low	26.9	12.3	44.6	3.9
National			31.8	38.1	18.2	3.4

Source: Conapo (2001) and IFE (2003)
* Chamber of Deputies (300 single-member districts)
** Includes the votes of the PRI-PVEM alliance

Table 4.10 Evolution of Poverty and Extreme Poverty in Mexico,
1984–1998 (Percentage of People)

	1984		1989		1992		1994		1996		1998	
Source	P*	EP*	P	EP	P	EP	P	EP	P	EP	P	EP
World Bank					40.0	14.9						
Lustig	28.5	13.9	32.6	17.1	31.3	16.1	31.8	15.5				
Aguilar Gutiérrez	38.8						73.3		78.7	24.4		
ECLAC			48	19			45	17	52	21	47	29

Sources: World Bank (2000, table 4), Lustig (1998, 202), Aguilar Gutiérrez (2000,
72–7), ECLAC (2000, 40, 42)
* P: poverty; EP: extreme poverty

Table 4.11 Tax Burden in Mexico, 1990–2003 (Federal Tax Income as a Percentage of GDP)

Year	Tax Burden	Year	Tax Burden
1990	10.8	1997	9.8
1991	10.8	1998	10.5
1992	11.3	1999	11.3
1993	11.4	2000	10.6
1994	11.3	2001	11.3
1995	9.3	2002	11.6
1996	8.9	2003	11.3

Source: Own calculation based on data from SHCP (2004) and INEGI (2004)

Table 5.1 Drug Production and Trafficking in Mexico, 1990–2002

Year	Arrests	Eradication (ha)		Seizures (mt)					Estimated Production (mt)*	
		Cannabis	Opium	Cannabis	Cocaine	Opium	Heroin	Methamphetamine*	Cannabis	Opium
1990	18,374	8,778.24	8,660.44	594.78	49.88	0.209	0.212		19,715	62
1991	8,762	12,702.25	9,342.36	254.96	50.27	0.095	0.146		7,775	41
1992	27,577	16,801.73	11,221.83	404.55	38.83	0.167	0.097		7,795	40
1993	17,626	16,645.21	13,015.17	494.66	46.16	0.129	0.062		6,283	49
1994	7,011	14,207.08	10,958.61	529.83	22.12	0.149	0.297	0.265	5,908	60
1995	9,902	21,573.30	15,389.22	780.17	22.16	0.223	0.203	0.496	12,400	53
1996	11,283	22,768.56	14,670.85	1,015.76	23.81	0.196	0.363	0.172	11,700	54
1997	10,742	23,576.07	17,732.23	1,038.47	34.95	0.343	0.115	0.039	8,600	46
1998	10,289	23,928.32	17,449.09	1,062.14	22.6	0.150	0.121	0.096	8,300	60
1999	10,732	33,351.32	15,746.54	1,471.96	34.62	0.801	0.260	0.358	6,700	43
2000	11,409	31,046.45	15,717.46	2,050.40	23.2	0.469	0.299	0.555	7,000	25
2001	9,844	28,699.2	19,115.7	1,838.8	30.0	0.516	0.269	0.396	7,400	71
2002	7,055	30,774.90	19,157.90	1,633.30	12.60	0.310	0.283	0.386	7,900	47

Source: Mexican Government (2003, 478)
* Up to 2000, data from BINLEA (2001); for 2001 and 2002, BINLEA (2003b)

Table 5.2 State Revenue in Mexico as a Percentage of Gross Domestic Product (Selected Years)

	Total Public Sector	Total Federal Government	Federal Taxes
1980	25.5	15.3	10.86
1985	30.36	16.86	10.21
1990	25.56	15.93	10.71
1995	22.99	15.24	9.26
1999	20.66	14.52	11.21

Source: Clavijo and Valdivieso (2000, 95)

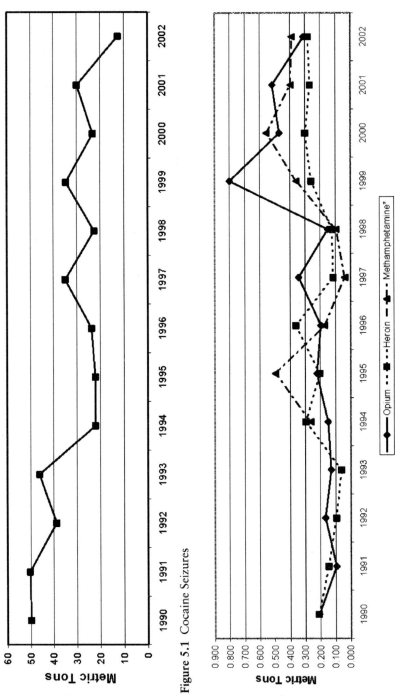

Figure 5.1 Cocaine Seizures

Figure 5.2 Opium, Heroin, and Methamphetamine Seizures

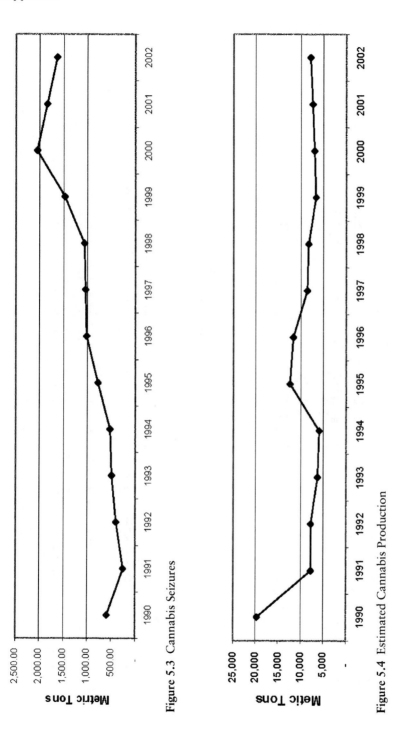

Figure 5.3 Cannabis Seizures

Figure 5.4 Estimated Cannabis Production

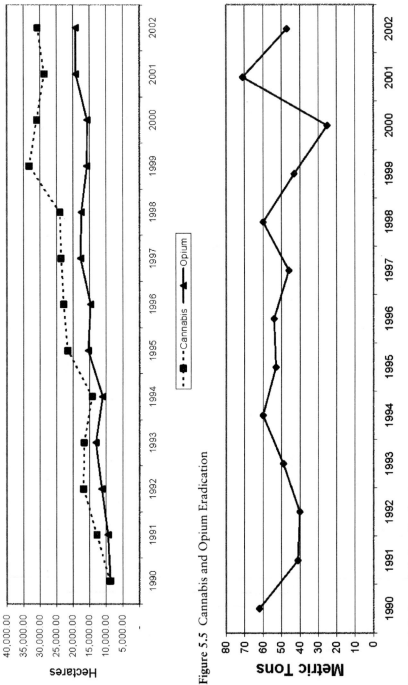

Figure 5.5 Cannabis and Opium Eradication

Figure 5.6 Estimated Opium Production

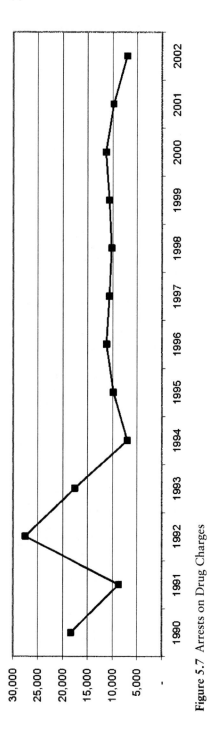

Figure 5.7 Arrests on Drug Charges

Notes

NOTES TO CHAPTER ONE

1. See chapter 6 (section 4).
2. The phrase "third wave" was made famous by Huntington (1991).
3. In the mainstream literature on democratic transition, *liberalization* means granting or extending rights such as the freedom of speech, the right to organize, and the freedom of the press. State *pluralization* takes place when politicians from different parties come to occupy different power positions in the structure of the state; it also results from legal changes that guarantee the separation of powers and the autonomy of the different branches of the state.
4. Among the most influential texts are O'Donnell, Schmitter, and Whitehead (1986), Diamond, Linz, and Lipset (1988/1989), Huntington (1991), Przeworski (1991) Linz and Stepan (1996), and Diamond (1999).
5. The acquiescence or support of decisive social forces—such as business, labor, and peasants—usually depended on the government's capacity to provide particular benefits. This "substantive" legitimacy was combined with a revolutionary and nationalist rhetoric.
6. In 1994, the "effective number of parties" was 2.8, the same as in 2000 (see table 2.1).
7. These figures include the Federal District, which politically is at least as important as a state.
8. See chapter 6, section 5. For a widely accepted definition of *liberalization*, see O'Donnell and Schmitter (1986).
9. As the U.S. State Department recognized, by 2003 the Mexican government "appeared to stall in its attempt to improve the domestic human rights situation, with a few exceptions" (BDHRL 2004). Most of the violations that this source reports took place in the states most affected by either insurgency or drug trafficking.
10. This book deals with changes that took place after 1977, but pays special attention to those that occurred in the 1990s. It also analyzes developments in the first post-PRI administration.
11. "During the transition it is always possible for some contestants to kick over the board. . . . This . . . is a threat employed frequently in the opening rounds of the game but one which loses credibility the longer play continues and the

more elaborate the rules become. Beyond a certain point, kicking or even pounding on the table may become counterproductive . . . and the committed players may well join forces to eliminate the obstreperous one" (O'Donnell and Schmitter 1986, 67).

12. "Terrorism, from having a central importance, has become a tragic aspect of life, mostly in the Basque country, but that cannot destabilize Spanish democracy" (Linz and Stepan 1996, 104).

13. The *Cristiada* (1926–29), a rural rebellion with a religious program that mobilized up to forty-five thousand combatants in western Mexico, was far more threatening. However, it took place before the consolidation of the post-revolutionary system.

14. See chapter 3, section 7.

15. To varying degrees, these practices exist in very different societies—modern or "traditional," democratic or undemocratic (Günes-Ayata 1994; Clark 1994). As the analysis of the Mexican case confirms, they all entail some kind of unequal political exchange and have deep roots in socioeconomic structures. Not surprisingly, they are more common in highly unequal societies where political participation is formally egalitarian (see chapter 6, section 5).

16. In all capitalist democracies, top business people exert far greater influence than ordinary citizens. In part, this is due to their privileged personal contacts with politicians and to their capacity to make decisions (investment, savings, and so on) that are crucial to the whole society (Lindblom 1977). It also results from their role as "political investors," providing parties and candidates with the resources necessary for modern electoral campaigns (Ferguson 1995). In countries like Mexico, with huge economic disparities, this situation seems compounded: parties and candidates are even more dependent on the support and acquiescence of the economic elite, and therefore more unwilling to undertake measures that would alter the prevailing distribution of economic assets.

17. These estimates come from Lustig (1998, 202), Aguilar Gutiérrez (2000, 72–7), and ECLAC (2000, 40, 42).

18. This figure is based on the estimation made in chapter 5 (section 2).

19. That was the title of a widely read text on Mexican politics published in the late 1990s (Oppenheimer 1998).

20. "During the transition, the property rights of the bourgeoisie are inviolable. . . . This is a fundamental restriction which leftist parties must accept if they expect to be allowed to play in the central parts of the board. . . . To the extent that the armed forces serve as the prime protector of the rights and privileges covered by [this] restriction, their institutional existence, assets, and hierarchy cannot be eliminated or even seriously threatened" (O'Donnell and Schmitter 1986, 69).

21. On the "social construction of democracy," see Andrews and Chapman (1995) and Rueschemeyer, Stephens, and Stephens (1992).

22. For an analysis of the destabilizing and corrupting effects of the U.S. "war on drugs" in Latin America and beyond, see Scott (2003) and Scott and Marshall (1998).

23. The predominance of neoliberal economics has a similar effect (see chapter 6, section 3).
24. As many analysts have pointed out, in the last decades of the twentieth century stability seemed to have been the overriding concern of U.S. policy toward Mexico (Pastor and Castañeda 1988; Erfani 1995; Baer 1999; Hakim 2001, 51–61). Moreover, since the 1980s, the United States has been a major, though often inconsistent, promoter of transition to procedural democracy in many parts of the world (see, for example, Carothers 1991, 2002; Whitehead 1996).
25. For specific proposals, see chapter 6, section 8.
26. At the beginning of the twenty-first century, the political crisis of Peru, Argentina, Bolivia, and Haiti showed the practical fragility of democratic procedures in Latin America.
27. On the weakness of popular support for democracy, see Canache (2002).
28. These and the following points are analyzed in chapter 6.

NOTES TO CHAPTER TWO

1. For references to the most well-known texts, see chapter 1.
2. In an influential text, liberalization is defined as the process of "redefining . . . extending . . . and making effective" such guarantees as the freedom of speech, the right to associate, freedom of the press, and so on (O'Donnell and Schmitter 1986, 7).
3. In another work, I made a comprehensive analysis of the mainstream literature on democratic transition (see Velasco Cruz 2003, chapter 1).
4. See, for example, the widely accepted definition made by O'Donnell and Schmitter (1986, 6).
5. The only important exception was the 1976 presidential election, when the PRI candidate was the only participant.
6. In most countries, political parties became important only after the new regime rules had been established. By contrast, political parties and elections played crucial roles at all stages of Mexico's "electoral route" to democracy (Klesner 1998).
7. See, for example, Middlebrook (1986), Woldenberg (2001, 152), Klesner (1998), Leiken (2001), and Bailey and Valenzuela (1997).
8. See Domínguez and McCann (1996, 50, 209), Domínguez and Poiré (1999, 2), Lawson (1997), Cornelius and Craig (1991, 1–4), Pastor (2000), and Levy (1990).
9. See, for example, Camp (1999a, 235–6), Domínguez and Poiré (1999, 5), Domínguez and McCann (1996, 209).
10. For widely influential characterizations of actors, see O'Donnell (1989, 64–5) and Huntington (1991, 108, 121).
11. On modes of transition, see O'Donnell (1989, 63–4), Huntington (1991, 114), Munck and Leff (1997), and Linz and Stepan (1996, 55–65).
12. Mexico's transition seems characterized by "multiple absences: no collapse, no foundational elections, no big pacts, no constitutional assembly, and no

alternation in power" (Schedler 2000, 6). Crespo (1999) analyzes several of these "absences."

13. The contradictory nature of Mexico's transition has also increased the opportunities for using democratic transition as an ideological and political weapon. Depending on their particular interests, politicians have either denounced the deficiencies of transition or hailed its advances. In doing so, each group has tried to present itself as the true promoter of democratic transition in the country (Whitehead 1994; Morris 1995, 35, 224).

14. Sources on this subject are numerous. The following review draws on Klesner (1987, 1997a, 1998, 1997b), Camp (1999b, Ch. 8), Craig and Cornelius (1995, 284–8, 290–7), Cornelius and Craig (1991, 80–3), Molinar Horcasitas (1989, 1991, 1996, 1998), Woldenberg (2001, 152), Becerra, Salazar, and Woldenberg (2000), Grayson (1998, 138–45), Lawson (1997, 15), and Domínguez and Poiré (1999, 5–10).

15. There were also minor changes in 1981–82. In December 2003, the Chamber of Deputies approved changes to the electoral legislation, augmenting the requirements for the creation of new political parties and forbidding new parties from participating in electoral alliances. In March 2004, the Mexican presidency proposed a new reform, aimed at reducing public financing to political parties; strengthening the authorities' capacity to oversee party finances; reducing the duration of electoral campaigns and party primaries; and somewhat coordinating the federal, statewide, and municipal electoral calendars (see Mexican Presidency 2004b).

16. All parties approved this reform at the constitutional stage. However, due to disagreements on party financing and coalition rules the consensus broke down when such changes were translated into ordinary laws. Nonetheless, this reform endured longer than any of its predecessors since 1977.

17. The percentage of seats allocated to any party cannot exceed in more than 8 points the percentage of votes such a party got in the elections.

18. The number of senators was doubled to 128—4 for each of the thirty-one states and the Federal District. In each state, 3 seats must go to the largest party and 1 to the second largest. After a new reform, in each state 2 seats are allocated to the largest party and 1 to the second largest party; the remaining 32 seats are allocated through proportional representation on a national basis.

19. "To prevent fraud," by 1992 Mexico had "thick books of regulations, thousands of election monitors, and a tightly centralized system." Yet, "perhaps all the laws and monitoring in Mexico [could not] compensate for the lack of confidence in the electoral process" (Pastor 2000, 20).

20. The only exception took place in 1991, when that party got 61.5 percent of the votes, 10 points above its 1988 score.

21. In the presidential contest of 1976, the "effective number of parties" was 1.1, which means that one party monopolized the votes, with the others playing an irrelevant role. In both 1994 and the year 2000, that number was 2.8 (see table 2.1). The effective number of legislative parties grew from 1.5 in 1976 to 2.8 in 1997 (see table 2.2).

22. Garrido (1982) remains the single most authoritative source on the historical origins of the PRI. For the evolution of the PRI in the 1980s and 1990s, see Morris (1995, 93–5), Camp (1999b, 172–5), Bailey (1987), Cornelius and Craig (1991, 59–73), Guillén López (1989), Hernández Rodríguez (1998), Arnaut (1997), Meyer (1989), and Garrido (1994).
23. On the PAN, see Loaeza (1989, 1997).
24. The best study of the PRD is that by Bruhn (1997a). For a quick review of the leftist forces that later joined the PRD, see Carr (1987). See also Valdés (1994) and Bruhn (1998).
25. "Although Mexico is a dozen years into a neoliberal economic restructuring program that has had great consequences for the distribution of income, for the number of Mexicans living in poverty, and for the penetration of foreign capital, goods, and services into the Mexican economy, neoliberalism was only peripherally an issue in [the 1997] election" (Klesner 1997a, 703). His analysis of the federal election of 2000 confirms this view (Klesner 2001).
26. As chapter 4 shall show, alongside this "procedural" cleanliness, there subsist important irregularities that are not strictly illegal, have some legitimacy, and relate to broad socioeconomic conditions rather than to technical aspects of the electoral process.
27. This includes the election of temporary governor for a state where "powers are declared disappeared." It also includes the election of the president and members of the Consultant Council of the National Commission for Human Rights (CNDH), the magistrates of the Electoral Tribunal, the governor of the Central Bank, and the ministers of the Supreme Court.
28. On Mexico's legislative, see Camp (1995a) and Pérez and Martínez (2000).
29. For a comprehensive analysis of the Mexican judiciary, see Fix-Zamudio and Cossío Díaz (1995).
30. Before the reform, justices were appointed by the president and ratified by the senate. After the reform, the Senate appoints—by a two-thirds majority—each justice by selecting from a three-member list proposed by the president.
31. On financial autonomy, see Domingo (2000, 715); on the CJF, see Fix-Zamudio and Cossío Díaz (1995, 552–3).
32. On the Electoral Tribunal, see Fix-Zamudio and Cossío Díaz (1995, 240–4) and Lujambio (2000, 100–12). On the judicial resolution of electoral controversies, see Eisenstadt 1999b.
33. Yet, only the Supreme Court may review the constitutionality of electoral laws approved by federal or state legislatures
34. As "the alarming persistence of human rights violations, high levels of inefficiency in the administration of justice, overburdened courts, and the continuing crises of corruption scandals" show, this "does not imply a better, more impartial and equitable administration of justice." Those deficiencies "are the consequence of deep-rooted structural problems which require more fundamental reforms at all levels of the justice apparatus and the political system" (Domingo 2000, 733).
35. For specific data, see Schedler 2000, 7 and Aguayo Quezada 2000, 260–2.

36. Figures for 1988 come from Lujambio (2000, 83–4); those for 2000 come from Aguayo Quezada (2000, 259).
37. See chapter 6, section 5.
38. A notorious exception seems to have taken place in 2000, in the election for governor of the state of Tabasco. The Federal Electoral Tribunal annulled the PRI victory, due to widespread allegations of fraud. New elections were held in 2001. Interestingly, the PRI candidate won again.
39. Scores vary from 1 (freest) to 7 (least free). For the Freedom House, "political rights" almost exclusively refer to voting, whereas "civil liberties" include "freedom of expression and belief," "association and organization rights," "rule of law and human rights," and "personal autonomy and economic rights" (Freedom House 2002a).
40. Yearly average for 1990–2001 was 3.7, whereas for 1972–80 it was 3.4. This means that, as measured by this index, Mexico's civil rights worsened during democratic transition. In 2000–01, the score was 3, the same as in 1972–73 (Freedom House 2002b).
41. A severe limitation is that both the state-level commissions and the CNDH may make only non-binding recommendations. Some CNDH recommendations, however, have had great political impact (see CNDH 1997–2003).
42. "In Mexico, where human rights abuses are a serious problem, the evidence is unequivocal that the poor are much more likely to be the victims than are members of the middle and upper classes" (Camp 1999b, 5).

NOTES TO CHAPTER THREE

1. As Childs (1995) demonstrates, Guevara dismissed this "democratic corollary" to his *foco* theory in 1963, three years after the theory's original formulation. The fact remains, however, that during the 1960s and early 1970s, leftist insurgencies were particularly unsuccessful in Latin American countries with comparatively more credible democratic credentials.
2. Another major actor is the United States. Its selective approach to illegal drugs—attacking leftist insurgents for their connections with the drug trade while supporting or tolerating right-wing paramilitary groups also involved in this trade—has been full of consequences (see Scott 2003; Scott and Marshall 1998; Chernick 1998).
3. On Colombia, see Leech (2002), Ruiz (2001), Téllez, Montes, and Lesmes (2002), Chernick (1999), Molano (2000), Vargas Meza (1998), and Pardo (2000); on Peru, see Palmer (1994) and Stern (1998).
4. In the mainstream literature, democratic transition is understood as relatively rapid, peaceful, and "procedural" political change, driven by elite pacts and competitive elections. Insurgency contradicts each of these claims. Historically, however, the Mexican case is hardly exceptional. Conflict and violence played a decisive role in the establishment of the most well-known democracies, including the United States, France, Germany, and Japan (see chapter 6, section 8).
5. This, of course, should not conceal the fact that insurgency can contribute to creating the conditions necessary for the construction of democracy. To

understand this, however, one has to dismiss core assumptions of the mainstream literature on democratic transition.

6. On the Spanish case, see also Reinares (1990).
7. See, for example, Harvey (1998) and Le Bot (1997).
8. See, for example, Gosner and Ouweneel (1996).
9. See section 2 below.
10. See section 6 below.
11. For a critical analysis of this view, as applied to Mexico, see Hellman (2000); for a more general analysis, see Kalyvas (2001).
12. Other factors, more closely related to Mexico's peculiarities, may contribute to this indecisiveness. One of them might be the desire to avoid repeating the 1968 experience, when the violent repression of the student movement severely hurt the legitimacy of the regime. Further, NAFTA and greater media coverage might have limited the options available to the Mexican state.
13. Cordoba (2000) cites two estimations of the number of EZLN combatants: 7,000 and 2,000; Wager and Schulz (1995, 10) estimate around "1,500 well-armed fighters, supported by several thousand others who are poorly armed and trained." With respect to the EPR and its offshoots, Cordoba (2000) estimates 500 combatants; Vázquez (1998) puts the number at 300; a report by U.S. News Online (1996) mentions between 200 and 2,000 fighters.
14. Compared to the EZLN, the EPR and its offshoots have smaller social bases, but have much better weapons, a more rigid military discipline, and better trained armed personnel. See Vázquez (1998), Turbiville (1997, 2000, 2001), and Simon (1996).
15. The smaller figure comes from Cordoba (2000), the larger from CIEPAC (2000). Mexican government sources usually recognize only three such groups: the EZLN, the EPR, and the ERPI.
16. They also have an important presence in the *Huasteca*, especially in the states of Hidalgo and Veracruz, a region sharing many of the socioeconomic features of Chiapas, Guerrero, and Oaxaca.
17. In its war declaration, issued on January 1, 1994, the EZLN put forward eleven demands: work, land, housing, food, health care, education, independence, liberty, democracy, justice, and peace; afterward, it has focused more on the struggle for Indian rights (see EZLN 1994a). On the EPR-ERPI, see Olmos (2001), Gutiérrez (1998, 304–16), Turbiville (1997, 88), and Lemoine (1998); the two organizations' basic documents can be seen in their respective web sites: http://burn.ucsd.edu/erpi/ and http://www.pengo.it/ PDPR-EPR/.
18. The most important instance was a bomb detonation in a Mexico City shopping center on January 8, 1994. The action, originally attributed to the EZLN, was eventually claimed by a group that later joined with several others to create the EPR (see Montemayor 1999, 34–5).
19. For an analysis of Mexico's insurgency in the 1960s and 1970s, see De Mora (1972).
20. From an exhaustive review of the literature on the subject, Coatsworth (1990) identifies six categories of illegal or extralegal rural rebellion. The Mexican insurgent movement of the 1990s does not fit any of these categories.

21. In this, Mexico's current wave of insurgency is similar to the 1810 and 1910 revolutionary movements, whose main actors had nationwide agendas, although their main social and military bases were usually rural. This, of course, should not obscure the obvious differences between those earlier movements and the current wave of insurgency in Mexico. Apart from being much larger, the Independence War and the Mexican Revolution had their main bases in some of the most developed areas of the country, whereas the 1990s insurgency developed in some of the most impoverished regions.

22. For the analysis of the EZLN's failed attempts to penetrate more urbanized regions, see Tello Díaz (2000) and Rico and De La Grange (1998). The EPR and related groups have better urban structures, but not nearly as well developed as their rural bases.

23. The figures cited above are calculated from data provided by INEGI (2001, 2000, 2004).

24. In Oaxaca and Guerrero live 3.5 percent and 3.2 percent of the country's population respectively, but their respective contributions to GDP are only 1.6 percent and 1.8 percent (INEGI 2001, 2003a).

25. In 1998, as a proportion of total employed population, rural workforce was 56.3 percent in Chiapas, 40.1 percent in Oaxaca, and 37.6 percent in Guerrero (INEGI 2000).

26. See, for example, Domínguez and Poire (1999).

27. The situation would be different if, as in post-war Japan, rural dwellers were "overrepresented." In Mexico, however, electoral districts are roughly equally populated. The presidential election is decided in a single, nationwide district.

28. The following paragraphs draw on Harvey (1994, 1998), Gramont (1996), Jones (1996), Gledhill (1996), and Pastor and Wise (1998).

29. Although it has a long history, the *ejido* sector in Mexico was a creation of the Mexican Revolution. While *ejido* land was privately exploited, private property had several restrictions. Therefore, it was considered a "social" form of land ownership.

30. "Most poor peasants are corn growers and most of the corn is grown by poor peasants" (Lustig 1992, 74).

31. General Plutarco E. Calles—one of the main founders of the post-revolutionary system—apparently understood very well the legitimating power of the *ejido* system: "This ejido question is the best way to control these people [the peasants]. You only have to tell them: 'If you want land, you have to support the government; if you are not with the government, then you will have no land'" (cited in Tobler 1990, 157).

32. As Montemayor (1999, 15–8) has pointed out, some of those regions have had recurring waves of insurgency in the last decades.

33. As a great revolutionist put it, "The mere existence of privations is not enough to cause an insurrection; if it were, the masses would be always in revolt" (Trotsky 1980, 495).

34. This situation has been somewhat modified after 1994, when the government improved the roads, presumably for military purposes.

35. See chapter 4, section 3.

36. On the crisis of the CNC, see Mackinlay (1996), Harvey (1998, 153–5), and Paz Paredes and Cobo (2000).
37. That happened with the *Ejido* Coalition in the *Costa Grande* (CECG) in Guerero and the Union of *Ejidal* and United Peasant Groups (UU) in Chiapas. See Harvey (1996, 270–5), Paz Paredes and Cobo (2000), and Legorreta Díaz (1998).
38. "Salinas was the most modern of Mexican presidents. Yet, despite pledges of reform and increased democratization, in Chiapas he chose to work with the existing (and retrogressive) power structure. Indeed, the president depended on these very elements for his own political fortunes" (Wager and Schulz 1995, 8).
39. Rojas (1995) aptly describes government repression in Chiapas before the Zapatista uprising.
40. Trying to prevent the emergence of a guerrilla group, the government of the state of Guerrero ordered the killing of seventeen unarmed peasants, most of them members of an independent organization, on June 28, 1995. Far from inhibiting political radicalization, the massacre increased the tensions in that state. For a description of the massacre, its antecedents, and immediate consequences, see Gutiérrez (1998, 119–203). See also Bartra (2000a, 2000b).
41. Harvey (1998), Tello Díaz (2000), Legorreta Díaz (1998), Wager and Schulz (1995, 5–6, 11–2), and J. Meyer (2000) analyze several facets of this intense organizational activity.
42. Two political organizations should be mentioned: the *Emiliano Zapata* National Independent Peasant Association (ANCIEZ), created by EZLN promoters in the early 1990s; and the State's Council of Peasant and Indigenous Organizations (CEOIC), created three weeks after the Zapatista uprising by sympathetic peasant organizations.
43. The best sources on these developments include Bartra (2000a), García (2000), Paz Paredes and Cobo (2000), and Gutiérrez (1998).
44. The PROCUP was founded in 1971 but its origins go back to the 1960s.
45. Officially, the EPR was the armed branch of the People's Revolutionary Democratic Party (PDPR). Lofredo (2004) makes a good description of the origins, evolution, and divisions of the EPR-PDPR.
46. According to Bruhn, who analyzed several EPR documents, "the EPR assigns an incongruously high saliency to 'elections' and 'voting,' evidently failing to see any contradiction between support for existing elections and active armed conflict. For the EPR, armed and unarmed movements are part of a seamless continuum pushing for change" (1999a, 38).
47. See Gutiérrez (1998, especially p. 234), Bartra (2000a), Lemoine (1998, especially p. 8), Rubín Bamaca (2000), Bartra (2000b, 73, 254–5, 261), and Sonnleitner (2000).
48. Solomon and Brett (1997, 25–31), Gutiérrez (1998, especially, pp. 45, 187, 201–3, and 236).
49. According to Wager and Schulz (1995, 32), the "ultimate contribution" of the EZLN might have been "that, at a critical moment in Mexican history, they forced reform on a reluctant president and an even more reluctant political system." This is also one of the main arguments in Harvey (1998).

50. For a description of the pre-electoral climate, see González Sandoval and González Graf (1995, 137–82), and Meyer (1996, 83).
51. See EZLN (1994b). Yet, the EZLN condemned the elections for governor of Chiapas held on the same day, and called for the establishment of a "transition government" in that state (Kampwirth 1996). In its efforts to make the EZLN accept or support the electoral process, the government went so far as to indirectly finance the National Democratic Convention convened by the EZLN in August 1994. See Oppenheimer (1998, 142–3).
52. For a detailed analysis of the EZLN's evolving attitude toward elections, see Viqueira and Sonnleitner (2000).
53. As chapter 5 will show, the increased presence of the military in Mexico's social life responds to two main phenomena, namely, illegal drug trafficking and insurgency. In practice, it is nearly impossible to separate the effects of each of these factors.
54. For additional analysis on the counterinsurgent role of the army, see Sierra Guzmán (2003a).
55. This figure seems clearly exaggerated, since it amounts to roughly one-third of Mexico's army. However, a review of the sources cited in this section and the author's personal observation make it clear that the government figure is an understatement.
56. For data on Oaxaca, the other Mexican state with greater incidence of insurgency, see Castro Soto (2000a).
57. For an analysis of the PFP counterinsurgent role, see Turbiville (2000, especially pp. 47–9). Formal cooperation between the army and police forces at the local level has resulted in the creation of Bases for Combined Operations (BOM). See López-Ménendez (2000, 85), Castro Soto (2000b, 110–11), and Gutiérrez (2000).
58. Many other "disappearances" occurred in the context of the government's anti-narcotics campaigns.
59. For a description and analysis of human rights abuses in the context of counterinsurgency, see AI (1998), Solomon and Brett (1997), Solomon (1999a, 1999b), and Cartwright (1999). According to the U.S. State Department, by 2003 "the Government generally respected many of the human rights of its citizens; however, serious problems remained in several areas, and in some states, especially Guerrero, Chiapas and Oaxaca, a poor climate of respect for human rights presented special concern" (BDHRL 2004).
60. See Womack (1999), Legorreta Díaz (1998), Bartra (2000a, 2000b), and Gutiérrez (1998).
61. Of course, a "third way" is also conceivable: a generous peace offer backed by decisive military action. As the following analysis implies, this option would require more, rather than less, government decisiveness.
62. See chapter 4.
63. Several authors have noticed this ambiguous situation, in which rebellion does not develop into full war but peace seems unachievable (Wager and Schulz 1995, 34–6; *Economist* 2000a; Lemoine 1998, 11).
64. See, for example, the *Commitments for Peace and Reconciliation* (reprinted in González Sandoval and González Graf 1995, 87–110)

65. For interpretations from people directly involved, see Ernesto Zedillo's letter to Luis D. Colosio (González Sandoval 1996, 118–21); Carlos Salinas' letter to the media (González Sandoval 1996, 129–34); and Manuel Camacho's letters resigning his position as peace commissioner (González Sandoval and González Graf 1995, 123–8). For a detailed description of intra-elite conflicts during 1994, see González Sandoval and González Graf (1995, 311–55).

66. For detailed description of intra-elite conflicts in that period, see González Sandoval (1996, 19–100). For an analysis of conflicts between governors and the presidency during those years, see Kaufman and Trejo (1997), Snyder (1999), and Eisenstadt (1999a).

67. The text of the law is reprinted in González Sandoval (1996, 326).

68. On August 28, 1996, the EPR attacked military and police positions in seven Mexican states (including Chiapas), leaving "at least eighteen people dead and more than two dozen wounded" (Turbiville 1997, 87). The EPR claimed to have killed at least forty-one members of the security forces and wounded another forty-eight (see Turbiville 1997, 87; EPR 1996).

69. Next on the list are Veracruz and Hidalgo, where insurgent groups have an important presence.

70. For a description of the data included into the "marginality" index, see chapter 4, section 2.

71. Indeed, it seems that the insurgent's incapacity to affect crucial business interests discourages the government from seeking any solution (military or negotiated) to the conflict. See Harvey (1999) and Conroy (1999).

72. The EZLN's thirty-four demands and the government responses are reprinted in González Sandoval and González Graf (1995, 87–110).

73. See chapter 6, section 3.

74. As of March 2004, the government's chief negotiator recognized that it would be impossible to end the conflict during Fox's presidential term. Overcoming the social and economic causes of the conflict, he affirmed, would take "decades" (Méndez and Garduño 2004).

75. See the EZLN communiqués issued on December 2, 2000, and April 29, 2001, both available online at http://www.ezln.org/documentos/.

76. See the communiqués issued on July 19–20 and August 4, 2003, available online at http://www.ezln.org/documentos/.

77. For an analysis of insurgency under the Fox administration, see Turbiville (2001, 6–7), Aranda and Bolaños (2000), and Lofredo (2004).

78. See, for example, Boyer's (1997) interview with Commandant *Antonio,* then a leader of the EPR and later the main founder of the ERPI. *Antonio* defined the current situation as one of "armed self-defense," an intermediate stage between peace and war, which "depending on circumstances . . . can last short or long." *Antonio* did not see a contradiction between armed struggle and elections. Instead, he defined armed struggle, elections, and peaceful mobilization as equally valid and complementary forms of popular struggle. See also Petrich 1997.

79. See section 2 above.

80. On the evolution of the "autonomist" movement, see Velasco (2003).

81. Many of the reasons behind the EZLN decision to define itself as an Indian organization are presented in Le Bot (1997). See also Harvey (1998, 217–23).
82. The current EPR has adopted a much more dogmatic program, calling for a Marxist revolution. Debate on this subject seems to have been a major issue leading to the division of that group. Documents of the current EPR are available online at http://www.pengo.it/PDPR-EPR/. See also Gutiérrez (1998, 305–15).
83. Relevant ERPI documents are available at http://burn.ucsd.edu/erpi/.
84. See the relevant documents at http://www.pengo.it/PDPR-EPR/.
85. For an illustrative description of these electoral costs, see Aguilar Zínser (1996).
86. Unlike many of its Latin American counterparts, Mexican insurgents in the 1970s lacked substantial international support, which surely was a major cause of their defeat. However, in that period Mexican insurgency developed within a "friendly" international environment, which gave it strong ideological justification.
87. The EPR and its offshoots have resorted to kidnapping and bank robberies to obtain funds for their military apparatus (Turbiville 2000, 48; Oppenheimer 1998). Some sources have suggested a connection between these groups and illegal drug activities, but no serious accusation or analysis has sustained these rumors (see Parker n.d.; Turbiville 2001, 6; Humphrey 2003, 5–6).
88. These casualties are probably comparable to those provoked by the direct conflict between insurgents and the government. According to a reasonable estimation, the EZLN uprising in early January 1994 left between 140 and 396 people killed (Womack 1999, 43–4). In February 2004, the EZLN issued a communiqué affirming that it lost 46 combatants and killed at least 27 members of the security forces during the 1994 uprising. A Mexican military document estimated that, as of December 1998, armed encounters between the EPR-ERPI and the security forces had left 76 people killed, 82 injured, and 169 prisoners (Marín 1999). A U.S. military document calculated that encounters between all the insurgents groups other than the EZLN and the security forces had produced an average of around 80 fatal casualties per year (Cordoba 2000).
89. Sources on the "paramilitary" groups include Womack (1999, 54–9, 340–54), Solomon and Brett (1997), Hidalgo Domínguez (2000), Castro Soto (2000b), CDHFBLC (1996), CDHMAPJ (1998), and PGR (1998).
90. Sources have documented up to ten "paramilitary" groups (Hidalgo Domínguez 2000, 153).
91. See, for example, CDHFBLC (2003). As of 2003, according to the U.S. State Department, "there were credible reports of violent incidents and killings allegedly committed by armed civilian groups and local political factions in Chiapas. . . . Human rights NGOs have accused the Chiapas state governor's administration of tolerating armed civilian groups" (BDHRL 2004).
92. Among the best-known critics are Montemayor (1999), Hidalgo Domínguez (2000), Castro Soto (2000b), López Astrain (1996), López y Rivas (2000).

93. On the evolution of the government military strategy, see Sierra Guzmán (2003a).
94. The best known case is that of "Peace and Justice." See Hidalgo Domínguez (2000, 52).
95. After 2000, when the candidate supported by the PRD was elected governor of Chiapas, there were mounting tensions between the EZLN and some followers of this party. A serious clash (leaving dozens of EZLN sympathizers injured) took place in April 2004 (see *La Jornada*, April 11).
96. This view is consistent with the case of Guerrero. The EPR and its offshoots do not control entire communities and have not concentrated their efforts in the "internal front." They have sought to engage the government forces in a more direct way; the government has adopted a similar attitude toward them. Therefore, the civilian population in Guerrero's rural areas has not had to pay the costs of a local "civil war."
97. The recent political history of Latin America might support this view. In several Southern Cone and Central American countries, democratic transition advanced only *after* the military governments had eliminated leftist radical opposition. Thus, the elimination of insurgency was a precondition rather than a result of democratic transition. This would account for the fact that these countries have not had a new wave of insurgency. However thin it might be, the consensus on electoral democracy had a firmer basis there: the radical left having been defeated, neither leftist uprising nor right-wing dictatorship finds significant supporters. Of course, extensive and careful research is needed to accept or reject this comparative hypothesis.

NOTES TO CHAPTER FOUR

1. For overview of these analyses, see Lijphart (1999) and Lijphart and Waisman (1996). On efforts at institutional reform in Latin America, see Domínguez (1998, 79–88). On the "risks" of presidential systems, see Linz and Valenzuela (1994) and Linz and Stepan (1996, 216–20). For an empirically oriented defense of the importance of regime types, see Przeworski et al. (1996, 45–8). O'Donnell (1994, 56; 1997, 46) holds that the "plebiscitary" tendencies of *delegative* democracies are largely a problem of formal "democratic institutions"; the elitist solution he proposes is worth citing: that a "decisive segment of the political leadership" realizes the "self-destructive" cycles provoked by delegative democracy and thus "agrees to change the terms on which they compete and govern" (1994, 68).
2. Wiarda has made a sustained effort to prove that the "Iberian culture" largely undermines Latin America's democratization efforts (see, for example, Wiarda 1974). One crucial question is, however, why Portugal and Spain—the cradle of the Iberian culture—have managed to establish apparently enduring democracies to a degree that seems impossible in most Latin America.
3. On this topic, see chapter 6, section 6.
4. These definitions are taken from Schmitter (1974, 93–8).

5. As section 4 below shall suggest, this authoritarian corporatism became more *social*—that is, less dependent upon the active support of the state—in the 1990s.

6. According to a very influential definition, clientelism is "a special case of dyadic (two person) ties involving a largely instrumental friendship in which an individual of higher socioeconomic status (patron) uses his own influences and resources to provide protection or benefits, or both, for a person of lower status (client) . . . who reciprocates by offering general support and assistance, including personal services, to the patron (Scott 1977, 125). See also Kurer (1997), Roniger (1990), Roniger and Günes-Ayata (1994), Eisenstadt and Roniger (1984), Eisenstadt and Lemarchand (1981), and Clapham (1984).

7. "Clientelism has been instrumental in determining the benefits that each state government receives from Mexico City. . . . The politically favored states tend to receive . . . special projects from the federal government. The central-state pattern is then duplicated at the state-municipality level" (Rodríguez 1997, 24). See also Ward (1998).

8. See also Schwerin (1973). The prominent role of violence in the above definition should not conceal the legitimacy of *caciquismo*, which comes from the *cacique*'s role as an intermediary, linking local people to national power structures (Friedrich 1977, 266).

9. Interestingly, the best study of Mexican *caciquismo* in the twentieth century is a fictional work—Juan Rulfo's *Pedro Páramo*.

10. Students of Mexican politics would hardly disagree with this other remark: "Patrimonialism gives free rein to the enrichment of the ruler himself, the court officials, favorites, governors, mandarins, tax collectors, influence peddlers, and the great merchants and financiers. . . . The ruler's favor and disfavor, grants and confiscations continuously create new wealth and destroy it again" (Weber 1978, p. 1099). See also (Kurer 1997, 74–7).

11. Thus defined, populism becomes an ideal scapegoat for current economic troubles and economic policy mismanagement. See, for example, Burki and Edwards (1996) and Dornbusch and Edwards (1991).

12. Latin American populism flourished during the period of import-substituting industrialization and found theoretical justification in Keynesian economics then in vogue (Conniff 1999, 4, 6). Nevertheless, in the late twentieth century there was a wave of neoliberal populism, with such leaders as Carlos Menem, Fernando Collor, and Alberto Fujimori (Kay 1996/1997; Weyland 1996).

13. Picking up and transporting large numbers of people to the voting booth (or to a political rally, demonstration, or the like). The PRI often resorted to this practice as a way to put pressure on voters and manipulate electoral results.

14. Coordinación Civil "Pro Elecciones Limpias" (2000). This coordinating group included nine organizations, with different political inclinations.

15. *Alianza Cívica* is perhaps the Mexican organization with most experience in electoral observation.

16. A national poll on vote buying and vote coercion found that 13.3 percent of the adult population "were reached by some social or political actor offer-

ing goods or services in exchange for their votes" or threatening them with sanctions if they failed to vote for a given party. Most of the affected people lived in poverty or "marginality" (Aparicio 2002, 95–7).

17. *Alianza Cívica* saw these perceptions about social welfare programs or secret voting as the terrain on which electoral manipulation could develop (Alianza Cívica 2000).

18. He also describes the justification given by a PRI local leader: "The law tells us that the vote should be free and secret . . . but it does not obligate the people to use the voting booth" (Sullivan 2000). Similar information is provided by Moore (2000a, 2000b), Dillon (2000), *Economist* (2000b), and Anderson (2000).

19. "Evidence from 2000 suggests that there has been a modernization of vote buying and vote coercion in Mexican elections." About "90 percent of such activities took place *before* the election day" (Cornelius 2002, 19).

20. Data on "marginality" come from Conapo/Progresa (1997). The marginality index combines data on illiteracy, educational level, availability of utilities, housing characteristics, and income level.

21. The following paragraphs partially draw on an analysis I published a few weeks after the presidential election (see Velasco Cruz 2000).

22. The correlation coefficient between marginality index and vote for the PRI candidate is 0.36, significant at the 5 percent level. This shows that the two variables are clearly associated: the more marginal a state was, the higher was its percentage of votes for the PRI. See table 4.4.

23. The correlation coefficient between marginality index and percentage of void votes is both very strong and statistically highly significant: 0.75, significant at the 1 percent level. See table 4.4.

24. See, for example, Domínguez and McCann (1996), who developed a "two-step" voting model to explain how Mexican voters made their electoral choices. See also Klesner (1997a), who underlines the "primacy of regime issues."

25. The correlation coefficient between marginality index and the combined vote for the PRI and the PRD is strong and statistically highly significant: 0.59, significant at the 1 percent level. See table 4.4.

26. In percentage terms, overall electoral support for the PRI in 1997 was astonishingly similar to that of the year 2000. This suggests that the PRI's defeat in 2000 resulted mainly from a shift within the non-PRI share of the vote, rather than from any significant reduction of the latter.

27. See, for example, Domínguez and McCann (1996).

28. This figure includes the Federal District.

29. According to an estimation made by Banamex (2000a), in the federal elections of 2000, the PRI got 43.3 percent of the votes in rural districts, compared to 30.9 percent in the urban areas.

30. Electoral data show considerable support for the PRI in Mexico City, by far the largest urban area in the country. Also significant is the fact that the percentage of votes for the PRI in this city remained virtually unchanged between 1997 and 2000 (23 percent and 24 percent, respectively). This suggests the existence of a hard nucleus of PRI supporters. The incidence of

urban marginality also supports this view: the PRI and PRD have been more successful in the two large urban areas with most marginality (Mexico City and Puebla). In contrast, the other two main urban areas of the country (Monterrey and Guadalajara) are traditional strongholds of the PAN. On urban "marginality," see Rubalcava and Chavarría 1999a, 1999b.

31. The poll was published by *Reforma* (July 3, 2000)

32. However, a statistical analysis of data colleted through a national survey of vote buying and vote coercion found no significant relation between age or sex and the incidence of these practices (see Aparicio 2002, 94).

33. Contradicting the argument that region is a major factor in explaining support or tolerance for authoritarian practices in Mexico, the year 2000 survey did not find any important regional difference.

34. The analysis of other surveys performed by Cornelius (2002) and Aparicio (2002) largely confirms this view.

35. The poll was published by *Reforma* (July 8, 2003).

36. Compared to the "welfare state" of the developed capitalist democracies, in Mexico and Latin America the expansionist state of the mid-twentieth century took on a more populist and clientelistic character.

37. For an analysis of the economic reform, see Lustig (1998); for an overview of the political side of the process, see Aitken et al. (1996).

38. This description of the PRI reform project is based on Hernandez Rodríguez (1998, 79–85), Domínguez and McCann (1996, 119–20), Colosio (1993), Arnaut (1997), Pacheco (1993), Peschard (1991), and Sales (1991).

39. "Only 4.3 percent of the PRI's 1991 candidates for the Chamber of Deputies and none of its candidates for the Senate were chosen through party primaries or nominating conventions" (Domínguez and McCann 1996, 120).

40. The first two figures come from Dresser (1991, 5), the third from Rodríguez (1997, 102).

41. See Dresser (1991), Rodríguez (1997, 76–82), Fox and Moguel (1995), and Kaufman and Trejo (1997).

42. See Bruhn (1995, 1996), Kaufman and Trejo (1997), Fox and Moguel (1995), and Cornelius, Craig, and Fox (1994).

43. In 1992, a top leader of PRONASOL boasted that the program had created over one hundred thousand committees, each with an average of 120 members. (See Fox and Moguel 1995, 192.)

44. For a full analysis of this, see Kauffman and Trejo (1997) and Snyder (1999).

45. Description of PROGRESA, taken from http://www.progresa.gob.mx/.

46. See Comisión Especial 2000 (2000). At least 42 percent of the denunciations that the Commission received involved the use of PROGRESA resources for electoral purposes. The final report presented by the Commission also denounced the use of PROGRESA resources in several state and local electoral processes in 1999 and 2000.

47. For systematic analyses of these subjects, see Eisenstadt (1999a) and Snyder (1999).

48. This election took place on February 24, 2002. The Mexican press widely documented the mutual accusations between the contenders. See, for instance, *Reforma* (February 22, 25, 28) and *La Jornada* (February 25–8).
49. See note 13 above.
50. PRI *caciquismo* also remains alive. At the turn of the century, it provoked two notorious crises. One was the "preventive" killing of seventeen peasants in June 1995, ordered by the governor of Guerrero (see chapter 3). The governor, a paradigmatic *cacique*, was removed from the post several months later, but suffered no legal punishment. In August 2000, a clash between two PRI factions for the control of a municipal government left at least ten people dead in the state of Mexico. A notorious female *cacique* was declared responsible and sentenced to jail. Yet, many other PRI caciques remained active in the country (see Cano, Nájar, and Pastrana 2000).
51. On this subject, see Middlebrook (1986, 1989, 1995), Collier (1992), Cornelius and Craig (1991, 88–92), Bellin (2000), and Murillo (2000).
52. See, for example, Middlebrook (1986, 201–2).
53. The top coordinating body within the official bloc was the Labor Congress (CT), whose main member was the Confederation of Mexican Workers (CTM). As part of his efforts to reform the PRI in the early 1990s, President Salinas proposed a "new unionism." While maintaining the alliance with the government, new unionism would be more representative of its affiliates. This proposal led to the foundation of the Goods and Services Unions Federation (FESEBES), which later provoked the division of the CT. When the FESEBES broke down in 1997, some of its organizations left the CT and allied with several independent unions to found the National Union of Workers (UNT). See Rendón Corona (2001) and Samstad (2001).
54. For an overview of changes in the Mexican labor sector during the 1990s, see Rendón Corona (2001), Samstad (2001), and Aguilar García (2002).
55. In aggregate terms, the PRI obtained more votes than any other party in state and municipal elections held in 2001 and 2002 (see Mexican Government 2003, 453–4).
56. In alliance with a minor party, the PRI obtained the largest share of the votes and the largest number of legislative seats. In both scores, its record was better than in 2000.
57. "The PRI devoted more effort than any other party to buying votes and coercing voters, but the PAN and PRD did not stay out of the game." Yet, "there are very interesting differences across parties in regard to the *effectiveness* of vote buying and vote coercion. It is clear that the PRI got the least benefit" (Cornelius 2002, 21).
58. The best analysis of this topic is Bruhn 1997b.
59. For an analysis of clientelistic practices within the PRD, see Sánchez (1999).
60. The internal election was held on March 14, 1999, annulled on April 1, and rescheduled for July 25. *La Jornada*, a Mexican newspaper sympathetic to the PRD, gave ample coverage to this process. See especially the March 15, April 2, and July 26 issues. See also Aguilar Camín (1999) and Montes (1999a).

61. The election took place on March 17, 2002. Due to numerous irregularities, the possibility of annulling it was seriously considered. *Reforma* (March 18–20) and *La Jornada* (March 17–20) published several notes on the theme.

62. Until 1997, the PRD had not won any state government and its government experience was confined to the municipality level—the lowest and weakest part of the Mexican state apparatus.

63. See, for example, Monge (2000). For a notorious case of clientelistic practices performed by PRD leaders in the Federal District, see Rascón (1999) and Montes (1999b). In March 2004, a media scandal broke out, disclosing allegedly illegal financial transactions made by René Bejarano, a PRD leader controlling a vast clientelistic network in Mexico City. Bejarano's electoral skills were widely appreciated in the PRD (Díaz 2004).

64. Baja California Sur, Chiapas, the Federal District, Nayarit, Tlaxcala, and Zacatecas. In strict sense, the Federal District is not a state but, politically, it is perhaps more important than a state.

65. There are two exceptions. One is A. M. López Obrador, who was elected mayor of the Federal District in 2000. He abandoned the PRI seven years before he got the PRD nomination. The other exception was Cuauhtémoc Cárdenas, the founder of the PRD, who deserted the PRI in 1987 and governed the Federal District from 1997 to 1999.

66. This is especially the case of Ricardo Monreal, the Zacatecas governor. The only partial exception is probably Pablo Salazar, elected governor of Chiapas in 2000, who sometimes came close to the PRD's positions in the Legislative Commission for Pacification in Chiapas (COCOPA).

67. The only exception to this trend took place in November 2001, when a PRD candidate who did not defect from the PRI won the governorship of Michoacán.

68. On the history of the National Action Party, see Loaeza (1989, 1997).

69. See, for example, Hernandez Rodríguez (1998, 72–7).

70. See Mizrahi (1995). This is why Camp concluded that, to expand its electoral base, the PAN will have to "alter its program" and "open up its recruitment practices to a larger social, geographic, and educational pool of Mexicans" (1995b, 79).

71. Analyzing the first years of PAN government in Baja California, Rodríguez and Ward (1994, 124) affirmed: "Having started its 1989 campaign with an official membership of minimal proportions, the PAN has not significantly developed its local membership." Mizrahi has argued that often the business groups with whom the PAN has established alliances have helped it win elections but have not contributed to strengthening the permanent structure of the party. Their contribution to PAN government has also been limited. See Mizrahi (1995 and 1998, 101–4).

72. "Notwithstanding the PAN's long political existence as an opposition party, it had an extremely precarious and fragile organizational structure. It operated with volunteers, had no paid professionals, had meager resources, and its cadres were mainly middle–class professionals without any administrative experience" (Mizrahi 1998, 101).

73. Ward (1995) analyzes how a combination of partial unwillingness and inability to "work within the traditional political machine" contributed to the PAN's incapacity to retain power in two very modern municipalities in Chihuahua (p. 142). However, he foresaw that electoral defeats would teach the party that "it needs to play the system a little more if it is to benefit in the longer term" (p. 144).

74. Something similar happened in other places. Mizrahi (1998, 108) cites a number of important municipalities, some in traditionally PAN areas, where the party failed to win "consecutive municipal elections."

75. Mizrahi (1998, 109). For the analysis of the Baja California case, see also Espinoza Valle (1999, especially pp. 78–82).

76. Oppenheimer (1998, 152) quotes opinion surveys according to which "political issues such as democracy and fair elections ranked low among people's concerns. Mexicans cared most about jobs, better education, better protection against crime, and even traffic jams." According to the data he quotes, unemployment, lack of money, and low wages are the top priorities of common Mexican citizens (pp. 151–5). Camp (1999a, 233–4) confirms this view: "Although Mexicans clearly express dismay with democratic processes, and with democracy as a model, they do not give its improvement very high priority compared to other, potential policy issues, namely economic concerns. . . . They ranked confronting inflation as most important, followed closely by increasing citizen participation, and maintaining order. Protecting freedom of speech ranked a distant fourth."

77. Scott (1977) made a very interesting analysis of the connection between clientelism and electoral competition. Clientelism, his analysis showed, is able to coexist with increased electoral competition. Indeed, it is capable not only of surviving, but also of becoming more influential when electoral competition becomes tighter. Hence its "inflationary character."

78. "Today's opposition movements . . . are inevitably faced with the choice between two uninviting alternatives. They may fall in with the regime. . . . In so doing, however, they will compromise their independence and foreclose the possibility of articulating a critique of the regime and its policies toward the poor. Alternatively, they may maintain a staunch independence from the regime but risk the loss of the popular support they command because members desperately need the benefits and concessions for which the organization is struggling and may not be able to afford the luxury of striking a more militant oppositionist stance. . . . Although the emergence of a new movement may challenge the old PRI-linked networks based on local caciques, it undermines the control of the caciques *only* by replacing the old networks with alternative channels that, generally speaking, are also clientelistic in their mode of operation" (Hellman 1994, 133, 128; emphasis in the original).

79. Hellman (1994) has argued that this contradiction also affects the internal life of the organizations. Most members of opposition groups are far more concerned with the organization's capacity to deliver goods than with internal democracy.

80. "The realities of pluralist politics, which reward the better organized and wealthier groups, do not justify confidence in the willingness or ability of domestic political institutions in fledgling democracies to promote the opportunities of those who are on the losing end of economic change" (Kapstein and Landa 2000).

81. See chapter 2, section 4.

82. "The problems of labor surplus and mass poverty mean that the minority of workers who are organized in the formal sector are likely to be privileged vis-à-vis the majority, an economic privilege jealously guarded by organized labor" (Bellin 2000, 184).

83. "Perhaps, and in a paradoxical way, democracy can provide the labor movement and unions in particular with a stronger negotiating power, which would allow them to resist change. Even after decades of gradual democratization, very few groups in the Mexican civil society have the same level of membership, organization, and economic resources as the [corporatist] union confederations" (Samstad 2001, 50).

84. "Capital and labor are *contingent* democrats for the very reason that they are *consistent* defenders of their material interests. Like their predecessors, capital and labor in late-developing countries will champion democratic institutions when these institutions are perceived as advancing their material interests" (Bellin 2000, 179; emphasis in the original).

85. What is important is the *combination* of widespread poverty and high inequality. In a society with massive poverty but low inequality, the members of the "elite" would have few resources to offer in exchange for political support; in a society with high inequality but little poverty, few people would feel the need to trade their votes for means of subsistence.

86. The situation of the middle and upper sectors can be very different. They do not necessarily expect direct assistance from the government; and, if they do, they have better opportunities to get it without forsaking their political rights. They have structural advantages in the political system, coming from their higher social visibility, their access to the media, and their relatively good education. People from the upper classes might also exploit the political advantages of their privileged economic position and their personal access to elected officials and the bureaucracy. In short, although people from these sectors might support authoritarian political forces, they can afford to be politically autonomous in a way that their counterparts from the lower sectors cannot.

87. See section 1 above.

88. All the estimations presented in table 4.10 are based on data from national surveys conducted by Mexico's National Institute for Statistics, Geography, and Informatics (INEGI). These data were collected through National Household Income and Spending Surveys (ENIGHs) conducted in 1984, 1989, 1992, 1994, 1996, and 1998.

89. Using two different poverty lines, Aguilar Gutiérrez (2000, tables 15 and 16) estimated that 92 percent or 75 percent of rural people lived in poverty in 1996. His corresponding estimates of urban poverty are 58 percent and 37 percent.

90. Inequality followed a similar pattern. According to Lustig (1998, 202), as measured by the Gini coefficient, inequality rose from 58.23 to 58.61 between 1984 and 1994. According to Aguilar Gutiérrez, the Gini coefficient grew from 48.4 to 63.5 between 1984 and 1996 (2000, 72–3, 76–7).

91. In June 2003, the 2002 ENIGH was made public (INEGI 2003c). According to it, average income decreased 2.6 percent from its 2000 level, but there was *also* a decrease in inequality: while the average income of the two top deciles decreased 10.5 percent, that of the eight lowest deciles increased between 1.9 percent and 7.2 percent. Based on these data, the Ministry for Social Development (SEDESOL) announced a decrease of 3.4 million in the number of people in poverty. Both the ENIGH data and the SEDESOL calculation were received with strong skepticism among academic specialists and the public. In part, the improvement may be an artifact of the measurement process: in 2002, the ENIGH questionnaire included a larger number of items and was applied to a larger sample of households than in the previous years. In so far as there was any improvement, it may have largely come from a notable increase in remittances from migrant workers in the United States. Several issues of *La Jornada* (June 18–20, 2003) and *Reforma* (June 18, 20, 2003) covered this theme. On the growth of remittances, see IADB (2003).

92. Székely (1998, 154). For his complete analysis of PRONASOL, see pp. 150–5. Lustig (1998) has also shown that, while "the poorest of the poor both in rural areas and urban areas fared better in 1994 than in 1989, this was not the case of the poorest" in the two most impoverished regions of the country, which however "were among the main targets of antipoverty programs" applied during that period (p. 205).

93. For description of the targeting mechanisms and objectives of the program, see PROGRESA (1999, 57–135).

94. For example, see Székely (1998, 105–6) and Aguilar Gutiérrez (2000, 98–9).

95. Unless otherwise indicated, all monetary figures are in U.S. dollars.

96. Bailey (1994, 97) puts the total PRONASOL budget in 1993 at 2.46 billion. Using this figure would add four cents to the average calculated above.

97. Calculations based on data provided by PROGRESA (2000, 7).

98. PROGRESA 2000 presents amounts in pesos. The following calculation is based on an exchange rate of 9.5 pesos per dollar.

99. The social policy of the Fox administration was an obvious continuation of that of the previous PRI governments (Novelo 2002; Zamarripa 2003; Lavielle, Ortiz, and Moreno 2003). It largely relied on two "targeted" antipoverty programs: *Oportunidades* (as PROGRESA was renamed) and PRO-CAMPO. No apparent effort was made to address the broad basis of poverty, especially the overall incentive structure of the economy. Even the leaders of *Oportunidades* recognize that the beneficiaries of this program may have become a large "political booty" (Guillén 2004). On January 20, 2004, the General Law for Social Development was enacted. Among other things, the law establishes that funding for poverty combat and per capita social spending must not be lower than in the preceding year and that the former must increase at least in the same proportion as the estimated GDP;

it also mandates the creation of a National Council for the Evaluation of Social Development Policy.

100. Figures for Latin America come from ECLAC (1999, 36). The other figures come from GFB (1999, 6).

101. See chapter 2. The PRI still had the majority of seats in the Senate. However, the opposition could use its majority in the Chamber of Deputies to block the Senate's decisions regarding the Federal Income Law, which would have forced the PRI to compromise. Moreover, the Chamber of Deputies' exclusive authority in determining the Federal Expenditure Budget increased the opposition's negotiating capacity in all budget issues.

102. For an overview of the debate in December 1999, see Banamex (2000b, 16, 19–20). Correa and Cruz Sáenz (2000) made a good description of the debate for the 2001 budget.

103. This analysis is based on data from Banamex (2000b), GFB (2000), Banamex (2001), and BBVA/Bancomer (2001).

104. A new special program was included in the 2000 budget to support state governments. It received the equivalent to 0.6 percent of the total budget. Compared to the budget proposed by the president, the one approved by the legislative in 1999 added 0.25 percent of the total budget to social security (retirement fund), 0.19 percent to education, and 0.1 percent to social development.

105. Compared to the budget proposed by the president, the legislative added 1.3 percent of the total budget to state and municipality funds, 0.3 percent to education, 0.3 percent to rural development, and 0.2 percent to social security (retirement fund). The congressional debate for the 2002 and 2003 budgets was very similar to that of the years analyzed here.

106. The final version of the proposal was renamed a "New Distributive Public Treasury." To ameliorate the regressive impact of the overall reform, this final version included two main compensatory elements: a monthly allotment of 108 pesos (around 11.37 U.S. dollars) to each of an estimated five million families in extreme poverty, and a "basic basket" of medicines exempt from VAT. That allotment would give each member of the selected extremely poor families around 0.08 dollars a day. For newspaper reports, see *El Economista* (April 1–5, 2001) and *La Jornada* (April 1–5, 2001); see also Mexican Presidency (2001a, 2001b).

107. On the revenue potential of the "special regimes," see OECD (1999a, 86–9).

NOTES TO CHAPTER FIVE

1. Unless otherwise indicated, all monetary figures in this chapter are in current U.S. dollars.

2. According to Smalc (2001) the illegal drug trade's estimated annual revenues of $100 to $300 billion favorably compares with automobile theft in the United States and Europe ($9 billion) and illegal people smuggling ($7 billion). The United Nations Drug Control Programme (UNDCP) estimates the drug business value at $400 billion (*Sources* 1999, 4). Das (1997, 131) cites a total estimation of $600 billion, with yearly profits of $100 billion.

3. Data from 1995 show that Colombia supplied 32 percent and Mexico 5 percent of the demand for heroin in the United States, placing total Latin American supply to the United States well below that of Southeast Asia (57 percent) (Farrel 1995, 137). As of 2000, Colombia supplied up to 65 percent and Mexico 17 percent of the demand for heroin in the United States (ONDCP 2001, 100). According to the U.S. State Department, Mexico supplied between 30 and 40 percent of the U.S. heroin market in 2003 (BINLEA 2004, 12).

4. According to U.S. sources, global cocaine production reached 715 metric tones in 1995 (Umberg 1999; DEA 1996).

5. "Though Mexico is the principal foreign supplier of methamphetamine and precursors for the United States, we also have our own domestic methamphetamine production, as demonstrated by DEA's seizure of over 1,810 methamphetamine laboratories in 2000. State authorities seized thousands more" (BINLEA 2001).

6. U.S. "cannabis crop . . . is worth up to $25 billion annually, which makes it one of the top three 'agricultural' products in the United States along with soya beans and corn" (*Sources* 1999, 4).

7. For an analysis of "transit" countries, see Friman (1995).

8. Typically, money laundering has three phases: "placing," "layering," and "integration." The first puts the "dirty" money into a financial institution; the second distributes the money among different institutions to conceal its illegal origin; and the third integrates the money into the legal economy. See Falco (1997, 33–6) and Blum (1999). For comprehensive overview of money laundering activities (as well as other drug activities), see BINLEA (2001) and OGD (2000).

9. Germany, The Netherlands, and the United States are among the eight countries that the U.S. State Department considers "major sources or precursors or essential chemicals" for the production of illegal drugs (BINLEA 2001).

10. "Transnational organized crime" is different from "domestic" organized crime, international crime, and "disorganized" crime. For clarification of these categories, see Williams (1995, 1998a) and Naylor (1997).

11. September 11, 2001, clearly changed this perception. The term "narcoterrorism," however, may maintain its appeal in the post 9/11 context. "Rarely well defined by its users," it has usually "served a more political than analytical purpose: to capitalize on popular fear of terrorists and drug traffickers in order to mobilize support for foreign interventions" (Scott and Marshall 1998, 23). It is interesting to notice in this context that in 2002, after the U.S. intervention, Afghanistan recovered its place as the world's largest heroin producer—a position it had lost in the last years of the Taliban regime. According to the U.S. International Narcotics Control Strategy Report (INCSR), opium production in Afghanistan jumped from 74 metric tons in 2001 to 1,278 in 2002. On the effects of the U.S. intervention on drug production, see Scott (2003).

12. The list of texts on the evolution of global crime is enormous. For "primary" data, see BINLEA (2001) and OGD (2000). Among the existing analyses,

see Keh and Farrell (1997), Flynn (2000), Lee III (1999), Williams (1995), McDonald (1995), and GDW (1998).

13. "Contrary to popular conceptions," most illegal drug "does not find its way into the United States on low-flying Cessnas, fast-moving 'cigarette' boats, or among the personal possessions of illegal immigrants. . . . Traffickers in illicit narcotics merely merge with the legitimate flows of goods, capital, and services within the marketplace, comfortable in the realization that governments have a shrinking capacity to separate the bad from the good" (Flynn 2000, 50, 54). See also Salzano and Hartman (1997). On the "internationalization" of criminal organizations, see Thornburgh (1995).

14. For an analysis of "offshore" banking, its importance for economic globalization and its effects on money laundering and global criminality, see Blum (1999).

15. Less tangibly, global economic flows might create "criminogenic" asymmetries that in several ways increase drug consumption (Passas 1998).

16. On this point, see UN (1995) and Gregory (1995).

17. On the connections between economic globalization and transnational crime, see Passas (1998, 1999), Lee III (1999), Keh (1996), Keh and Farrell (1997), Farrel (1995), McFarlane (1998), Flynn (2000), and Lintner (1998).

18. Of course, the counterfactual question is whether the previous authoritarian or totalitarian regimes would have performed better than their successors. The question has to remain open. On the connections between worldwide "democratization" and the growth of global criminality, with emphasis on the Russian case, see Naylor (1995), Turbiville (1995), Voronin (1996), Porteous (1996), Lee III (1995), Williams (1996), Dunn (1996), Shelley (1996), Ulrich (1997), and Burlingame (1997).

19. Regarding the U.S. influence on Mexico's drug business and anti-drug efforts during most of the 20th Century, see Astorga (2003).

20. The Reagan approach also entailed using illegal drugs as a counterinsurgent tool, actively supporting or tolerating right-wing drug groups, while branding leftist groups as "narcoterrorists." The use of drug revenues to subsidize right-wing subversion was particularly notorious in the "Contra" war in Nicaragua (see Scott and Marshall 1998). As the analysis of Indochina, Afghanistan, and Colombia shows, this has been part of an enduring pattern (see Scott 2003).

21. The "narcotics certification process"—as modified in September 2002—requires the U.S. president to submit to Congress a list identifying all major drug producing and drug-transit countries and signaling those nations that "have demonstrably failed to make substantial efforts" to fulfill "their obligations under international counternarcotics agreements" and take "the counternarcotics measures specified in U.S. law." "Decertified" countries are not entitled, save when "vital U.S. national interests" are concerned, to many forms of foreign assistance. Mexico is part of this "majors list" (see BINLEA 2003a). "Decertification" has obvious implications for the international standing of affected countries.

22. These observations and those of the following paragraph are based on the review of many texts focusing on the U.S. "war on drugs." For an overview

of the U.S. anti-drug policies, see among others, BINLEA (2001), ONDCP (2001), Perl (1995), Falco (1997), *Economist* (1999), Tullis (1995, 89–133), Dermota (1999/2000), and Mainwaring (1994). For critical assessments and alternatives to the current approach, see Scott and Marshall (1998), Bertram et al. (1996), Massing (1998), Falco (1998), and Zirnite (1998). On U.S. demand, see Reuter (1998).

23. Coca cultivation in Peru and Bolivia dramatically reduced in the 1990s, but this has been offset by growing cultivation in Colombia. See BINLEA (2001) and Boyer (2001).

24. According to calculations made by ONDCP (2003, 54, table 41), a pure gram of cocaine sold at $212 in the U.S. retail market in 2000, compared to $423 in 1981; purity was estimated at 61 percent in 2000, compared to 36 percent in 1981. A pure gram of heroin cost $2,088 in 2000, down from $3,295 in 1981; purity was estimated at 25 percent in 2000, up from 4 percent in 1981. For figures showing the growth of worldwide drug production, see ibid. (tables 44–6).

25. "Cutting off their supply has been, and will continue to be, our principal international counternarcotics goal. . . . Our objective is to reduce and ultimately cut off the flow of illegal drugs to the United States" (BINLEA 2004, 11–6).

26. For an analysis of how the United States supported the Cali group against its Medellin rivals, see Scott and Marshall (1998, 79–103).

27. This problem is well described in Bertram, et al. (1996), Naylor (1995, 1997), and Boyer (2001).

28. Examples of this selective approach are legion. The Colombian government sought the collaboration of the Cali group to destroy the Medellin traffickers. The United States conveniently targets left-wing Colombian groups that intervene in coca cultivation, implicitly tolerating or supporting right-wing groups that also participate in the drug business. In practice, governments in the rich consumer countries show a relatively tolerant attitude toward legal financial institutions that get involved in money laundering, including "offshore" banks. See Bertram et al. (1996), *Economist* (1999), Dermota (1999/2000), Falco (1997), and Boyer (2001).

29. On the nature of drug groups, see Naylor (1995; 1997, 39–42), Lupsha (1996), Williams (1998a, 1998b), Halstead (1998), and Jackson, Herbrink, and Jansen (1996).

30. With more demanding assumptions, based on U.S. consumption data, these authors admitted that Mexico's drug income could be as low as $2.1 billion.

31. Reuter and Ronfeldt's estimation (1992) used two "export prices" per pound of marijuana: $136 and $455. According to the U.S. Office for National Drug Control Policy (ONDCP 2001, 15–9), heroin prices declined moderately during the 1990s, while those of marijuana remained basically stable. For a review of long-term price trends, see Bertram et al. (1996, 266–7).

32. See, for example, Scott (2003, 89).

33. Data quoted by Bertram et al. (1996) show that a cocaine kilo would cost $2,500 in Colombia, between $16,000 and $25,000 at the entry point in the

United States, and between $70,000 and $300,000 on American streets. The difference between the export price in Colombia and the import price in the United States is at least $13,500. The "transshipment margin" mentioned above assumes that Mexican traffickers get less than half of this amount.

34. Among other things, this calculation assumes that Mexicans do not participate in drug trafficking (at the intermediate or retail level) within the United States, an assumption that the U.S. government would strongly reject. U.S. official sources insist that Mexican organizations control drug trafficking in the United States down to the retail level (see, e.g., BINLEA 2004, 160). This calculation assumes, in addition, that Mexican traffickers get only about 3 percent of the value of the U.S. cocaine market, estimated at around $40 billion (ONDCP 2001, 140; Reuter 1998, 34).

35. "In recent years, international money launderers have turned increasingly to Mexico for initial placement of drug proceeds into the global financial system." This has continued so, even after Mexico enacted its 1996 reforms that "provide the legal framework for more effective control of money laundering" (BINLEA 2001). See also Falco (1997), U.S. House (1997), Dermota (1999/2000), and Blum (1999).

36. This would imply that Mexican producers and traffickers get less than one-fifth of the U.S. methamphetamine market, officially estimated at $1.6 billion (ONDCP 2001, 140). Loret de Mola (2001, 134) estimated Mexico's *profits* from methamphetamines to be at least $630 million. On money laundering in Mexico, see Graver (1999).

37. For further assessment of Mexico's drug income, see Smith (1999), Toro (1995), Toro (1998), Andreas (1998a, 1998b), and Lupsha (1995).

38. According to the World Bank (2001a), Mexico's GDP in 1999 equaled $470 billion.

39. Yearly Mexican exports averaged $101 billion between 1993 and the year 2000 (SE 2001).

40. This includes forestry, hunting, fishing, crop cultivation, and livestock production (SAGARPA 2001).

41. For an overview of organized crime in Mexico's northern border, see Molina Ruiz (2000).

42. In the mid 1990s, 55 percent of total drug eradication took place in these three states.

43. The war denied the United States access to East Asian morphine, at the same time increasing the need for this powerful pain killer (Toro 1995, 7, 11; Reuter and Ronfeldt 1992, 92).

44. As Andreas (1998a) shows, NAFTA created new opportunities for Mexican drug traffickers. Increased and less regulated legal trade also facilitates the flow of illegal products.

45. OGD (1996) identifies six drug "cartels" in Mexico, most of them based on the north.

46. This number assumes that 5 people can make a living from one hectare planted with cannabis or opium poppy, and that an average of forty thousand hectares is cultivated yearly. A document prepared by the Mexican and U.S. Governments (1997) affirms that the total cultivated area is about fifty

thousand hectares. If this is the case, the potential number of people living off drug cultivation may be 250,000.

47. Loret de Mola (2001, 99) affirms that Mexico's drug business employs between 365,000 and 730,000 direct workers. This would imply, calculating three dependants for every worker, that the number of Mexicans living off the drug industry ranges between 1.1 million and 2.2 million.

48. Such a study would surely have to draw on the methodology and approach applied by Thoumi (1995) to the Colombian case (see also Thoumi 1999).

49. For additional data on this regard, see Loret de Mola (2001, 28) and Toro (1998, 138).

50. The analysis presented by Kennedy, Reuter, and Riley (1994) confirms this assertion. Data cited by Bertram et al. (1996, 15, 20) show that cocaine produced in the Andes multiplies its price by seven once it enters the United States and by sixty-six when it reaches its final consumers. For comparisons of wholesale and retail drug prices within the United States, see ONDCP (2001, 12–9).

51. To a large extent, illegal drugs do not compete but rather supplement the legal economy, giving opportunities to people and regions that the latter leaves aside.

52. In half of the indigenous municipalities identified by INI (2001) as involved in illegal drug activities, the main drug activity is cultivation; in 20 percent of those municipalities, the predominant drug activity is trafficking.

53. This topic is analyzed in Kennedy, Reuter, and Riley (1994).

54. "Drug organizations possess and wield the ultimate instrument of corruption: money. The drug trade has access to almost unimaginable quantities of it. No commodity is so widely available, so cheap to produce and so easily renewable as illegal drugs" (BINLEA 2004, 18).

55. In 1985, the Federal Security Direction (DFS) was entirely disbanded given its undeniable involvement in drug trafficking. The Mexican government had tolerated this involvement as long as the DFS contributed to uprooting the 1970s Mexican insurgency (Pimentel 2000, 68–9). For an analysis of the DFS's connections with the illegal drug trade, its counterinsurgent tasks, and its links with the DEA and the CIA, see Scott and Marshall (1998, 33–42). Two generals that occupied commanding positions in the DFS were indicted of drug trafficking in 1998 and eventually arrested two years later (Boyer 2001, 144–7, 358).

56. For a systematic analysis of drug-related corruption in Mexico, see Pimentel (2000).

57. This was probably the case of several top politicians, including the president's brother, in the Salinas administration (1988–94). Allegations of drug corruption also reached the personal assistant of President Zedillo (1994–2000) and probably even one of Zedillo's brothers (see Boyer 2001, 124–56; Smith 1999, 204).

58. It is hard to make a systematic assessment of drug corruption in Mexico. For overviews of the subject, see Andreas (1998b) and Lupsha (1995). Bailey and Godson (2000, 33–8) propose four alternative models to understand

the problem, which range from "contained corruption" to centralized control of the drug business by the country's top authorities.

59. As an example, he cites the "payroll" of a notorious drug lord captured in 1995. He also suggests that, in the 1980s and early 1990s, the "clientelistic and centralized" nature of the PRI regime forced drug traffickers to subordinate themselves to—or obtain the permission of—central authorities of the country. This association, according to him, enabled Mexican drug traffickers to rapidly accumulate large amounts of power and wealth, thus outdoing their Colombian partners (Andreas 1998b, 163).

60. For newspaper analysis on the subject, see Dillon (1998), and Castillo and Zúñiga (2001).

61. Additionally, it has been estimated that, out of distrust on the efficiency or honesty of the criminal system, over 50 percent of total crimes went unreported (Bailey and Godson 2000, 27).

62. See, for example, Toro (1995, 1998), Fernández Menéndez (2001, 34), and Reuter and Ronfeldt (1992).

63. This distinguishes them from politically motivated terrorist organizations of any ideological inclination (Schmid 1996). Not even Colombian drug lords sought to take over the government in the late 1980s and early 1990s: they fought only a defensive war to prevent the government from attacking them and to avoid extradition.

64. In the 1990s, as a proportion of GDP, the illegal drug trade was more important in Bolivia than in Colombia, but its political consequences were stronger in the latter. The economic explanation of this is that, in Bolivia, drug income went to a large number of farmers, whereas in Colombia it was monopolized by small groups that accumulated important means of violence (Thoumi 1995; Cano 2001; Najar 2001).

65. According to Tullis (1995, 104–5), the main goal of Mexico's anti-drug policies has been to eliminate political threats from large drug organizations.

66. "Decapitation" (a preferred strategy in the current "war on drugs") is powerless against a multi-headed enemy. Their flexible and informal links make drug organizations more efficient and resilient (Lee III 1999).

67. "Business disputes between smugglers may be resolved by killing rather than suing each other" (Andreas 1999, 91).

68. For insightful remarks on the "business-like" nature of illegal drug groups, see Zabludoff (1997).

69. "While some smugglers attempt to intimidate or violently neutralize the state, the general rule is that they may buy off key state officials because they cannot entirely bypass or bully them" (Andreas 1999, 92; see also Williams 1998a, 71).

70. The "Condor Operation," launched in 1975, remains the single most important campaign of this kind in Mexico (see Toro 1995, 15–8; Reuter and Ronfeldt 1992).

71. "Law enforcement officials may overlook the activities of one smuggler in exchange for information that leads to the busting of other smuggler" (Andreas 1999, 94).

72. "The lucrative payoffs from the drug trade" provoke "intense competition within and between law enforcement agencies" (Andreas 1998b, 162). "Some of the bloodiest battles in the war on drugs were not between the police and the criminals, but between bands of corrupted members of the security force" (Oppenheimer 1998, 301). On these combinations, see also Smith (1999, 204), Lee III (1999, 23), and Boyer (2001, 115–7).

73. For instances of government officials' responsiveness to drug organizations, see Andreas (1998b).

74. "Between September 2001 and June 2002, the PFP witnessed a twenty-five percent increase in its ranks thanks to the addition of 1,700 newly hired agents and the incorporation of 826 new recruits for the Federal Support Forces (FFA), which are composed entirely of military police and members of the navy. Whole army units were transferred to the FFA to make a current total of eight . . . and 1,600 members of several navy battalions were also added to the PFP. Top positions in the PFP are also held by military officers: The FFA is led by a general, and the PFP as a whole is led by a retired brigadier general" (Sierra Guzmán 2003b, 4).

75. As of August 2001, Mexican defense minister affirmed that between 26,000 and 28,000 members (about 15 percent) of the army and the air force take part in anti-drug operations on any given day (Aranda and Pérez 2001).

76. See Mexican Government (2003, 448). The United States has strongly advocated military involvement in anti-drug affairs (BINLEA 2001). For analysis on the U.S. efforts to "militarize" the drug on war in Latin America, see Zirnite (1998), Mainwaring (1994), Ferreyra and Segura (2000), and Youngers (2002).

77. "In only six years [from 1997 to 2003] persecuting organized crime, tens of military men have met the same fate as the commandants and agents of the Federal Security Direction and the Federal Judicial Police, who preceded them in this task." Corruption has affected personnel at different levels and departments of the Army, including five generals (Barajas 2003).

78. "The U.S. government's 'war on drugs' . . . hinders efforts to put civilian-military relations on a new footing. It is detrimental to efforts to reduce military roles and missions, to eliminate its role in maintaining internal public order, to enhance civilian control over military forces and to increase both the transparency and accountability of military forces" (Youngers 2002, 1).

79. This trend continued under the Fox administration. As the U.S. State Department recognized, by 2003 "the military played a large role in some law enforcement functions, primarily counternarcotics. . . . Elected civilian officials maintained effective control over the police and the military; however, corruption was widespread within police ranks and also was a problem in the military. . . . Military personnel and police officers committed human rights abuses" (BDHRL 2004).

80. According to Nelleman and Goulka (1999, 34), in the late 1990s, incidence of forced "disappearance" reached a level similar to that of the 1970s, when the government launched its toughest counterinsurgency campaign. According to them, "no other country has so many drug-related disappearances. . . . Some Mexican authorities have . . . acknowledged to the media

that in 1997 there have been more than 100 cases of 'disappearances" in the state of Chihuahua alone." A similar situation is evident in Baja California and Sinaloa, two northern states heavily involved in illegal drug activities (AI 1998, 28).

81. For further data on militarization and its consequences for corruption and human rights, see Sierra Guzmán (2003b).

82. "Organized crime thrives in a weak state." This is particularly true of weak states that act as if they were strong, pretending to regulate and tax private activity. Corruption risks are greater in such a situation (Farer 1999, 251).

83. The unequal effects of recent economic globalization might have increased the vulnerability of some states. As Jordan (1999, 7, 12) points out, seeing their authority decline, some Third World states might find drug resources attractive. This combines with financial shortages and the need for foreign investment, which have been particularly strong in many "developing" nations. On the links between economic reform and criminal threats, see Saba and Manzetti (1999), Farer (1999, 266–7), and Treverton (1999).

84. "Long term efforts by the GOM [Government of Mexico] to address the climate of corruption have been stymied by administrative shortcomings in its law enforcement agencies such as a lack of police operational funds, lack of equipment and training, low salaries, and limited career trajectories" (BIN-LEA 2001). For evidence on how Mexican law enforcers have had to rely on illegal drug money, see Pimentel (2000, 64–5), Arzt (2000, 169), and Cassel (1999, 4).

85. The weakness of the civilian apparatus of the state has been a major motivation for militarization in Mexico (Benítez Manaut 2000, 221).

86. This section covers up to the year 2000. For the ensuing period, see section 5.

87. In 1995, the Mexican government complained that the country's drug problem had worsened "in spite of the resources invested in drug eradication and interdiction" (Mexican Government 1995, 5).

88. Seemingly, in the late 1970 and early 1980s, the DFS made great progress in controlling Mexico's illegal drug trade. According to a well informed source, it "did more than simply protect the most notorious traffickers. It brought them together as a cartel, centralized and rationalized their operation, snuffed out competitors, and, through its connections with the CIA, provided the international protection needed to ensure their success" (Scott and Marshall 1998, 40).

89. "Formerly, the police apparatus was rather successful in keeping criminals at bay. Now, that same police apparatus, without leadership, is one of the main sources of criminality" (Meyer 1995, 231).

90. Intra elite conflicts largely contributed to the unprecedented indictment on drug charges of Mario Villanueva, governor of Quintana Roo, in 1999 (Fernández Menéndez 2001, 235–79).

91. The problem of mounting criminality shows one of the most pathetic paradoxes in Latin America: "The same economic reforms and the same move toward representative democracy that have weakened the really existing

states need strong states to function and neutralize the perverse or unforeseen effects they have unleashed" (Castañeda 1998).

92. For an ample analysis of the links between political and fiscal decentralization, see Rodríguez (1997).

93. In 1994, articles 21 and 73 of the Constitution were amended. In 1995, the legislative branch approved a law that provided for the creation of a National System of Public Security's Coordinating Body. In December 2000, the president created the Public Security Ministry, whose chief would also head the National Council for Public Security (SNSP 2001). In March 2004, the president proposed a new amendment to articles 21 and 73 of the Constitution, reinforcing the legal basis of the SNSP (see Mexican Presidency 2004a).

94. See, for example, Avila (2000), Urrutia, et al. (2000), and Cornejo and Venegas (2000).

95. As the national press widely documented, in April 2004 a major scandal broke out, disclosing links between the police apparatus (including the Attorney General) of the state of Morelos and drug trafficking groups. The state governor (from the PAN) was also involved in the scandal.

96. In 1994, incoming president Zedillo appointed Antonio Lozano, from an opposition party (PAN), as head of the PGR. The experiment lasted two years, and was suspended among mounting accusations of corruption and inefficiency. For an analysis sympathetic to that experiment, see Arzt (2000).

97. These figures refer to "ordinary" public financing, which is doubled in election years. Therefore, in election years, single private contributions and total private funding to any party may not be superior to 0.025 percent and 5 percent, respectively, of total public financing to all the parties.

98. Party public financing in the year 2000 was forty-four times as high as that of 1989 (Lujambio 2001, 10).

99. That is, 5 percent and 0.025 percent of $322 million (total public financing to political parties in 2000).

100. In March 2004, the president proposed a series of changes to the electoral legislation, with the stated aim of cutting the cost of elections. The initiative sought to reduce "ordinary" public financing to political parties by an estimated 29 percent. It also proposed to cut "campaign" financing, which, according to the current law, gives each party an amount equal to its ordinary funding; the reform would reduce this to 75 percent for general federal elections and to 50 percent for midterm elections. The proposal also sought to regulate party primary elections. Finally, it intended to increase the IFE's capacity to oversee party finances. However, it did not add any explicit regulation to media payments, which, as mentioned above, are both the most important and the most difficult to oversee. Regulations to private financing would also remain unchanged (see Mexican Presidency 2004b). Opposition parties quickly criticized the initiative and put forward several competing proposals (Guerrero 2004).

101. Allegations of large-scale financial irregularities committed by the PAN and PRI in the presidential contest of the year 2000 occupied a prominent place in the public debate between 2000 and 2003. Eventually, the IFE imposed

fines of nearly 100 million U.S. dollars on the PRI and almost 50 million on the parties that supported Vicente Fox (PAN and PVEM). In March 2004, a great scandal broke out, disclosing apparently illegal financial transactions made by leaders of the PRD. The illegal funds were seemingly spent in the party's internal contest of 2002 and the federal election of 2003.

102. For a comprehensive overview of cases, see Curzio (2000).
103. In 2000, each of these three parties got between 20 percent and 30 percent of total public funding (Lujambio 2001, 13).
104. As shown above, parties other than the PRI are also vulnerable to drug-related corruption. As their prospects to seize power become greater, they are likely to receive higher and more frequent monetary offers from drug dealers.
105. However, in October 2001, the Mexican Supreme Court ruled against extraditing a person who may face life imprisonment.
106. "While the idea was to eradicate corruption, torture and other human rights violations from the federal police, the AFI incorporated 3,500 agents from the disbanded Federal Judicial Police and agents from other PGR offices. By incorporating the same personnel into the new structure, there is a risk that the old practices of abuse, corruption and impunity will be replicated. There have been alarming allegations of torture and corruption with the new AFI" (Sierra Guzmán 2003b).
107. In March 2004, the president sent to Congress a reform initiative that would affect several institutional aspects of the justice system. Among other things, it sought to replace the PGR by a Federal Office of Public Prosecutions (Fiscalía General de la Federación), replace the SSP by a Ministry of the Interior, and merge the PFP and AFI into a Federal Police (see Mexican Presidency 2004a; Castillo García 2004).
108. At the programmatic level, the continuity is virtually complete. While recognizing the advantages of an "integral approach," the *National Program for Drug Control 2001–2006* gives priority to punitive rather than preventive actions, emphasizes the control of drug supply rather than demand reduction, and shows an overriding concern with curtailing drug exports. See Mexican Government (2002).
109. The U.S. government recognized that in 2002 Mexico remained the major transit route for cocaine entering the United States, accounting for 65 percent of total cocaine supply in this country (see BINLEA 2003b).
110. As reported by Barajas and Ortega (2004), these crimes killed seventy-four people in the first twenty-six days of 2004.
111. "Far from being a short-term solution, militarization seems to have taken on a permanent character, surviving as a policy from one administration to the next and systematically transferring military units, weapons, and logistical resources to the police forces" (Sierra Guzmán 2003b, 16).
112. The only exception to this was the disbanding of the PJF. Cleaning operations within the PJF had been very frequent in the past.
113. Drug-related corruption in the armed forces has persisted, and perhaps increased. Barajas (2003) reported that, between 1997 (when military men began to take charge of civilian police agencies) and early 2003, almost 100

members of the Army—including seven generals—had been convicted on drug crimes. From the ranks of the army have emerged some important drug leaders—the most notorious case being Alcides Magaña, captured in June 2001.

114. For a positive assessment of increased Mexican "collaboration" with the U.S. anti-drug efforts, see BINLEA (2003b).

115. On Peru, see Palmer (1992, 1996) and McClintock (1988); on Central America, see Arana (2001); on Chile, see Boyer (2001, 179–201).

116. The number of illegal drug users in Mexico grew significantly in the 1980s and 1990s. See Mexican Government (1995, 4–11; 2002, 30–4), BINLEA (2001), and OGD (2000, 137–9).

117. For reflections on a new anti-drug strategy for Mexico, see Toro (1995, 67–72).

NOTES TO CHAPTER SIX

1. The record on human, civil, and political rights partially contradicts the expectations of the mainstream literature. However, this evolution is congruent with the predominant pattern in the "third wave" of democratization (see section 5 below).

2. Analyzing changes in Latin American politics, Chalmers et al. (1997) found a similar pattern of state and regime weakness, but they call it "dispersion of political decision making" or—even more positively—"multi-centric decision making." While recognizing that this dispersion is not necessarily conducive to democracy, they emphasize its positive consequences: "In the increasingly polycentric states in [Latin America], popular representation—and political representation more generally—is increasingly taking place through a different structure of representation, the associative network. . . . These structures arise out of and rest on purposive, non-hierarchical 'acts of association.'" However, dispersed state authority and a weak political regime can be serious obstacles to addressing basic nationwide problems like the ones analyzed here.

3. For the analysis of some ways in which "elite" democratization can harm "democracy from below," see Eckstein (1990).

4. Active behavior in favor of the business elite has also been abundant. The most notorious case was the bailout of banks in 1995, when the need to confront an economic emergency coupled with the voracity of the economic elite and the complicity of political leaders. By mid 2003, the public debt generated by the bailout amounted to U.S. $89.35 billion, equivalent to 14 percent of GDP (González Amador 2003). In spite of all subsequent political pluralization, the issue has not been clarified and nobody has been legally punished. (For an analysis of the bailout, its antecedents and consequences, see Solís Rosales 2003.)

5. Przeworski et al. (1996, 42–3) affirm that, once democracy is established, declining levels of inequality make it more likely to survive, but there is no distinguishable relation between inequality and the establishment of democracy. Huntington (1989, 20) suggests that inequality is scarcely relevant for

the analysis of democratic transition, since "democracy is clearly compatible with inequality in both wealth and income and, in some measure, it may be dependent upon such inequality" (see also Huntington 1991, 59–72). This view was already evident in some forerunners of the transition literature. Lipset (1959) suggested that economic development contributes to democratization mainly by raising the living standards of the lower class. Yet, none of his indexes of economic development includes data on economic inequality. Dahl (1971, 103–4) also contributed to this ambiguity: while asserting that extreme economic inequality is "unfavorable to competitive politics and to polyarchy," he stressed democracy's capacity to survive in highly unequal societies.

6. In the 1990s, extreme poverty affected between 14.9 percent and 29 percent of the population (see table 4.10). For details on the different estimations of poverty, see chapter 4, section 5.

7. See chapter 4.

8. Data presented in this paragraph result from averaging several Gini coefficient and poverty estimations made by ECLAC (2002) for the 1989–2000 period. This source does not include Haiti and Cuba.

9. A comparison with countries from other regions may also be instructive. According to estimations for the 1990s given by the World Bank (2001b, table 5), the Gini coefficient was 0.315 in Canada, 0.408 in the United States, 0.250 in Belgium and Sweden, 0.327 in France, 0.300 in Germany, 0.249 in Japan, 0.378 in India, and 0.403 in China.

10. For Uruguay, ECLAC (2002) only gives data on urban (not total) poverty. According to this source, urban poverty in Uruguay is lower than in any other Latin American nation.

11. As chapter 5 analyzes, anti-drug campaigns have been a major cause of gross human rights violations in Mexico. Something similar has happened in other countries and regions. As the analysis of Indochina, Afghanistan, and Colombia made by Scott (2003) shows, this is part of a global pattern.

12. In reality, as will be mentioned below, democratic transition in Spain was not purely procedural; it involved many structural changes.

13. The "third wave," in Huntington's original analysis, started in 1974 and had three main stages: Southern Europe (Portugal, Greece, and Spain) in the mid 1970s, South America in the 1980s, and the former communist bloc of Eastern Europe and the Soviet Union in the late 1980s and early 1990s.

14. Between 1970 and 1991, social spending (as a percentage of GDP) doubled in Spain and Portugal and tripled in Greece. Not surprisingly, "economic differences among regions and people decreased" in all three countries under the new democratic regimes (Maravall 1995, 135–7).

15. These remarks, however, do not apply to communist countries (notably China) where transition to capitalism has not been accompanied by *democratic transition*.

16. See, for instance, Linz and Stepan (1996, 434–57), Kopstein and Reilly (2000, 1), King (2000), and World Bank (2002, 98).

17. The World Bank found a major difference between Central European and Baltic States (CBS), on the one hand, and former Soviet Union countries, on

the other. In the former group, "strong social transfers and redistribution mechanisms have dampened the rise in education premiums and wage dispersion." This did not happen in the latter group of countries, which at the end of the 1990s were more unequal and had worse democratic records (World Bank 2002, xiv).

18. See, for example, Hartlyn and Valenzuela (1998, 11). While they include Colombia among the most democratic countries, their analysis confirms that, prior to the 1980s, the Colombian regime hardly deserved to be considered democratic: it had civilian governments, but its electoral processes were severely limited in practice.

19. Chile has a high level of income inequality; as measured by the Gini coefficient, it averaged 0.555 in the 1990s, slightly higher than in Mexico. However, its percentage of people living in poverty is one of the lowest in Latin America, only comparable to those of Uruguay and Costa Rica (ECLAC 2002). As measured by the Foster, Greer y Thorbecke (FGT) index—which estimates both poverty and income distribution—Chile has one of the best social situations in Latin America (ECLAC 2000, 40).

20. According to the widely recognized Latinobarometro (2003) survey, only 53 percent of Mexicans agreed that democracy was preferable to any other form of government; 44 percent were classified as "non-democrats"; 82 percent were dissatisfied with how democracy works; 63 percent would not object to an undemocratic government if it were able to solve the economic problems of the country. The fate of the first post-PRI government is illustrative. As reported by *Reforma* (Feb. 28, 2003), immediately after taking office, President Fox enjoyed the support of about three-thirds of the population. More than two years later, the situation had changed drastically: in February 2003, only 46 percent of Mexicans believed "much" or "something" of what the president said. The rest of Latin American is in a similar situation. The percentage of people believing that democracy is preferable to any other form of government decreased from 61 percent to 53 percent between 1996 and 2003. In 2003, 52 percent of the population affirmed that they "would not care if an undemocratic government came to power, if it were able to solve economic problems" (Latinobarometro 2003). For an analysis of deficient popular support in "fragile" democracies, see Canache (2002).

21. W.B. Gallie, quoted in Collier and Levitsky (1997, 433). As Skinner (1973, 299) put it, *democracy* is a "term that necessarily commends what it describes."

22. As two sympathetic authors put it, "positive political assessments" linked to democratic transition may "cushion against painful economic restructuring" (Linz and Stepan 1996, 439).

23. On the last point, see Carothers (1991).

24. Indeed, the ideological power of democracy is so strong that it can be used to legitimize even openly anti-democratic regimes. This, for example, was the implication of the analysis made by Kirkpatrick (1979). In her view, democracy is difficult to obtain in most of the Third World. Yet, during the Carter administration, the U.S. government was hostile to all the non-dem-

ocratic regimes. By so doing, it indirectly favored the enemies of its non-democratic friends. Therefore, it was necessary to distinguish between authoritarian and totalitarian (communist) regimes. According to her, the former might develop into democracy, while the latter are impermeable to democratic change. Therefore, she concluded, there were good democratic grounds for supporting authoritarianism.

25. A study by the World Bank, assessing ten years of transition in twenty-six former communist countries, found seven "competitive democracies" (Hungary, Czech Republic, Poland, Estonia, Slovenia, Lithuania, and Latvia), eight "concentrated political regimes," seven "war-torn regimes," and four "noncompetitive political regimes" (2002, 98).

26. On this point, see also Kopstein and Reilly (2000).

27. According to Crossette (2000), a new category has entered the political lexicon: *rogue democracies,* that is to say, "democratic governments that go off the rails, either in aggressiveness toward neighbors, cruelty to citizens or backtracking on the promise that democracy will foster liberty and equality." The United Nations Development Program (UNDP 2000, 56, 59) affirms that, in many countries, democratic transition "remains imperiled, insecure, fragile. . . . Many democracies . . . fail to protect or promote human rights," and in "extreme cases of illiberal majoritarian democracy, the human rights of several groups have worsened."

28. The developing and institutionalization of political parties, another key institution of procedural democracy, shows a similarly divergent trend across countries. See, for example, Mainwaring and Scully (1995) and Mainwaring (1998).

29. Collier and Levitsky (1997) identified up to 150 such "diminished subtypes." See also Diamond (1999, 32–60).

30. "Many countries that policy makers and aid practitioners persist in calling 'transitional' are not in transition to democracy, and of the democratic transitions that are under way, more than a few are not following the model. . . . It is time to recognize that the transition paradigm has outlived its usefulness and to look for a better lens" (Carothers 2002, 6). Carothers' critique of the "transition paradigm" is extremely interesting. However, he fails to refer the analytical shortcomings that he identifies to the core of the "paradigm": the procedural definition of democracy. As this book has shown, the central analytical and practical limitations of the transition literature stem from this unrealistic definition.

31. This limited conception of democracy has had a profound influence in the study of political "development." The best source on this topic is Gendzier (1995).

32. Instead of the distinction between "transition" and "consolidation," some authors have proposed different pairs (delegative/representative democracy, illiberal/liberal democracy, etc.), which however perform the same basic analytical function (O'Donnell 1994, 1997, 1999; Zakaria 1997).

33. See, for example, O'Donnell and Schmitter (1986, 6–8) and Przeworski (1991, 37–9).

34. As a master of satire put it, "arbitrary power is the natural object of temptation to a prince, as wine or women to a young fellow, or a bribe to a judge, or vanity to a woman" (Jonathan Swift, cited by Brogan 1962, xviii).
35. For an interesting analysis of the "state system," see Miliband (1969).
36. Between 1976 and 1986, the number of seats in the Chamber of Deputies grew from 238 to 500. Most of the new seats are allocated through proportional representation. A similar change was evident in the Senate, whose number of seats grew from 64 to 128 in 1993. State legislatures evolved in a similar way (Lujambio 2000, 43–66). While useful to pluralize the legislatures, proportional representation also has negative consequences: it breaks the link between voters and legislators and increases the influence of party bureaucracies (Taylor 1997, 319).
37. If passed, the electoral reform initiative that the government sent to Congress in March 2004 would reduce the duration of electoral campaigns and somewhat unify the electoral calendars of the country. It proposed that all statewide and municipal contests taking place in the same year as the federal elections must be held on the federal election-day (see Mexican Presidency 2004b). Opposition parties quickly criticized this proposal (Guerrero 2004).
38. See, among others, Hibbs (1977) and Boix (2000).
39. As a student of social democracy put it, "labor's power advantage lies in its numbers; its disadvantage in the scant, and unevenly distributed, resources among wage earners. . . . Labor movements cannot afford to ignore the fact that economic insecurity, poverty, and unemployment weaken proletarian solidarity and impede class mobilization" (Esping-Andersen 1985, 10, 22).
40. Traditionally, Mexican labor has been weak (Bellin 2000; Murillo 1997). As measured by the proportion of workers in the formal sector, the rate of unionization, and the centralization of union strength, it became even weaker in the 1990s (Aguilar García 2002).
41. "Simply changing the type of structure of representation obviously does not mean that the popular sectors will be taken more seriously or that their claims necessarily will be satisfied. . . . Associative networks, like clientelistic relations, corporatist institutions, class-based parties, and populist movements, can be manipulated by elites to entrench or reinvent inequalities or mystify people about their real interests" (Chalmers et al. 1997).
42. See chapter 4, section 5. Moreover, targeted anti-poverty programs may also have negative effects on social solidarity—breeding "discontent between those who pay and those who receive"—and may stigmatize welfare recipients (see Esping-Andersen 1985, 33, 145–9).
43. "A comprehensive strategy for greater equality and less poverty must include *consistent* actions on a broad front, involving macroeconomic and institutional policies that determine the overall pattern of development, as well as microeconomic interventions to directly enhance the capabilities of poor households. . . . Fostering economic growth through policies that steer resources away from poor areas and people, and then trying to compensate with a poverty alleviation program, turns out to have been an ineffective

overall strategy for coping with poverty" (Khan and Riskin 2001, 121, 123; emphasis in the original).

44. "The dynamic process of democratization itself is set off by a prolonged and inconclusive political struggle." The protagonists of this struggle "represent well-entrenched forces (typically social classes), and the issues have profound meaning to them" (Rustow 1970, 352).

45. From their "empirical study" of crime rates in Latin America, Fajnzylber, Lederman, and Loayza (1998, 19–20) conclude: "Countries with more unequal distribution of income tend to have higher crime rates than those with more egalitarian patterns of income distribution." Thus, "policy makers facing a crime wave should . . . consider a combination of counter-cyclical re-distributive policies and increases in the resources devoted to apprehending and convicting criminals."

46. Through their emphasis on "associative networks," Chalmers et al. (1997) suggest a more "cooperative" approach to inequality alleviation: "The elaboration of associative networks changes the context of political action, in part because it encourages an elite view of popular sectors as partners in finding solutions, as opposed to being either enemies or objects of all-or-nothing co-optation." However, the analysis made here shows that significantly reducing inequality necessarily entails *redistributing* income and sources of income; therefore, some level of conflict is clearly inevitable.

Bibliography

Aguayo Quezada, ed. 2000. *El almanaque mexicano*. Mexico City: Grijalbo, Proceso, and Hechos Confiables.

Aguilar Camín, Héctor. 1999. "Las elecciones del PRD." *La Jornada,* April 4.

Aguilar García, Javier. 2002. *La población trabajadora y sindicalizada en México en el período de la globalización*. Mexico City: IIS (UNAM) and Fondo de Cultura Económica.

Aguilar Gutiérrez, Genaro. 2000. *Desigualdad y Pobreza en México: ¿Son Inevitables?* Mexico City: UNAM-Miguel Angel Porrúa.

Aguilar Zínser, Adolfo. 1996. "Apocalypse Now! La rencontre Marcos-Cardenas." In *Mexique: de Chiapas à la crise financière,* edited by L. E. Gómez. Paris: L'Harmattan.

Aitken, Rob, Nikki Craske, Gareth A. Jones, and David E. Stansfield, eds. 1996. *Dismantling the Mexican State?* London and New York: St. Martin's Press.

Alianza Cívica. 2000. "Boletín de prensa," May 28.

Ambriz, Agustín. 2001. "Oculta Fox al IFE el origen de fondos para su campaña." *Proceso,* July 15.

Amnesty International (AI). 1998. *Mexico: "Disappearances": A Black Hole in the Protection of Human Rights*. New York: Amnesty International.

Anderson, John W. 2000. "Rural Mexico Stays Behind Ruling Party." *Washington Post,* May 2.

Anderson, John W., and Molly Moore. 2000. "Two Mexicos Go to the Polls." *Washington Post,* July 2.

Andreas, Peter. 1998a. "The Paradox of Integration: Liberalizing and Criminalizing Flows across the U.S.-Mexican Border." In *The Post-NAFTA Political Economy: Mexico and the Western Hemisphere,* edited by C. Wise. University Park: The Pennsylvania State University Press.

———. 1998b. "The Political Economy of Narco-Corruption in Mexico." *Current History* 97, no. 168: 160–5.

———. 1999. "Smuggling Wars: Law Enforcement and Law Evasion in a Changing World." In *Transnational Crime in the Americas,* edited by T. Farer. New York and London: Routledge.

Andrews, George R., and Herrick Chapman, eds. 1995. *The Social Construction of Democracy: 1870–1990*. New York: New York University Press.

Aparicio, Ricardo. 2002. "La magnitud de la manipulación del voto en las elecciones federales del año 2000." *Perfiles Latinoamericanos* 10, no. 20: 79–99.

Aponte, David. 2000. "El gobierno panista sólo negociará con el EZLN: Fox." *La Jornada,* March 15.

Arana, Ana. 2001. "The New Battle for Central America." *Foreign Affairs* 80, no. 6: 88–101.

Aranda, Jesús, and Angel Bolaños. 2000. "Atraerá PGR pesquisa sobre el ataque a la PFP en Cuajimalpa." *La Jornada,* July 25.

Aranda, Jesús, and Ciro Pérez Silva. 2001. "Descarta Vega García que soldados mexicanos participen en acciones de paz en el extranjero." *La Jornada,* August 28.

Aristotle. 1981. *The Politics.* Trans. T.A. Sinclair. Harmondsworth and New York: Penguin.

Arnaut, Alberto. 1997. "The Partido Revolucionario Institucional." In *Mexico: Assessing Neo-Liberal Reform,* edited by M. Serrano. London: Institute of Latin American Studies, University of London.

Arnson, Cynthia J., ed. 1999. *Comparative Peace Processes in Latin America.* Washington, D.C. and Stanford: Woodrow Wilson Center and Stanford University Press.

Arzt, Sigrid. 2000. "Alcances y límites de un acto de buena fe: la experiencia del PAN al frente de la Procuraduría General de la República." In *Crimen organizado y gobernabilidad democrática: México y la franja fronteriza,* edited by J. Bailey and R. Godson. Mexico City: Grijalbo.

Astorga, Luis. 2000. "Crimen organizado y la organización del crimen." In *Crimen organizado y gobernabilidad democrática: México y la franja fronteriza,* edited by J. Bailey and R. Godson. Mexico City: Grijalbo.

———. 2001. "La seguridad dependiente." *Bien común y gobierno* 7, no. 77: 5–12.

———. 2003. *Drogas sin fronteras: los expedientes de una guerra permanente.* Mexico City: Grijalbo.

Avila, José J. 2000. "Debe intervenir la federación para frenar la violencia: alcalde de Juárez." *La Jornada,* 29 Februrary.

Baer, M. Delal. 1999. "Mexico's Coming Backlash." *Foreign Affairs* 78, no. 4: 90–104.

Bailey, John. 1987. "Can the PRI Be Reformed? Decentralizing Candidate Selection." In *Mexican Politics in Transition,* edited by J. Gentleman. Boulder: Westview Press.

———. 1994. "Centralism and Political Change in Mexico: The Case of National Solidarity." In *Transforming State-Society Relations in Mexico: The National Solidarity Strategy,* edited by W. A. Cornelius, A. L. Craig, and J. Fox. La Jolla: Center for U.S.-Mexican Studies, University of California, San Diego.

Bailey, John, and Arturo Valenzuela. 1997. "The Shape of the Future." *Journal of Democracy* 8, no. 4: 43–57.

Bailey, John, and Roy Godson, eds. 2000. *Crimen organizado y gobernabilidad democrática: México y la franja fronteriza.* Mexico City: Grijalbo.

Banamex. 2000a. *Estudios económicos y socio-políticos de México: Entorno sociopolítico,* no. 14.

———. 2000b. *Examen de la situación económica de México* 76, no. 889.

———. 2001. *Examen de la situación económica de México* 77, no. 901.

Barajas, Abel. 2003. "Contamina a Ejército combate al narco." *Reforma,* April 13.
Barajas, Abel, and Maricela Ortega. 2004. "Estalla narcocrisis." Reforma, January 28.
Bartra, Armando. 2000a. *Guerrero bronco: Campesinos, ciudadanos y guerrilleros en la Costa Grande.* Mexico City: Era.
———, ed. 2000b. *Crónicas del sur: Utopías campesinas en Guerrero.* Mexico City: Era.
Basurto, Jorge. 1999. "Populism in Mexico: From Cárdenas to Cuauhtémoc." In *Populism in Latin America,* edited by M. Conniff. Tuscaloosa and London: The University of Alabama Press.
BBVA/Bancomer. 2001. *Informe Económico/Economic Report.* January.
Becerra, Ricardo, Pedro Salazar, and José Woldenberg. 2000. *La mecánica del cambio político en México: elecciones, partidos y reformas.* Mexico City: Cal y Arena.
Bellin, Eva. 2000. "Contingent Democrats: Industrialists, Labor, and Democratization in Late-Developing Countries." *World Politics* 52, no. 2: 175–205.
Benítez Manaut, Raúl. 2000. "La contención de grupos armados, el narcotráfico y el crimen organizado en México: El papel de las fuerzas armadas." In *Crimen organizado y gobernabilidad democrática: México y la franja fronteriza,* edited by J. Bailey and R. Godson. Mexico City: Grijalbo.
Bertram, Eva, Morris Blachman, Kenneth Sharpe, and Peter Andreas. 1996. *Drug War Politics: The Price of Denial.* Berkeley: University of California Press.
Blum, Jack A. 1999. "Offshore Money." In *Transnational Crime in the Americas,* edited by T. Farer. New York and London: Routledge.
Boix, Carles. 2000. "Partisan Governments, the International Economy, and Macroeconomic Policies in Advanced Nations, 1960–93." *World Politics* 53, no. 1: 38–73.
Borón, Atilio A. 1998. "Faulty Democracies? A Reflection on the Capitalist 'Fault Lines' in Latin America." In *Fault Lines of Democracy in Post-Transition Latin America,* edited by F. Agüero and J. Stark. Miami: University of Miami's North-South Press.
Boyer, Jean François. 1997. "Entrevista al EPR." *La Jornada,* May 31.
———. 2001. *La guerra perdida contra las drogas: Narcodependencia del mundo actual.* Mexico City: Grijalbo.
Brogan, D.W. 1962. "Preface" to *On Power: Its Nature and the History of Its Growth,* by Bertrand de Jouvenel. Boston: Beacon Press.
Browne T. Barry, and B. Sims. 1994. *Crossing the Line: Immigrants, Economic Integration, and Drug Enforcement on the U.S. Mexican Border.* Albuquerque: Resource Center Press.
Bruhn, Kathleen. 1995. "Governing under the Enemy: The PRD in Michoacán." In *Opposition Government in Mexico,* edited by V. E. Rodríguez and P. M. Ward. Albuquerque: University of New Mexico Press.
———. 1996. "Social Spending and Political Support: The 'Lessons' of the National Solidarity Program in Mexico." *Comparative Politics* 28, no. 2: 151–77.

———. 1997a. *Taking on Goliath: The Emergence of a New Left Party and the Struggle for Democracy in Mexico.* University Park: The Pennsylvania State University Press.

———. 1997b. "The Seven-Month Itch? Neoliberal Politics, Popular Movements, and the Left in Mexico." In *The New Politics of Inequality in Latin America: Rethinking Participation and Representation,* edited by D. A. Chalmers et al. Oxford: Oxford University Press.

———. 1998. "The Partido de la Revolución Democrática: Diverging Approaches to Competition." In *Governing Mexico: Political Parties and Elections,* edited by M. Serrano. London: Institute of Latin American Studies, University of London.

———. 1999a. "Antonio Gramsci and the *Palabra Verdadera*: The Political Discourse of Mexico's Guerrilla Forces." *Journal of Interamerican Studies and World Affairs* 41, no. 2: 29–55.

———. 1999b. "PRD Local Governments in Michoacan: Implications for Mexico's Democratization Process." In *Subnational Politics and Democratization in Mexico,* edited by W. A. Cornelius, T. A. Eisenstadt, and J. Hindley. La Jolla: Center for U.S.-Mexican Studies, University of California, San Diego.

Burki, Shahid J., and Sebastian Edwards. 1996. *Dismantling the Populist State: The Unfinished Revolution in Latin America and the Caribbean.* Washington, D.C.: The World Bank.

Burlingame, Timothy M. 1997. "Criminal Activity in the Russian Banking System." *Transnational Organized Crime* 3, no. 3: 46–72.

Camp, Roderic Ai. 1992. *Generals in the Palacio: The Military in Modern Mexico.* Oxford: Oxford University Press.

———. 1995a. "Mexico's Legislature: Missing the Democratic Lockstep?" In *Legislature and Democratic Transformation in Latin America,* edited by D. Close. Boulder: Lynne Rienner.

———. 1995b. "The PAN's Social Bases: Implications for Leadership." In *Opposition Government in Mexico,* edited by V. E. Rodríguez and P. M. Ward. Albuquerque: University of New Mexico Press.

———. 1999a. "Democracy through Mexican Lenses." *Washington Quarterly* 22, no. 3: 229–42.

———. 1999b. *Politics in Mexico: The Decline of Authoritarianism.* 3d ed. New York and Oxford: Oxford University Press.

Canache, Damarys. 2002. *Venezuela: Public Opinion and Protest in a Fragile Democracy.* Coral Gables: North-South Center Press.

Cano, Arturo. 2001. "La sociedad paga el precio." *Masiosare,* May 6.

Cano, Arturo, Alberto Nájar, and Daniela Pastrana. 2000. "Los *lobos* del PRI." *Masiosare,* August 27.

Cárdenas, Cuauhtémoc, Andrés M. López Obrador, Rosario Robles et al. 2000. "Por la refundación y la regeneración del Partido de la Revolución Democrática." *La Jornada,* October 28.

Carothers, Thomas. 1991. *In the Name of Democracy: U.S. Policy toward Latin America in the Reagan Years.* Berkeley: University of California Press.

———. 2002. "The End of the Transition Paradigm." *Journal of Democracy* 13, no. 1: 5–21.

Carr, Barry. 1987. "The PSUM: The Unification Process on the Mexican Left." In *Mexican Politics in Transition*, edited by J. Gentleman. Boulder: Westview Press.

Cartwright, William, ed. 1999. *Mexico: Facing the Challenges of Human Rights and Crime*, Ardsley, NY: Transnational Publishers.

Cassel, Douglas. 1999. "Human Rights: General Report." In *Mexico: Facing the Challenges of Human Rights and Crime*, edited by W. Cartwright. Ardsley, NY: Transnational Publishers.

Castañeda, Jorge. 1993. *Utopia Unarmed: The Latin American Left After the Cold War.* New York: Knopf.

———. 1998. "El problema del ascenso de la criminalidad," February 19. Available online at http://epn.org/castan/jc980219.html.

———. 1999. *La herencia: arqueología de la sucesión presidencial en México.* Mexico City: Alfaguara.

Castellanos, Laura. 1998. "Tres décadas de contrainsurgencia en Guerrero." *La Jornada*, January 25.

Castillo García, Gustavo. 2004. "Busca Fox dar autonomía a PGR y convertirla en fiscalía de la nación." *La Jornada*, March 26.

Castillo, Gustavo, and Juan A. Zúñiga. 2001. "Aumentó la incidencia delictiva por la introducción ilegal de armas de fuego." *La Jornada*, July 16.

Castro Soto, Gustavo E. 2000a. "El plan contrainsurgente para Oaxaca." In *Siempre cerca, siempre lejos: Las fuerzas armadas en México*, edited by R. Benítez Manaut et al. Mexico City: CIEPAC, CENCOS, and Global Exchange.

———. 2000b. "Las fuerzas armadas en Chiapas." In *Siempre cerca, siempre lejos: Las fuerzas armadas en México*, edited by R. Benítez Manaut et al. Mexico City: CIEPAC, CENCOS, and Global Exchange.

Centro de Derechos Humanos "Fray Bartolomé de las Casas" (CDHFBLC). 1996. *Ni Paz ni Justicia*, San Cristóbal, Mex.: CDHFBLC.

———. 2003. "Amenazas de grupos paramilitares: Boletín de prensa," December 20. Available online at http://www.laneta.apc.org/cdhbcasas/Boletines/2003.

Centro de Derechos Humanos "Miguel Agustín Pro Juárez" (CDHMAPJ). 1998. *Chiapas, la guerra en curso.* Mexico City: CDHMAPJ.

Centro de Investigaciones Económicas y Políticas de Acción Comunitaria (CIEPAC). 2000. *Boletín Chiapas al día*, no. 200. Available online at http://www.ciepac.org/bulletins/200–300/bolec200.html.

Cepeda Ulloa, Fernando. 1998. "Introduction" to *Latin America and the Multinational Drug Trade*, edited by E. Joyce and C. Malamud. New York: St. Martin's Press.

Cervantes, Jesusa. 2002. "El sindicalismo, peor que nunca." *Proceso*, February 17.

Chalmers, Douglas A., Scott B. Martin, and Kerianne Piester. 1997. "Associative Networks: New Structure of Representation for the Popular Sectors." In *The New Politics of Inequality in Latin America: Rethinking Participation and Representation*, edited by D. A. Chalmers et al. Oxford: Oxford University Press.

Chernick, Marc C. 1998. "The Paramilitarization of the War in Colombia." *NACLA Report on the Americas* 31, no. 5: 28–33.

———. 1999. "Negotiating Peace and Multiple Forms of Violence: The Protracted Search for a Settlement to the Armed Conflicts in Colombia." In *Comparative Peace Processes in Latin America,* edited by C. J. Arnson. Washington, D.C. and Stanford: Woodrow Wilson Center and Stanford University Press.

Childs, Matt D. 1995. "An Historical Critique of the Emergence and Evolution of Ernesto Che Guevara's *Foco* Theory." *Journal of Latin American Studies* 27, no. 3: 593–624.

Clapham Cristopher, ed. 1984. *Private Patronage and Public Power: Political Clientelism in the Modern State.* New York: St. Martin's Press.

Clark, Thomas. 1994. "Clientelism, U.S.A.: The Dynamics of Change." In *Democracy, Clientelism, and Civil Society,* edited by L. Roniger and A. Günes-Ayata. Boulder: Lynne Rienner.

Clavijo, Fernando, and Susana Valdivieso. 2000. "Reformas estructurales y política macroeconómica." In *Reformas económicas en México, 1982–1999,* edited by F. Clavijo. Mexico City: Fondo de Cultura Económica-CEPAL-EAEC.

Cleary, Edward L. 1995. "Human Rights Organizations in Mexico: Growth in Turbulence." *Journal of Church and State* 37 (Autumn): 793–812.

Cleaver, Harry. 2000. "The Virtual and Real Chiapas Support Network." Available online at http://www.eco.utexas.edu/faculty/Cleaver/anti-hellman.html.

Coatsworth, John H. 1990. "Patrones de rebelión rural en América Latina: México en una perspectiva comparativa." In *Revuelta, rebelión y revolución: La lucha rural en México del siglo XVI al siglo XX,* edited by F. Katz. Vol.1. Mexico City: ERA.

Collier, David, and Steven Levitsky. 1997. "Democracy with Adjectives: Conceptual Innovation in Comparative Research." *World Politics* 49, no. 3: 430–51.

Collier, Paul. 2000. "Economic Causes of Civil Conflict and their Implications for Policy." Available online at http://www.worldbank.org/research/conflict/papers/civil conflict.pdf.

Collier, Ruth B. 1992. *The Contradictory Alliance: State-Labor Relations and Regime Change in Mexico.* Berkeley: University of California.

Colosio, Luis D. 1993. "Why the PRI Won the 1991 Elections." In *Political and Economic Liberalization in Mexico,* edited by R. Roett. Boulder: Lynne Riener.

Comisión especial encargada de vigilar que no se desvíen recursos públicos federales en el proceso federal electoral del año 2000 (Comisión Especial 2000). 2000. "Informe final," August 23.

Comisión Nacional de los Derechos Humanos (CNDH). 1997–2003. *Informe Anual de Actividades.* Mexico City: CNDH.

Conniff, Michael, ed. 1999. *Populism in Latin America.* Tuscaloosa and London: The University of Alabama Press.

Conroy, Michael. 1999. "Reflections." In *Comparative Peace Processes in Latin America,* edited by C. J. Arnson. Washington, D.C. and Stanford: Woodrow Wilson Center and Stanford University Press.

Consejo Nacional de Población (Conapo). 2001. *Indices de marginación, 2000.* Mexico City: Conapo.

Consejo Nacional de Población and Programa de Educación, Salud y Alimentación (Conapo/Progresa). 1997. *Indices de marginación 1995.* Mexico City: Conapo.

Constantine, Thomas A. 1996. Testimony on drug control in the Western Hemisphere before the Subcommittee on the Western Hemisphere of the House International Relations Committee. 104th Cong., 2d sess. June 6.

Coordinación Civil Pro Elecciones Limpias. 2000. "Boletín de Prensa," July 12.

Cordoba, José de. 2000. "U.S. Sees Rebels as Posing a Threat to Mexican Vote." *Wall Street Journal,* February 14.

Cornejo, Jorge A., and Juan M. Venegas. 2000. "Con o sin apoyo de la Federación, BC combatirá al crimen organizado." *La Jornada,* March 1.

Cornelius, Wayne A. 1973. "Contemporary Mexico: A Structural Analysis of Urban Caciquismo." In *The Caciques: Oligarchical Politics and the System of Caciquismo in the Luso-Hispanic World,* edited by R. Kern. Albuquerque: University of New Mexico Press.

———. 2002. "La eficacia de la compra y coacción del voto en las elecciones mexicanas de 2000." *Perfiles Latinoamericanos* 10, no. 20: 11–31.

Cornelius, Wayne A., and Ann L. Craig. 1991. *The Mexican Political System in Transition.* La Jolla: Center for U.S.-Mexican Studies, University of California, San Diego.

Cornelius, Wayne A., Ann L. Craig, and Jonathan Fox, eds. 1994. *Transforming State-Society Relations in Mexico: The National Solidarity Strategy.* La Jolla: Center for U.S.-Mexican Studies, University of California, San Diego.

Correa, Guillermo and César Cruz Sáenz. 2000. "El ejecutivo propuso . . . y el legislativo se impuso." *Proceso,* December 30.

Cosío Villegas Daniel. 1976. *El sistema político mexicano.* Mexico City: Joaquín Mortiz,

Craig, Ann L., and Wayne A. Cornelius. 1995. "Houses Divided: Parties and Political Reform in Mexico." In *Building Democratic Institutions: Party Systems in Latin America,* edited by S. Mainwaring and T. R. Scully. Stanford: Stanford University Press.

Craig, Richard. 1980. "Human Rights and Mexico's Anti-Drug Campaign." *Social Science Quarterly* 60, no. 4: 691–701.

Crespo, José Antonio. 1999. *Fronteras democráticas en México: retos, peculiaridades y comparaciones.* Mexico City: Océano.

Crossette, Barbara. 2000. "The World: A Different Kind of Rogue; When Democracy Runs Off the Rails." *New York Times,* June 4, Week in Review section.

Curzio Gutiérrez, Leonardo. 2000. "Crimen organizado y financiamiento de campañas políticas en México." In *Crimen organizado y gobernabilidad democrática: México y la franja fronteriza,* edited by J. Bailey and R. Godson. Mexico City: Grijalbo.

Dahl, Robert A. 1971. *Polyarchy: Participation and Opposition,* New Haven: Yale University Press.

Das, Dilip K. 1997. "Organized Crime: A World Perspective (Executive Summary of the Third International Police Executive Symposium, Yokohama, Japan, 1996)." *Transnational Organized Crime* 3, no. 3: 126–46.

De Mora, Juan Miguel. 1972. *Las guerrillas en México y Jenaro Vázquez Rojas.* Mexico City: Editora Latinoamérica.

Demarest, Geoffrey. 1995. "Geopolitics and Urban Armed Conflict in Latin America." *Small Wars and Insurgencies* 6, no. 1: 44–67.

Dermota, Ken. 1999/2000. "Snow Business: Drugs and the Spirit of Capitalism." *World Policy Journal* 16, no. 4: 15–24.

Diamond, Larry. 1999. *Developing Democracy: Toward Consolidation.* Baltimore and London: The Johns Hopkins University Press.

Diamond, Larry, Juan Linz, and Seymour Martin Lipset, eds. 1988/1989. *Democracy in Developing Countries.* 4 vols. Boulder: Lynne Rienner.

Díaz, Gloria L. 2000. "Aguas Blancas: la pesadilla no termina." *Proceso,* special online edition available at http://www.proceso.com.mx/especiales/aguasblancas/texto01.html.

———. 2004. "El precio de la ambición." *Proceso,* March 7.

Dillon, Sam. 1998. "What Went Wrong? Mexico Can't Fathom Its Rising Crime." *New York Times,* June 28.

———. 2000. "Clean Vote in Mexico, but Fraud Dies Hard." *New York Times,* June 27.

Dix, Robert H. 1984. "Why Revolutions Succeed and Fail." *Polity* 16, no. 3: 423–46.

Domingo, Pilar. 2000. "Judicial Independence: The Politics of the Supreme Court in Mexico." *Journal of Latin American Studies* 32, no. 3: 705–35.

Domínguez, Jorge I. 1998. *Democratic Politics in Latin America and the Caribbean.* Baltimore: The Johns Hopkins University Press.

Domínguez, Jorge I., and Alejandro Poire, eds. 1999. *Toward Mexico's Democratization: Parties, Campaigns, Elections, and Public Opinion.* New York and London: Routledge.

Domínguez, Jorge I., and James A. McCann. 1996. *Democratizing Mexico: Public Opinion and Electoral Choices,* Baltimore: The Johns Hopkins University Press.

Dornbusch, Rudiger, and Sebastian Edwards, eds. 1991. *The Macroeconomics of Populism in Latin America,* Chicago: The University of Chicago Press.

Dresser, Denise. 1991. *Neopopulist Solutions to Neoliberal Problems: Mexico's National Solidarity Program.* La Jolla: Center for U.S.-Mexican Studies, University of California, San Diego.

Drug Enforcement Administration (DEA). 1996. "The South American Cocaine Trade: An 'Industry' in Transition." Available online at http://www.usdoj.gov/dea/pubs/intel/cocaine.htm.

Dunn, Guy. 1996. "Major Mafia Gangs in Russia." *Transnational Organized Crime* 2, no. 2/3: 63–87.

Eckstein, Susan. 1990. "Formal Versus Substantive Democracy: Poor People's Politics in Mexico City." *Mexican Studies/Estudios Mexicanos* 6, no. 2: 213–301.

Economic Commission for Latin America and the Caribbean (ECLAC). 1999. *Economic Survey of Latin America and the Caribbean 1998–1999.* Santiago, Chile: ECLAC.

————. 2000. *Panorama social de América Latina*, Santiago, Chile: ECLAC.

————. 2002. *Panorama social de América Latina*, Santiago, Chile: ECLAC.

Economist. 1996. "Mexico: Enter, Left," vol. 340, September 7: 39–40.

————. 1999. "Uncle Sam's War on Drugs," vol. 350, February 20: 33–4.

————. 2000a. "An Uneasy Waiting Game for Mexico, and Marcos," vol. 354, January 8: 34–5.

————. 2000b. "Mexico's Election: The Beginning of the End of the Longest-Ruling Party," vol. 355, June 24: 25–7.

Eisenstadt, Todd A. 1999a. "Electoral Federalism or Abdication of Presidential Authority? Gubernatorial Elections in Tabasco." In *Subnational Politics and Democratization in Mexico,* edited by W. A. Cornelius, T. A. Eisenstadt, and J. Hindley. La Jolla: Center for U.S.-Mexican Studies, University of California, San Diego.

————. 1999b. "Instituciones judiciales en un régimen en vías de democratización: solución legal frente a solución extralegal de los conflictos poselectorales en México." *Foro Internacional* 39, no. 156–7: 295–326.

Eisenstadt, S.N., and Luis Roniger. 1984. *Patron, Clients and Friends: Interpersonal Relations and the Structure of Trust in Society.* Cambridge: Cambridge University Press.

Eisenstadt, S.N., and Rene Lemarchand, eds. 1981. *Political Clientelism, Patronage, and Development,* Beverly Hills: Sage Publications.

Ejército Popular Revolutionario (EPR). 1996. "Parte militar," August 28. Available online at http://www.pengo.it/PDPR-EPR/comunicados/c_280896.htm.

————. 2000. "Comunicado revolucionario: posición política ante el nuevo gobierno de Vicente Fox," August 28. Available online at http://www.pengo.it/PDPR-EPR/comunicados/c_280800.htm.

Ejército Zapatista de Liberación Nacional (EZLN). 1994a. "Declaración de la Selva Lacandona." Available online at http://www.ezln.org/documentos/1994/199312xx.en.htm.

————. 1994b. "Segunda Declaración de la Selva Lacandona." Available online at http://www.ezln.org/documentos/1994/19940610.es.htm.

Erfani, Julie A. 1995. *The Paradox of the Mexican State: Rereading Sovereignty from Independence to NAFTA.* Boulder: Lynne Rienner.

Esping-Andersen, Gosta. 1985. *Politics against Markets: The Social Democratic Road to Power.* Princeton: Princeton University Press.

Espinoza Valle, Victor A. 1999. "Alternation and Political Liberalization: The PAN in Baja California." In *Subnational Politics and Democratization in Mexico,* edited by W. A. Cornelius, T. A. Eisenstadt, and J. Hindley. La Jolla: Center for U.S.-Mexican Studies, University of California, San Diego.

Fajnzylber, Pablo, Daniel Lederman, and Norman Loayza. 1998. *Determinants of Crime Rates in Latin America: An Empirical Assessment.* Washington, D.C.: The World Bank.

Falco, Mathea. 1998. "America's Drug Problem and Its Policy of Denial." *Current History* 97, no. 168: 145–49.

————, ed. 1997. *Rethinking International Drug Control: New Directions for U.S. Policy.* Washington: Council on Foreign Relations.

Farer, Tom. 1999. "Fighting Transnational Organized Crime: Measures Short of War." In *Transnational Crime in the Americas*, edited by T. Farer. New York and London: Routledge.

Farrel, Graham. 1995. "The global Rate of Interception of Illicit Opiates and Cocaine 1980–1994." *Transnational Organized Crime* 1, no. 4: 134–49.

Ferguson, Thomas. 1995. *The Golden Rule: The Investment Theory of Party Competition and the Logic of Money-Driven Political Systems*. Chicago: The University of Chicago Press.

Fernández de Cevallos et al. 1995. "Acuerdo por la Paz, Democracia y la Justicia." Reprinted in *Los límites rotos: Anuario político*, edited by J. P. González Sandoval, and J. González Graf. Mexico City: Océano.

Fernández Menéndez, Jorge. 2001. *El otro poder: las redes del narcotráfico, la política y la violencia en México*. Mexico City: Aguilar.

Ferreyra, Aleida, and Renata Segura. 2000. "Examining the Military in the Local Sphere: Colombia and Mexico." *Latin American Perspectives* 27 no. 2: 18–35.

Fix-Zamudio, Héctor, and José R. Cossío Díaz. 1995. *El Poder Judicial en el ordenamiento mexicano*. Mexico City: Fondo de Cultura Económica.

Flynn, Stephen E. 2000. "The Global Drug Trade versus the Nation-State." In *Beyond Sovereignty: Issues for a Global Agenda*, edited by M. K. Cusimano. Boston and New York: Bedford and St. Martin's.

Fox, Jonathan, and Julio Moguel. 1995. "Pluralism and Anti-Poverty Policy: Mexico's National Solidarity Program and Left Opposition Municipal Governments." In *Opposition Government in Mexico*, edited by V. E. Rodríguez and P. M. Ward. Albuquerque: University of New Mexico Press.

Freedom House. 2000. "Democracy's Century: A Survey of Global Political Change in the Twentieth Century." Available online at http://freedomhouse.org/reports/century.pdf.

———. 2002a. *Freedom in the World, 2001–2002*. Available online at http://freedomhouse.org/research/freeworld/2002/.

———. 2002b. "Freedom in the World Country Ratings, 1972–73 to 2000–01." Available online at http://www.freedomhouse.org/research/freeworld/FH-SCORES.xls.

Friedrich, Paul. 1977. "The Legitimacy of a Cacique." In *Friends, Followers, and Factions*, edited by W. Schmidt et al. Berkeley: University of California Press.

Friman, H. Richard. 1995. "Just Passing Through: Transit States and the Dynamics of Illicit Transshipment." *Transnational Organized Crime* 1, no. 1: 65–83.

Fuentes, Carlos. 1994. "Chiapas: Latin America's First Post-Communist Rebellion." *New Perspectives Quarterly* 11, no. 2: 54–8.

García, Carlos. 2000. "Inventario de las organizaciones campesinas." In *Crónicas del sur: utopías campesinas en Guerrero*, edited by A. Bartra. Mexico City: Era.

Garman, Christopher, Stephan Haggard, and Eliza Willis. 2001. "Fiscal Decentralization: A Political Theory with Latin American Cases." *World Politics* 53, no. 2: 205–36.

Garrido, Luis Javier. 1982. *El partido de la revolución institucionalizada: la formación del nuevo estado en México (1928–1945)*. Mexico City: Siglo XXI.

———. 1994. "Reform of the PRI: Rhetoric and Reality." In *Party Politics in an Uncommon Democracy,* edited by N. Harvey and M. Serrano. London: Institute of Latin American Studies, University of London.

Gendzier, Irene L. 1995. *Development against Democracy: Manipulating Political Change in the Third World.* Hampton, CT and Washington, DC: The Tyrone Press.

Geopolitical Drug Watch (GDW). 1998. "A Drug Trade Primer for the Late 1990s." *Current History* 97, no. 168: 150–3.

Gledhill, John. 1996. "The State, the Countryside . . . and Capitalism." In *Dismantling the Mexican State?* edited by R. Aitken et al. London and New York: St. Martin's Press.

Godínez, Víctor M. 2000. "La economía de las regiones y el cambio estructural." In *Reformas económicas en México, 1982–1999,* edited by F. Clavijo. Mexico City: Fondo de Cultura Económica-CEPAL-EAEC.

Gómez Tagle, Silvia. 1997. *La transición inconclusa. Treinta años de elecciones en México.* Mexico City: Colmex.

González Amador, Roberto. 2003. "Los fracasos de particulares han costado al país 109 mil 214 mdd." La Jornada, July 25.

González Sandoval, ed. 1996. *El año del vacío: anuario político.* Mexico City: Océano.

González Sandoval, Juan Pablo, and Jaime González Graf, eds. 1995. *Los límites rotos: Anuario político.* Mexico City: Océano.

González, Cecilia, and Marcela Turati. 2001. "Etnias y Narco." *Reforma,* February 21.

Gosner, Kevin, and Arij Ouweneel, eds. 1996. *Indigenous Revolts in Chiapas and the Andean Highlands.* Amsterdam: CEDLA.

Gramont, Hubert C., ed. 1996. *Neoliberalismo y organización social en el campo mexicano.* Mexico City: Plaza y Valdés.

Graver, David. 1999. "Drug-Money Laundering in Mexico." In *Mexico: Facing the Challenges of Human Rights and Crime,* edited by W. Cartwright. Ardsley, NY: Transnational Publishers.

Grayson, George W. 1998. *Mexico: From Corporatism to Pluralism?* Fort Worth: Harcourt Brace College Publishers, 1998.

Gregory, Frank. 1995. "Transnational Crime and Law Enforcement Cooperation: Problems and Process between East and West in Europe." *Transnational Organized Crime* 1, no. 4: 105–33.

Grupo Financiero Bancomer (GFB). 1999. *Reforma Tributaria Federal.* Mexico City: Bancomer.

———. 2000. *Informe Economico/Economic Report,* January.

Guerrero, Claudia. 2004. "Emprenden diputados pleito por propuesta." *Reforma,* March 23.

Guevara, Che. 1997. *Guerrilla Warfare.* 3d ed. Wilmington: SR Books.

Guillén López, Tonatiuh. 1989. "The Social Basis of the PRI." In *Mexico's Alternative Political Futures,* edited by W. A. Cornelius, J. Gentleman, and P. H. Smith. La Jolla: Center for U.S.-Mexican Studies, University of California, San Diego.

Guillén, Guillermina. 2004. "Pelean millones de votos vía Oportunidades." *El Universal,* February 9.

Günes-Ayata, Ayse. 1994. "Clientelism: Predomodern, Modern, Postmodern." In *Democracy, Clientelism, and Civil Society,* edited by L. Roniger and A. Günes-Ayata. Boulder: Lynne Rienner.

Gurr, Ted R. 1970. *Why Men Rebel.* Princeton: Princeton University Press.

Gutiérrez, Alejandro. 2004. "El sofisticado ejército del narco." *Proceso,* January 18.

Gutiérrez, Maribel. 1998. *Violencia en Guerrero,* Mexico City: La Jornada.

———. 2000. "Las fuerzas armadas en Guerrero." In *Siempre cerca, siempre lejos: Las fuerzas armadas en México,* edited by R. Benítez Manaut et al. Mexico City: CIEPAC, CENCOS, and Global Exchange.

Hagopian, Frances. 1998. "Democracy and Political Representation in Latin America in the 1990s: Pause, Reorganization, or Decline?" In *Fault Lines of Democracy in Post-Transition Latin America,* edited by F. Agüero and J. Stark. Miami: University of Miami's North-South Press.

Hakim, Peter. 2001. "The Uneasy Americas." *Foreign Affairs* 80, no. 2: 46–61.

Halstead, Boronia. 1998. "The Use of Models in the Analysis of Organized Crime and Development Policy." *Transnational Organized Crime* 4, no. 1: 1–24.

Hartlyn, Jonathan, and Arturo Valenzuela. 1998. "Democracy in Latin America since 1930." In *Latin America: Politics and Society since 1930,* edited by L. Bethell. Cambridge, U.K.: Cambridge University Press.

Harvey, Neil. 1994. *Rebellion in Chiapas: Rural Feforms, Campesino Radicalism, and the Limits to Salinismo.* San Diego: Center for U.S.-Mexican Studies, University of California.

———. 1996. "Nuevas formas de representación en el campo mexicano: La Unión Nacional de Organizaciones Regionales Campesinas Autónomas (UN-ORCA)." In *Neoliberalismo y organización social en el campo mexicano,* edited by H. C. Gramont. Mexico City: Plaza y Valdés.

———. 1998. *The Chiapas Rebellion: The Struggle for Land and Democracy.* Durham and London: Duke University Press.

———. 1999. "The Peace Process in Chiapas: Between Hope and Frustration." In *Comparative Peace Processes in Latin America,* edited by C. J. Arnson. Washington, D.C. and Stanford: Woodrow Wilson Center and Stanford University Press.

Hellman, Judith A. 1994. "Mexican Popular Movements, Clientelism, and the Process of Democratization," In *Latin American Perspectives* 21, no. 2: 124–42.

———. 2000. "Real and Virtual Chiapas: Magic Realism and the Left." In *Necessary and Unnecessary Utopias: Socialist Register 2000,* edited by L. Panitch and C. Leys. Suffolk, UK, and New York: Merlin Press and Monthly Review Press.

Henríquez Arellano, Edmundo. 2000. "Usos, costumbres y pluralismo en los Altos de Chiapas." In *Democracia en tierras indígenas: Las elecciones en Los Altos de Chiapas (1991–1998),* edited by J. P. Viqueira and W. Sonnleitner. Mexico City: CIESAS, Colmex, and IFE.

Henríquez, Cristina, and Melba Pría. 2000. *Regiones indígenas tradicionales. Un enfoque geopolítico para la seguridad nacional.* Mexico City: INI.

Hernández Rodríguez, Rogelio. 1998. "The Partido Revolucionario Institucional." In *Governing Mexico: Political Parties and Elections,* edited by M. Serrano. London: Institute of Latin American Studies, University of London.

Hibbs, Douglas. 1977. "Political Parties and Macroeconomic Policy." *American Political Science Review* 71, no. 4: 1467–87.

Hidalgo Domínguez, Onécimo. 2000. "La paramilitarización en Chiapas." In *Siempre cerca, siempre lejos: Las fuerzas armadas en México,* edited by R. Benítez Manaut et al. Mexico City: CIEPAC, CENCOS, and Global Exchange.

Horn, Michael T. 1997. Testimony on violent drug mafias before the Subcommittee on Western Hemisphere, Peace Corps, Narcotics, and Terrorism of the Senate Foreign Relations Committee. 105th Cong., 1st sess. July 16.

Humphrey, Christopher. 2003. "Narcotics, Economics, and Poverty in the Southern States." In *Mexico Southern States Development Strategy,* edited by G. Hall et al. Washington, D.C.: World Bank. Available online at http://wbln0018.worldbank.org/LAC/LAC.nsf/ECADocbyUnid/541D538865DA825A85256DC500 7A7BC8?Opendocument.

Huntington, Samuel P. 1989. "The Modest Meaning of Democracy." In *Democracy in the Americas: Stopping the Pendulum,* edited by R. A. Pastor. New York: Holmes and Meier Publishers.

———. 1991. *The Third Wave: Democratization in the Late Twentieth Century.* Norman and London: University of Oklahoma Press.

———. 1997. "Democracy for the Long Haul." In *Consolidating the Third Wave Democracies: Themes and Perspectives,* edited by L. Diamond et al. Baltimore: The Johns Hopkins University Press.

INEGI. 2000. "Población ocupada por sector de actividad económica según entidad federativa, 1998." Available online at http://www.inegi.gob.mx.

———. 2001. *XII Censo general de población y vivienda.* Aguascalientes: INEGI.

———. 2003a. "Banco de Información Económica. Producto Interno Bruto por Entidad Federativa." Available online at http://dgcnesyp.inegi.gob.mx/ BDINE/M15/M15.HTM.

———. 2003b. "Banco de Información Económica: Inversión Extranjera Directa, nueva metodología." Available online at http://dgcnesyp.inegi.gob.mx/BDINE/K10/K1000001.HTM.

———. 2003c. "El INEGI da a conocer los resultados de la Encuesta Nacional de Ingresos y Gastos de los Hogares correspondientes al Año 2002." Press release, no. 064. Available online at http://www.inegi.gob.mx/inegi/ contenidos/espanol/prensa/Boletines/Boletin/Comunicados/Especiales/2003/Junio /cp_64.doc.

———. 2004. "Banco de Información Económica. Producto Interno Bruto Trimestral." Available online at http://dgcnesyp.inegi.gob.mx/BDINE/A10/ A10.HTM.

Instituto Federal Electoral (IFE). 1997. "Estadística de las elecciones federales de 1997 y locales en el D. F. de 1997." Available online at http://www.ife.org.mx/.

———. 2000. "Estadística de las elecciones federales de 2000." Available online at http://www.ife.org.mx/.

———. 2003. "Estadística de las elecciones federales de México, 2003." Available online at http://www.ife.org.mx/.

Instituto Nacional Indigenista-Subdirección de Investigación (INI). 2001. Unpublished Document on Production, Trafficking, and Use of Illegal Drugs in Indian Communities.

Inter-American Development Bank (IADB). 2003. *Sending Money Home: An International Comparison of Remittance Markets.* Washington, DC: IADB.

Irízar, Guadalupe. 2001. "Ubican a siete grupos armados en el país." *Reforma,* July 21.

Jackson, Janet L., Janet C.M. Herbrink, and Robert W.J. Jansen. 1996. "Examining Criminal Organizations: Possible Methodologies." *Transnational Organized Crime* 2, no. 4: 83–105.

Jones, Gareth A. 1996. "Dismantling the *Ejido:* A Lesson in Controlled Pluralism." In *Dismantling the Mexican State?* edited by R. Aitken et al. London and New York: St. Martin's Press.

Jordan, David C. 1999. *Drug Politics: Dirty Money and Democracies.* Norman: University of Oklahoma Press.

Kalyvas, Stathis N. 2001. "'New' and 'Old' Civil Wars: A Valid Distinction?" *World Politics* 54, no. 1: 99–118.

Kampwirth, Karen. 1996. "Creating Space in Chiapas: An Analysis of the Strategies of the Zapatista Army and the Rebel Government in Transition." *Bulletin of Latin American Research* 15, no. 2: 261–76.

Kapstein, Ethan B., and Dimitri Landa. 2000. "Democracy and the Market: The Case of Globalization." In *Freedom in the World 1999–2000,* edited by Freedom House. Available online at http://www.freedomhouse.org/survey/2000.

Kaufman, Robert R., and Guillermo Trejo. 1997. "Regionalism, Regime Transformation, and PRONASOL: The Politics of the National Solidarity Programme in Four Mexican States." *Journal of Latin American Studies* 29, no. 3: 717–45.

Kay, Bruce H. 1996/1997. "Fujipopulism" and the Liberal State in Peru, 1990–1995." *Journal of Interamerican Studies and World Affairs* 38 no. 4: 55–98.

———. 1999. "Violent Opportunities: The Rise and Fall of 'King Coca' and Shining Path." *Journal of Inter-American Studies and World Affairs* 41, no. 3: 97–127.

Keh, Douglas I. 1996. "Economic Reform and Criminal Finance." *Transnational Organized Crime* 2, no. 1: 66–80.

Keh, Douglas I., and Graham Farrell. 1997. "Trafficking Drugs in the Global Village." *Transnational Organized Crime* 3, no. 2: 90–110.

Kennedy, Michael, Peter Reuter, and Kevin J. Riley. 1994. *A Simple Economic Model of Cocaine Production.* Santa Monica, CA: RAND.

Kern, Robert, and Ronald Dolkart. 1973. "Introduction" to *The Caciques: Oligarchical Politics and the System of Caciquismo in the Luso-Hispanic World,* edited by R. Kern. Albuquerque: University of New Mexico Press.

Khan, Azizur Rahman, and Carl Riskin. 2001. *Inequality and Poverty in China in the Age of Globalization.* Oxford: Oxford University Press.

King, Charles. 2000. "Post-Postcommunism: Transition, Comparison, and the End of "Eastern Europe." *World Politics* 53, no. 1: 143–72.

Kirkpatrick, Jeane. 1979. "Dictatorships and Double Standards." *Commentary* 68, no. 5: 34–45.

Klesner, Joseph L. 1987. "Changing Patterns of Electoral Participation and Official Party Support in Mexico." In *Mexican Politics in Transition,* edited by J. Gentleman. Boulder: Westview Press.

———. 1997a. "Democratic Transition? The 1997 Mexican Elections." *PS: Political Science and Politics* 30, no. 4: 703–11.

———. 1997b. "Electoral Reform in Mexico's Hegemonic Party System: Perpetuation of Privilege or Democratic Advance?" Available on line at http://www2.Kenyon.edu/Depts/Psci/Fac/Klesner/Electoral_Reform_in_Mexi co.htm.

———. 1998. "An Electoral Route to Democracy? Mexico's Transition in Comparative Perspective." *Comparative Politics* 30, no. 4: 477–97.

———. 2001. "The End of Mexico's One Party Regime." *PS: Political Science and Politics* 34, no. 1: 107–14.

Knight, Alan. 2000. "Cultura política y caciquismo." *Letras libres,* no. 24.

Kopstein, Jeffrey, and David A. Reilly. 2000. "Geographic Diffusion and the Transformation of the Postcommunist World." *World Politics* 53, no. 1: 1–37.

Kurer, Oskar. 1997. The Political Foundations of Development Policies. Lanham, Md.: University Press of America.

Laakso, Murkuu and Rein Taagepera. 1979. "'Effective' Number of Parties: A Measure with Application to West Europe." *Comparative Political Studies* 12, no. 1: 3–27.

Latinbarómetro. 2003. "Informe–Resumen: La Democracia y la Economía." Available online at http://www.latinobarometro.org/.

Lavielle, Briseida, Alejandro Ortiz, and Rocío Moreno. 2003. "Omisiones e ineficiencias." *Enfoque,* June 15.

Lawson, Chappell. 1997. "The elections of 1997." *Journal of Democracy* 8, no. 4: 13–27.

Le Bot, Yvon. 1997. *Subcomandante Marcos: El sueño zapatista.* Mexico City: Plaza y Janés.

Lee III, Rensselaer W. 1995. "Drugs in Communist and Former Communist States." *Transnational Organized Crime* 1, no. 2: 193–205.

———. 1999. "Transnational Organized Crime: An Overview." In *Transnational Crime in the Americas,* edited by T. Farer. New York and London: Routledge.

Leech, Garry. M. 2002. *Killing peace: Colombia's conflict and the failure of U.S. intervention.* New York: Information Network of the Americas (INOTA).

Legorreta Díaz, M. del Carmen. 1998. *Religión, política y guerrilla en Las Cañadas de la Selva Lacandona.* Mexico City: Cal y Arena.

Leiken, Robert S. 2001. "With a Friend like Fox." *Foreign Affairs* 80, no. 5: 91–104.

Lemoine, Maurices. 1998. "Mexico's New Guerrillas: First Chiapas, Now Guerrero." *Le Monde Diplomatique,* online edition available at http://www.en.monde-diplomatique.fr/1998/11/08.

Levy, Daniel C. 1990. "Mexico: Sustained Civilian Rule without Democracy." In *Politics in Developing Countries,* edited by L. Diamond, J. Linz, and S. M. Lipset. Boulder: Lynne Rienner.

Levy, Santiago, and Sweder Van Wijnbergen. 1995. "Transition Problems in Economic Reform: Agriculture in the North American Free Trade Agreement." *The American Economic Review* 85, no. 4: 738–54.

Lijphart, Arend. 1999. *Patterns of Democracy: Government Forms and Performance in Thirty-Six Countries*. New Heaven: Yale University Press.

Lijphart, Arend, and Carlos Waisman, eds. 1996. *Institutional Design in New Democracies: Eastern Europe and Latin America*. Boulder: Westview Press.

Lindblom, Charles. 1977. *Politics and Markets: The World's Political Economic Systems*. New York: Basic Books.

Lintner, Bertil. 1998. "Global Reach: Drug Money in the Asia Pacific." *Current History* 97, no. 168: 179–82.

Linz, Juan, and Alfred Stepan. 1996. *Problems of Democratic Transition and Consolidation: Southern Europe, South America, and Post-Communist Europe*. Baltimore: The Johns Hopkins University Press.

Linz, Juan, and Arturo Valenzuela, eds. 1994. *The Failure of Presidential Democracy*. Baltimore: The Johns Hopkins University Press.

Lipset, Seymour M. 1959. "Some Social Requisites of Democracy: Economic Development and Political Legitimacy." *The American Political Science Review* 53, no. 1: 69–105.

Loaeza, Soledad. 1989. *El llamado de las urnas*. Mexico City: Cal y Arena.

———. 1997. "Partido Acción Nacional: Opposition and the Government in Mexico." In *Mexico: Assessing Neo-Liberal Reform*, edited by M. Serrano. London: Institute of Latin American Studies, University of London.

Lofredo, Jorge. 2004. "La guerrilla mexicana: de la unidad a la ruptura." *Memoria*, no. 180: 12–20.

López Astrain, Martha Patricia. 1996. *La guerra de baja intensidad en México*. Mexico City: Plaza y Valdés/Univ. Iberoamericana.

López Monjardín, Adriana. 1996. "A contracorriente: Expresiones de resistencia a las reformas de la legislación agraria." In *Neoliberalismo y organización social en el campo mexicano*, edited by H. C. Gramont. Mexico City: Plaza y Valdés.

López y Rivas, Gilberto. 2000. "Los cuatro conflictos armados en México."*La Jornada*, January 17.

López-Ménendez, Marisol. 2000. "El ejército y la seguridad pública." In *Siempre cerca, siempre lejos: Las fuerzas armadas en México*, edited by R. Benítez Manaut et al. Mexico City: CIEPAC, CENCOS, and Global Exchange.

Loret de Mola, Carlos. 2001. *El negocio: La economía de México atrapada por el narcotráfico*. Mexico City: Grijalbo.

Lujambio, Alonso. 2000. *El poder compartido: Un ensayo sobre la democratización mexicana*. Mexico City: Océano.

———. 2001. "Dinero y democratización: El financiamiento y la fiscalización de los partidos políticos en la transición mexicana a la democracia, 1988–2000." Paper presented at the seminar "Dinero y contienda político-electoral: Retos para la democracia." Mexico City, June 5–8.

Lupsha, Peter A. 1995. "Transnational Narco-Corruption and Narco Investment: A Focus on Mexico." *Transnational Organized Crime* 1, no. 1: 84–101.

———. 1996. "Transnational Organized Crime and the Nation State." *Transnational Organized Crime* 2, no. 1: 21–48.

Lustig, Nora. 1992. Mexico, the Remaking of an Economy. Washington, D.C.: The Brookings Institution.

———. 1998. *Mexico: The Remaking of an Economy.* 2d ed. Washington: Brookings Institution Press.

Mackinlay, Horacio. 1996. "La CNC y el 'nuevo movimiento campesino.'" In *Neoliberalismo y organización social en el campo mexicano,* edited by H. C. Gramont. Mexico City: Plaza y Valdés.

Mainwaring, Max G. 1994. "National Security Implications of Drug Trafficking for the USA and Colombia." *Small Wars and Insurgencies* 5, no. 3: 379–408.

Maiwnwaring, Scott. 1998. "Party Systems in the Third Wave." *Journal of Democracy* 9, no. 3: 67–81.

Mainwaring, Scott, and Timothy R. Scully. 1995. "Introduction: Party Systems in Latin America." In *Building Democratic Institutions: Party Systems in Latin America,* edited by S. Mainwaring and T. R. Scully. Stanford: Stanford University Press.

Malkin, Victoria. 2001. "Narcotrafficking, Migration, and Modernity in Rural Mexico." *Latin American Perspectives* 28, no. 4: 101–28.

Maravall, José María. 1995. *Los resultados de la democracia: Un estudio del sur y el este de Europa.* Madrid: Alianza.

Marín, Carlos. 1999. "Reporte de inteligencia militar." *Proceso,* January 3.

Martínez Rodríguez, Antonia. 1998. "Parliamentary Elites and the Polarisation of the Party System in Mexico." In *Governing Mexico: Political Parties and Elections,* edited by M. Serrano. London: Institute of Latin American Studies, University of London.

Massing, Michael. 1998. *The Fix.* New York: Simon and Schuster.

Maxfield, Sylvia. 1990. *Governing Capital: International Finance and Mexican Politics.* Ithaca: Cornell University Press.

———. 2000. "Capital Mobility and Democratic Stability: Comparing East Asia and Latin America." *Journal of Democracy* 11, no. 4: 95–106.

McClintock, Cynthia. 1984. "Why Peasants Rebel: The Case of Peru's Sendero Luminoso." *World Politics* 37, no. 1: 48–84.

———. 1988. "The War on Drugs: The Peruvian Case." *Journal of Interamerican Studies and World Affairs* 30, no. 2/3: 127–42.

McDonald, William. 1995. "The Globalization of Criminology: The New Frontier is the Frontier." *Transnational Organized Crime* 1, no. 1: 1–22.

McFarlane, John. 1998. "Transnational Crime, Corruption, and Crony Capitalism in the Twenty-First Century: An Asia-Pacific Perspective." *Transnational Organized Crime* 4, no. 2: 1–30.

Méndez, Enrique, and Roberto Garduño. 2004. "Luis H. Alvarez: el gobierno foxista no resolverá el conflicto con el EZLN." *La Jornada,* March 25.

Mexican Government. 1995. *Programa Nacional para el Control de Drogas 1995–2000.* Mexico City: Poder Ejecutivo Federal.

———. 2002. *Programa Nacional para el Control de Drogas 2001–2006.* Mexico City: Poder Ejecutivo Federal.

————. 2003. *Tercer Informe de Gobierno. Anexo Estadístico.* Mexico City: Poder Ejecutivo Federal.

Mexican and U.S. Governments. 1997. *United States/Mexico Binational Drug Threat Assessment.* Washington, DC: The White House.

Mexican Presidency. 2001a. "Exposición General de la propuesta de la Nueva Hacienda Pública Distributiva." April. Available online at http://www.shcp.gob.mx/docs/nhpd/em.pdf.

————. 2001b. "Iniciativa de Decreto que Establece, Reforma, Adiciona y Deroga Diversas Disposiciones Fiscales." April. Available online at http://www.shcp.gob.mx/docs/nhpd/pi01.pdf.

————. 2004a. "Iniciativa de decreto que reforma y adiciona diversas disposiciones de la Constitución Política de los Estados Unidos Mexicanos." March 29. Available online at http://seguridadyjusticia.presidencia.gob.mx/.

————. 2004b. "Iniciativa de Reformas Electorales del Ejecutivo Federal." March 22. Available online at http://sil.gobernacion.gob.mx/Archivos/Documentos/ REFORMASELECTORALESEJEC.pdf.

Mexico Working Group. 2000. "Democracy: The Long Winding Road—Report of the Mexico Working Group Delegation to Observe the 2000 Mexican Elections." July.

Meyer, Jean. 2000. *Samuel Ruiz en San Cristóbal.* Mexico City: Tusquets.

Meyer, Lorenzo. 1989. "Democratization of the PRI: Mission Impossible?" In *Mexico's Alternative Political Futures,* edited by W. A. Cornelius, J. Gentleman, and P. H. Smith. La Jolla: Center for U.S.-Mexican Studies, University of California, San Diego.

————. 1995. *Liberalismo autoritario. Las contradicciones del sistema político mexicano.* Mexico City: Océano.

————. 1996. "Trois moments, trois impressions." In *Mexique: de Chiapas à la crise financière,* edited by L. E. Gómez. Paris: L'Harmattan.

————. 2000. "Los caciques: ayer, hoy ¿y mañana?" *Letras libres,* no. 24.

Middlebrook, Kevin. 1986. "Political Liberalization in an Authoritarian Regime: The Case of Mexico." In *Transitions from Authoritarian Rule,* edited by G. O'Donnell, P. C. Schmitter, and L. Whitehead. Vol 2, *Latin America.* Baltimore: The Johns Hopkins University Press.

————. 1989. "The CTM and the Future of Government-Labor Relations." In *Mexico's Alternative Political Futures,* edited by W. A. Cornelius, J. Gentleman, and P. H. Smith. La Jolla: Center for U.S.-Mexican Studies, University of California, San Diego.

————. 1995. *The Paradox of Revolution: Labor, the State, and Authoritarianism in Mexico.* Baltimore: The Johns Hopkins University Press.

Midlarsky, Manus I. 1988. "Rulers and the Ruled: Patterned Inequality and the Onset of Mass Political Violence." *American Political Science Review* 82, no. 2: 491–509.

Miliband, Ralph. 1969. *The State in Capitalist Society.* New York: Basic Books.

Mizrahi, Yemile. 1995. "Entrepreneurs in the Opposition: Modes of Political Participation in Chihuahua." In *Opposition Government in Mexico,* edited by V. E. Rodríguez and P. M. Ward. Albuquerque: University of New Mexico Press.

———. 1998. "The Costs of Electoral Success: The Partido Acción Nacional." In *Governing Mexico: Political Parties and Elections,* edited by M. Serrano. London: Institute of Latin American Studies, University of London.

Molano, Alfredo. 2000. "The Evolution of the FARC: A Guerrilla Group's Long History." *NACLA Report on the Americas* 34, no. 2: 23–31.

Molina Ruiz, Francisco Javier. 2000. "Crimen organizado y la gobernabilidad democrática en la frontera México-Estados Unidos." In *Crimen organizado y gobernabilidad democrática: México y la franja fronteriza,* edited by J. Bailey and R. Godson. Mexico City: Grijalbo.

Molinar Horcasitas, Juan. 1989. "The Future of the Electoral System." In *Mexico's Alternative Political Futures,* edited by W. A. Cornelius, J. Gentleman, and P. H. Smith. La Jolla: Center for U.S.-Mexican Studies, University of California, San Diego.

———. 1991. *El tiempo de la legitimidad. Elecciones, autoritarismo y democracia en México.* Mexico City: Cal y Arena.

———. 1996. "Changing the Balance of Power in a Hegemonic Party System." In *Institutional Design in New Democracies: Eastern Europe and Latin America,* edited by A. Lijphart and C. Waisman. Boulder: Westview Press.

———. 1998. "Renegociación de las reglas del juego: el estado y los partidos políticos." In *La reconstrucción del estado: México después de Salinas,* edited by M. Serrano, and V. Bulmer-Thomas. Mexico City: Fondo de Cultura Económica.

Monge, Raúl. 2000. "Cárdenas y Robles gastaron más que Espinosa Villarreal." *Proceso,* November 26.

Montemayor, Carlos. 1999. *Guerrilla recurrente.* Mexico City: Universidad Autónoma de Ciudad Juárez.

Montes, Eduardo. 1999a. "Lo que no debe continuar en el PRD." *La Jornada,* March 27.

———. 1999b. "Oportunidad para el PRD." *La Jornada,* February 13.

Moore, Molly. 2000a. "In Mexico, Ballots and Bullets." *Washington Post,* June 28.

———. 2000b. "Mexico's Middle Class Fortifies Opposition." *Washington Post,* June 20.

Morley, Samuel A. 1995. *Poverty and Inequality in Latin America: The Impact of Adjustment and Recovery in the 1980s.* Baltimore: The Johns Hopkins University Press.

Morris, Stephen D. 1995. *Political Reformism in Mexico: An Overview of Contemporary Mexican politics,* Boulder and London: Lynne Rienner Publishers.

Muller, Edward N., and Mitchell A. Seligson. 1987. "Inequality and Insurgency." *American Political Science Review* 81, no. 2: 425–52.

Munck, Gerardo L. and Carol S. Leff. 1997. "Modes of Transition and Democratization: South America and Eastern Europe in Comparative Perspective." *Comparative Politics* 29, no. 3: 343–62.

Murillo, M. Victoria. 1997. "A Strained Alliance: Continuity and Change in Mexican Labour Politics." In *Mexico: Assessing Neo-Liberal Reform,* edited by M. Serrano. London: Institute of Latin American Studies, University of London.

————. 2000. "From Populism to Neoliberalism: Labor Unions and Market Reforms in Latin America." *World Politics* 52, no. 2: 135–74.

Nademan, Ethan A. 1999. "Global Prohibition Regimes: The Evolution of Norms in International Society." In *Transnational Crime,* edited by N. Passas. Dartmouth: Ashgate.

Najar, Alberto. 2001. "Lecciones sin aprender." *Masiosare,* May 6.

National Democratic Institute for International Affairs (NDI). 2000a. "International Visitors Laud Electoral Advances but Urge Action to Remedy Voter-Coercion and Media Bias." NDI Press Release. Mexico City, June 9.

————. 2000b. "Statement of the NDI International Delegation to Mexico's July 2, 2000 Elections." Press Bulletin. Mexico City, July 3.

Naylor, R. Thomas. 1995. "From Cold War to Crime War: The Search for a New 'National Security' Threat." *Transnational Organized Crime* 1, no. 4: 37–56.

————. 1997. "Mafias, Myths, and Markets: On the Theory and Practice of Enterprise Crime." *Transnational Organized Crime* 3, no. 3: 1–45.

Nelleman, Steven, and Jeremiah Goulka. 1999. "Drugged Law Enforcement: The Influence of Drug Trafficking on the Rule of Law and Human Rights in Mexico." In *Mexico: Facing the Challenges of Human Rights and Crime,* edited by W. Cartwright. Ardsley, NY: Transnational Publishers.

Novelo, Federico. 2002. *La política económica y social de la alternancia: Revisión crítica,* Mexico City: M. A. Porrúa and UAM-X.

O'Donnell, Guillermo. 1989. "Transitions to Democracy: Some Navigation Instruments." In *Democracy in the Americas: Stopping the Pendulum,* edited by R. A. Pastor. New York: Holmes and Meier Publishers.

————. 1994. "Delegative Democracy." *Journal of Democracy* 5, no. 1: 55–69.

————. 1997. "Illusions about Consolidation." In *Consolidating the Third Wave Democracies: Regional Challenges,* edited by L. Diamond et al. Baltimore: The Johns Hopkins University Press.

————. 1999. "Polyarchies and the (Un)Rule of Law in Latin America: A Partial Conclusion." In *The (Un)Rule of Law and the Underprivileged in Latin America,* edited by J. E. Méndez, G. O'Donnell, and P. S. Pinheiro. Notre Dame, Indiana: University of Notre Dame Press.

O'Donnell, Guillermo, and Philippe C. Schmitter. 1986. *Transitions from Authoritarian Rule: Tentative Conclusions about Uncertain Democracies.* Baltimore: The Johns Hopkins University Press.

O'Donnell, Guillermo, Philippe C. Schmitter, and Lawrence Whitehead, eds. 1986. *Transitions from Authoritarian Rule.* Baltimore: The Johns Hopkins University Press.

Observatoire Géopolitique des Drogues (OGD). 1996. *Atlas Mondial des Drogues.* Paris: PUF.

————. 2000. *La Géopolitique Mondiale des Drogues 1998/1999 : Rapport Annuel.* Paris: OGD.

Office of National Drug Control Policy (ONDCP). 2001. *The National Drug Control Strategy: 2001 Annual Report.* Washington, DC: US Government Printing Office.

————. 2003. *The National Drug Control Strategy: Data Supplement.* Washington, DC: US Government Printing Office.

Olmos, Jose G. 2000. "Pruebas de que el *narco* infiltró al PRI, pide Labastida." *La Jornada,* March 1.

———. 2001. "Movimientos armados desafían a Fox." *Proceso,* June 3.

Oppenheimer, Andres. 1998. *Bordering on Chaos: Mexico's Roller-Coaster Journey Toward Prosperity.* Boston: Little Brown.

Organization for Economic Cooperation and Development (OECD). 1999a. *OECD Economic Surveys, 1998–1999: Mexico.* Paris: OECD.

———. 1999b. *Revenue Statistics, 1965–1998.* Paris: OECD.

Pacheco, Guadalupe. 1993. "Construir la nueva organización territorial del PRI." *Examen,* May.

Palmer, David S. 1992. "Peru, the Drug Business and Shining Path: Between Scylla and Charybdis?" In *Journal of Interamerican Studies and World Affairs* 34, no. 3:65–88.

———. 1994. *The Shining Path of Peru.* New York: St. Martin's Press.

———. 1996. "Peru, Drugs, and the Shining Path." In *Drug Trafficking in the Americas,* edited by B. M. Bagley and W. O. Walker III. Coral Gables: North-South Center Press.

Panagides, Alexis. 1994. "Mexico." In *Indigenous People and Poverty in Latin America,* edited by G. Psacharopoulos and H. A. Patrinos. Washington, D.C.: The World Bank.

Pardo, Rafael. 2000. "Colombia's Two Front War." *Foreign Affairs* 79, no. 4: 64–73.

Parker, Richard n.d. "Mexico's Poor Trading Machetes for AK-47s." *Albuquerque Journal,* special report available on line at http://www.abqjournal.com/news/drugs/276489056@Bottom1.

Passas, Nikos. 1998. "Globalization and transnational Crime: Effects of Criminogenic Asymmetries." *Transnational Organized Crime* 4, no. 3/4: 22–55.

———, ed. 1999. *Transnational Crime,* Dartmouth: Ashgate.

Pastor, Manuel, and Carol Wise. 1998. "State Policy and Distributional Stress." In *The Post-NAFTA Political Economy: Mexico and the Western Hemisphere,* edited by C. Wise. University Park: The Pennsylvania University Press.

Pastor, Robert A. 2000. "Mexico's Victory: Exiting the Labyrinth." *Journal of Democracy* 11, no. 4: 20–4.

Pastor, Robert A., and Jorge G. Castañeda. 1988. *Limits to friendship.* New York: Knopf.

Paternorstro, Silvana. 1995. "Mexico as a Narco-Democracy." *World Policy Journal* 12: 41–7.

Paz Paredes, Lorena, and Rosario Cobo. 2000. "Café Caliente." In *Crónicas del sur: utopías campesinas en Guerrero,* edited by A. Bartra. Mexico City: Era.

Pérez, Germán, and Antonia Martínez, eds. 2000. *La Cámara de Diputados en México.* Mexico City: FLACSO, Miguel Angel Porrúa, Cámara de Diputados.

Perl, Raphael F. 1995. "United States Foreign Narcopolicy: Shifting Focus to International Crime?" *Transnational Organized Crime* 1, no. 1: 33–46.

Peschard, Jacqueline. 1991. "El PRI: una descentralización dirigida." *Estudios Políticos,* no. 8: 55–70.

Petrich, Blanche. 1997. "Entrevista al EPR." *La Jornada,* February 6.

Pimentel, Stanley. 2000. "Los nexos entre política y crimen organizado." In *Crimen organizado y gobernabilidad democrática: México y la franja fronteriza*, edited by J. Bailey and R. Godson. Mexico City: Grijalbo.

Piñeyro, José Luis. 1998. "El narcotráfico y la seguridad nacional de México: Cambios, críticas y propuestas." *Revista de Administración Pública*, no. 98: 101–15.

Porteous, Samuel D. 1996. "The Threat from Transnational Crime: An Intelligence Perspective." *Transnational Organized Crime* 2, no. 4: 153–65.

Power, Timothy J., and Mark J. Gasiorowski. 1997. "Institutional Design and Democratic Consolidation in the Third World." *Comparative Political Studies* 30, no. 2: 123–55.

Procuraduría General de la República (PGR). 1998. *El libro blanco de Acteal*. Mexico City: PGR.

Programa de Educación, Salud y Alimentación (PROGRESA). 1999. *Más oportunidades para las familias pobres: Evaluación de resultados del Programa de Educación, Salud y Alimentación*. Mexico City: SEDESOL.

———. 2000. *¿Está dando buenos resultados Progresa? Informe de los Resultados de una Evaluación Realizada por el IFPRI, 2000*, Mexico City: SEDESOL.

Przeworski, Adam. 1991. *Democracy and the Market: Political and Economic Reform in Eastern Europe and Latin America*. Cambridge: Cambridge University Press.

Przeworski, Adam, Michael Alvarez, José A. Cheibub, and Fernando Limongi. 1996. "What Makes Democracies Endure?" *Journal of Democracy* 7, no. 1: 39–55.

Psacharopoulos, George, and Harry Anthony Patrinos, eds. 1994. *Indigenous People and Poverty in Latin America*. Washington, D.C.: The World Bank.

Public Citizen. 2001. *Down on the Farm: NAFTA's Seven-Years War on Farmers and Ranchers in the U.S., Canada, and Mexico*. Available online at http://www.citizen.org/pctrade/nafta/reports/naftaAG/NAFTAREPORT.html.

Purcell, Susan K. 1981. "Mexico: Clientelism, Corporatism, and Political Stability." In *Political Clientelism, Patronage, and Development*, edited by S.N. Eisenstadt and R. Lemarchand. Beverly Hills: Sage Publications.

Ramos, Rolando. 2000. "Bloqueará el PRI intento de aplicar IVA a alimentos y medicinas." *El Economista*, December 8.

Rascón, Marco. 1999. "La vía láctea." *La Jornada*, January 31.

Reding Andrew. 1995. *Democracy and Human Rights in Mexico*. Available online at http://worldpolicy.org/americas/mexico/mexico95.html.

Reina, Ana María. 1999. "The Human Rights Situation in Mexico." In *Mexico: Facing the Challenges of Human Rights and Crime*, edited by W. Cartwright. Ardsley, NY: Transnational Publishers.

Reinares, Fernando. 1990. "Sociogénesis y evolución del terrorismo en España." In *España: Sociedad y política*, edited by S. Giner. Madrid: Espasa-Calpe.

Rendón Corona, Armando. 2001. "El corporativismo sindical y sus transformaciones." *Nueva Antropología* 53, no. 59: 11–30.

Reuter, Peter. 1998. "Foreign Demand for Latin American Drugs: The USA and Europe." In *Latin America and the Multinational Drug Trade*, edited by E. Joyce and C. Malamud. New York: St. Martin's Press.

Reuter, Peter, and David Ronfeldt. 1992. "Quest for Integrity: The Mexican-US Drug Issue in the 1980s." *Journal of Inter-American Studies and World Affairs* 34, no. 3: 89–153.

Rico, Maite, and Bertrand De La Grange. 1998. *Marcos, la genial impostura.* Mexico City: Aguilar.

Rodríguez, Victoria E. 1997. *Decentralization in Mexico: From Reforma Municipal to Solidaridad, to Nuevo Federalismo.* Boulder: Westview Press.

Rodríguez, Victoria E., and Peter M. Ward. 1994. *Political Change in Baja California: Democracy in the Making?* La Jolla: Center for U.S.-Mexican Studies, University of California, San Diego.

Rojas, Rosa. 1995. *Chiapas: la paz violenta.* Mexico City: La Jornada.

Ronfeldt, David, John Arquilla, Graham E. Fuller, and Melissa Fuller. 1998. *The Zapatista Social Netwar in Mexico.* Santa Monica, CA: RAND Arroyo Center.

Roniger, Luis. 1990. *Hierarchy and Trust in Modern Mexico and Brazil.* New York: Praeger.

Roniger, Luis, and Ayse Günes-Ayata, eds. 1994. *Democracy, Clientelism, and Civil Society.* Boulder: Lynne Rienner.

Rosas, Ana M. 2000a. "Más impuestos a empresas: PRD." *El Economista,* December 8.

———. 2000b. "Rechazará el PRI cualquier aumento al IVA." *El Economista,* December 4.

Rubalcava, Rosa María, and Jorge Chavarría. 1999a. "La marginación en Puebla, Guadalajara y Monterrey." In *Atlas Demográfico de Mexico,* edited by G. Garza. Mexico City: Conapo-Progresa.

———. 1999b. "La marginación metropolitana de la Ciudad de México." In *Atlas Demográfico de Mexico,* edited by G. Garza. Mexico City: Conapo-Progresa.

Rubalcava, Rosa María, and Juan Carlos Ordaz. 1999. "La marginación metropolitana." In *Atlas Demográfico de Mexico,* edited by G. Garza. Mexico City: Conapo-Progresa.

Rubín Bamaca, Homero W. 2000. "El abstencionismo en los Altos de Chiapas: La otra cara de las elecciones." In *Democracia en tierras indígenas: Las elecciones en Los Altos de Chiapas (1991–1998),* edited by J. P. Viqueira and W. Sonnleitner. Mexico City: CIESAS, Colmex, and IFE.

Rueschemeyer, Dietrich, Evelyne H. Stephens, and John D. Stephens. 1992. *Capitalist Development and Democracy.* Chicago: University of Chicago Press.

Ruiz, Bert. 2001. *The Colombian civil war,* Jefferson, N.C.: McFarland.

Rustow, Dankwart A. 1970. "Transitions to Democracy: Toward a Dynamic Model." *Comparative Politics* 2, no. 3: 337–63.

Ryan, Jeffrey J. 1994. "The Impact of Democratization on Revolutionary Movements." *Comparative Politics* 27, no. 1: 27–44.

Saba, Roberto P., and Luigi Manzetti. 1999. "Privatization in Argentina: The Implications for Corruption." In *Transnational Crime,* edited by N. Passas. Dartmouth: Ashgate.

SAGARPA. 2001. "Balanza comercial agroalimentaria," Mexico City: SAGARPA-Centro de Estadística Agropecuaria.

Sales, Carlos. 1991. "Estructura territorial del partido." *Examen,* June.

Salzano, Julie, and Stephen W. Hartman. 1997. "Cargo Crime." *Transnational Organized Crime* 3, no.1: 39–49.

Samstad, James G. 2001. "El movimiento obrero mexicano después de Fidel Velázquez: la erosión del corporativismo en el sexenio de Zedillo." *Nueva Antropología* 53, no. 59: 31–52.

Sánchez, Marco Aurelio. 1999. *PRD: La elite en crisis*, Mexico City: Plaza y Valdés.

Schedler, Andreas. 2000. "Mexico's Victory: the Democratic Revelation." *Journal of Democracy* 11, no. 4: 5–19.

Schmid, Alex P. 1996. "The Links between Transnational Organized Crime and Terrorist Crimes." *Transnational Organized Crime* 2, no. 4: 40–82.

Schmitter, Philippe C. 1974. "Still the Century of Corporatism?" *The Review of Politics* 36, no. 1: 85–131.

Schumpeter, Joseph A. 1947. *Capitalism, Socialism and Democracy.* 3d ed. New York: Harper & Row.

Schwerin, Karl H. 1973. "The Anthropological Antecedents: Caciques, Cacicazgos, and Caciquismo." In *The Caciques: Oligarchical Politics and the System of Caciquismo in the Luso-Hispanic World,*" edited by R. Kern. Albuquerque: University of New Mexico Press.

Scott, James C. 1977. "Patron-Client Politics and Political Change in Southeast Asia." In *Friends, Followers, and Factions*, edited by W. Schmidt et al. Berkeley: University of California Press.

Scott, Peter Dale. 2003. *Drugs, Oil, and War: The United States in Afghanistan, Colombia, and Indochina.* Lanham, MD: Rowman and Littlefield.

Scott, Peter Dale, and Jonathan Marshall. 1998. *Cocaine Politics: Drugs, Armies, and the CIA in Central America.* Berkeley and Los Angeles: University of California Press,

Secretaría de Economía (SE). 2001. "Exportaciones totales de México." Available online at http://www.economia-snci.gob.mx/Estad_stica/Expmx.htm.

Secretaría de Hacienda y Crédito Público (SHCP). 2004. "Sistema de Finanzas Públicas, Ingresos tributarios." Available online at http://www.shcp.gob.mx/eofp/seriesm/consultam.asp?opc=0.

Serrano, Mónica. 1998. "Introduction" to *Governing Mexico: Political Parties and Elections*, edited by M. Serrano. London: Institute of Latin American Studies, University of London.

Shelley, Louise I. 1996. "Post-Soviet Organized Crime: A New Form of Authoritarianism." *Transnational Organized Crime* 2, no. 2/3: 122–38.

Sierra Guzmán, Jorge Luis. 2003a. *El enemigo interno: contrainsurgencia y fuerzas armadas en México.* Mexico City: CEEAN, UIA, and Plaza y Valdés.

———. 2003b. "Mexico's Military in the War on Drugs." Available online at http://www.wola.org/publications/ddhr_mexico_brief.pdf.

Simon, Joel. 1996. "Militarization of Mexico: Part I. Mexican Army Escalates Patrols in Reputed Rebel Stronghold." Available online at http://www.pacific-news.org/jinn/stories/2.18/960828-rebel.html.

SIPAZ. 1998. "Acteal, un año después." Available online at http://www.nonviolence.org/sipaz/vol3no5/acteals.htm.

Sistema Nacional de Seguridad Pública (SNSP). 2001. "Presentación." Available online at http://www.ssp.gob.mx/application?pageid=snsp_sub_2&docName=Antecedente s&docId=37.

Skinner, Quentin. 1973. "The Empirical Theorists of Democracy and Their Critics: A Plague on Both Their Houses." *Political Theory* 1, no. 3: 287–306.

Skocpol, Theda. 1979. *States and Social Revolutions.* New York: Cambridge University Press.

Smale, Alison. 2001. "The Dark Side of the Global Economy." *New York Times,* August 16.

Smith, Peter H. 1999. "Semiorganized International Crime: Drug Traffickers in Mexico." In *Transnational Crime in the Americas,* edited by T. Farer. New York and London: Routledge.

Snyder, Richard. 1999. "After the State Withdraws: Neoliberalism and Subnational Authoritarian Regimes in Mexico." In *Subnational Politics and Democratization in Mexico,* edited by W. A. Cornelius, T. A. Eisenstadt, and J. Hindley. La Jolla: Center for U.S.-Mexican Studies, University of California, San Diego.

Solís Rosales, Ricardo, ed. 2003. *Del FOBAPROA al IPAB: Testimonios, análisis y propuestas.* Mexico City: UAM-Plaza y Valdés.

Solomon, Joel A. 1999a. "Mexican Human Rights Policy and Practice in the 1990s." In *Mexico: Facing the Challenges of Human Rights and Crime,* edited by W. Cartwright. Ardsley, NY: Transnational Publishers.

———. 1999b. *Systemic Injustice: Torture, "Disappearance," and Extrajudicial Execution in Mexico.* New York: Human Rights Watch.

Solomon, Joel A., and Sebastian Brett. 1997. *Implausible Deniability: State Responsibility for Rural Violence in Mexico.* New York: Human Rights Watch.

Sonnleitner, Willibald. 2000. "Promesas y desencantos de una democratización electoral incipiente pero inacabada (1991–1998)." In *Democracia en tierras indígenas: Las elecciones en Los Altos de Chiapas (1991–1998),* edited by J. P. Viqueira and W. Sonnleitner. Mexico City: CIESAS, Colmex, IFE.

Sources. 1999. "The Globalization of the Drug Trade," no. 111 (April).

Sterling, Claire. 1994. *Thieves' World.* New York: Simon and Schuster.

Stern, Steve J. 1998. *Shining and Other Paths: War and Society in Peru, 1980–1995.* Durham: Duke University Press.

Stiglitz, Joseph E. 2002. *Globalization and Its Discontents.* New York and London: W. W. Norton.

Sullivan, Kevin. 2000. "A Not So Secret Ballot in Rural Mexico." *Washington Post,* July 3.

Székely, Miguel. 1998. *The Economics of Poverty, Inequality and Wealth Accumulation in Mexico.* New York: St. Martin's Press.

Taylor, Michael C. 1997. "Constitutional Crisis: How Reforms to the Legislature Have Doomed Mexico." *Mexican Studies* 13, no. 2: 299–324.

Téllez, Edgar, Oscar Montes, and Jorge Lesmes. 2002. *Diario íntimo de un fracaso: historia no contada del proceso de paz con las FARC.* Bogotá: Planeta.

Tello Díaz, Carlos. 2000. *La rebelión de las cañadas: Origen y ascenso del EZLN.* 2d ed. Mexico City: Cal y Arena.

Thornburgh, Dick. 1995. "The Internationalization of Business Crime." *Transnational Organized Crime* 1, no. 1: 23–32.

Thoumi, Francisco E. 1995. *Political Economy and Illegal Drugs in Colombia.* Boulder: Lynne Rienner.

———. 1999. "The Impact of the Illegal Drug Industry on Colombia." In *Transnational Crime in the Americas*, edited by T. Farer. New York and London: Routledge.

Tilly, Charles. 1978. *From Mobilization to Revolution.* Reading, MA: Addison-Wesley.

Tobler, Hans Werner. 1990. "Los campesinos y la formación del estado revolucionario, 1910–1940." In *Revuelta, rebelión y revolución: La lucha rural en México del siglo XVI al siglo XX*, edited by F. Katz. Vol.1. Mexico City: ERA.

Toro, Maria Celia. 1995. *Mexico's "War" on Drugs: Causes and Consequences.* Boulder: Lynne Rienner.

———. 1998. "The Political Repercussions of Drug Trafficking in Mexico." In *Latin America and the Multinational Drug Trade*, edited by E. Joyce and C. Malamud. New York: St. Martin's Press.

Treverton, Gregory F. 1999. "International Organized Crime, National Security, and the Market State." In *Transnational Crime in the Americas*, edited by T. Farer. New York and London: Routledge.

Trotsky, Leon. 1980. *History of the Russian Revolution.* 3 vols. New York: Pathfinder.

Tullis, LaMond. 1995. *Unintended Consequences: Illegal Drugs and Drug Policies in Nine Countries.* Boulder: Lynne Rienner.

Turbiville Jr., Graham. 1995. "Organized Crime and the Russian Armed Forces." *Transnational Organized Crime* 1, no. 4: 57–104.

———. 1997. "Mexico's Other Insurgents." *Military Review* 77, no. 3: 81–90.

———. 2000. "Mexico's Multidimensional Force for Internal Security." *Military Review* 80, no. 4: 41–9.

———. 2001. "Mexico's Evolving Security Posture." *Military Review* 81, no. 3, on-line edition available at http://www-cgsc.army.mil/milrev/English/MayJun01/turb.htm.

U.S. House. 1996. Committee on Banking and Financial Services. *Money Laundering Activity Associated with the Mexican Narco-Crime Syndicate: Hearing before the Subcommittee on General Oversight and Investigations of the Committee on Banking and Financial Services.* 104th Cong., 2d sess. September 5.

———. 1997. *Money Laundering Activity Associated with the Mexican Narco-Crime Syndicate.* Washington, DC: US Government Printing Office.

U.S. State Department's Bureau for International Narcotics and Law Enforcements Affairs (BINLEA). 1998. *International Narcotics Control Strategy Report, 1997.* Available online at http://www.state.gov/g/inl/rls/nrcrpt/1997/.

———. 2001. *International Narcotics Control Strategy Report, 2000.* Available online at http://www.state.gov/g/inl/rls/nrcrpt/2000/.

———. 2002. *International Narcotics Control Strategy Report, 2001.* Available online at http://www.state.gov/g/inl/rls/nrcrpt/2001/.

———. 2003a. "FY 2003 Narcotics Certification Process," January 31. Available online at http://www.state.gov/g/inl/rls/fs/17010.htm.

———. 2003b. *International Narcotics Control Strategy Report, 2002.* Available online at http://www.state.gov/g/inl/rls/nrcrpt/2002/.

———. 2004. *International Narcotics Control Strategy Report, 2003.* Available online at http://www.state.gov/g/inl/rls/nrcrpt/2002/.

U.S. State Department's Bureau of Democracy, Human Rights, and Labor (BDHRL). 2004. *Country Reports on Human Rights Practices, 2003: Mexico.* Available online at http://www.state.gov/g/drl/rls/hrrpt/2003.

Ulrich, Christopher. 1997. "Transnational Organized Crime and Law Enforcement Cooperation in the Baltic States." *Transnational Organized Crime* 3, no. 2: 111–30.

Umberg, Thomas J. 1999. Testimony on anti-narcotics efforts in the Western Hemisphere and implementation of the Western Hemisphere Drug Elimination Act before the Subcommittee on the Western Hemisphere of the House Committee on International Relations, 106th Cong., 1st sess. March 3.

United Nations (UN). 1995. "Report to the Secretary-General: Implementation of General Assembly Resolution 49/150 on the Naples Political Declaration and Global Action Plan against Organized Transnational Crime." *Transnational Organized Crime* 1, no. 3: 169–79.

United Nations Development Programme (UNDP). 2000. *Human Development Report, 2000.* New York and Oxford: Oxford University Press.

Urrutia, Alonso et al. 2000. "Se reforzará el combate al crimen organizado en Juárez y Tijuana." *La Jornada,* March 1.

U.S. News Online. 1996. "Rebellion, Mexican Style." Available online at http://www.usnews.com/usnews/issue/23mexi.htm.

Valdés, Leonardo. 1994. "Partido de la Revolución Democrática: The Third Option in Mexico." In *Party Politics in "An Uncommon Democracy,"* edited by N. Harvey and M. Serrano. London: Institute of Latin American Studies, University of London.

Valle, Eduardo. 1995. *El segundo disparo: La narcodemocracia mexicana.* Mexico City: Océano.

Vanderbush, Walt. 1999. "Assessing Democracy in Puebla: The Opposition Takes Charge of Municipal Government." *Journal of Interamerican Studies and World Affairs* 41, no. 2: 1–27.

Vargas Meza, Ricardo. 1998. "The FARC, the War, and the Crisis of the State." *NACLA Report on the Americas* 31, no. 5: 22–7.

Vázquez, Felipe. 1998. "Politics-Mexico: Government's Hidden War with Maoists." *IPS World News,* online edition available at http://www.oneworld.net/external/?url=http%3A%2F%2Fwww.oneworld.org%2Fips2%2Fjune98%2F04_11_013.html.

Velasco Cruz, José L. 2000. "La derrota de los pobres: Análisis post-electoral." *La Jornada,* July 23.

———. 2003. Beyond Democratic Transition: Political Change in Late Twentieth-Century Mexico. Ph.D. diss., Boston University.

Velasco, Saúl. 2003. *El movimiento indígena y la autonomía en México.* Mexico City: UNAM-UPN.

Viqueira, Juan Pedro, and Willibald Sonnleitner, eds. 2000. *Democracia en tierras in-dígenas: Las elecciones en Los Altos de Chiapas (1991–1998)*. Mexico City: CIESAS, Colmex, and IFE.

Voronin, Yuriy A. 1996. "The Emerging Criminal State: Economic and Political Aspects of Organized Crime in Russia." *Transnational Organized Crime* 2, no. 2/3: 53–63.

Wager, Stephen J., and Donald E. Schulz. 1995. "Civil-Military Relations in Mexico: The Zapatista Revolt and Its Implications." *Journal of Inter-American Studies and World Affairs* 37, no. 1: 1–42.

Waller, Michael. 1999. "Mexican Standoff: The Narcostate Next Door." *Insight on the News*, December 27, online edition available at http://www.insightmag. com/news/1999/12/27/World/Mexican.Standoff.The.Narcostate.Next.Door-208352.shtml.

Ward, Peter M. 1995. "Policy Making and Policy Implementation among Non-PRI governments: The PAN in Ciudad Juarez and in Chihuahua." In *Opposition Government in Mexico*, edited by V. E. Rodríguez and P. M. Ward. Albuquerque: University of New Mexico Press.

———. 1998. "De clientelismo a tecnocracia: cambios recientes en la gestión munic-ipal en México." *Política y Gobierno* 5 (January-June): 95–133.

Weber, Max. 1978. *Economy and Society*. Edited by G. Roth and C. Wittich. Berkeley: University of California Press.

Weyland, Kurt. 1996. "Neopopulism and Neoliberalism in Latin America: Unexpected Affinities." *Studies in Comparative International Development* 31, no. 3: 3–31.

Whitehead, Laurence. 1994. "The peculiarities of Transition 'a la Mexicana.'" In *Party Politics in "An Uncommon Democracy,"* edited by N. Harvey and M. Serrano. London: Institute of Latin American Studies, University of London.

———, ed. 1996. *The International Dimensions of Democratization: Europe and the Americas*. Oxford: Oxford University Press.

Wiarda, Howard J. 1974. *Politics and Social Change in Latin America: The Distinct Tradition*. Amherst: University of Massachusetts Press.

Williams, Phil. 1995. "Problems and Dangers Posed by Organized Transnational Crime in the Various Regions of the World." *Transnational Organized Crime* 1, no. 3: 1–41.

———. 1996. "Introduction: How Serious a Threat is Russian Organized Crime." *Transnational Organized Crime* 2, no. 2/3: 1–26.

———. 1998a. "Organizing Transnational Crime: Networks, Markets, and Hierarchies." *Transnational Organized Crime* 4, no. 3/4: 57–87.

———. 1998b. "The Nature of Drug-Trafficking Networks." *Current History* 97, no. 168: 154–9.

Woldenberg, José. 1997. "The Future of the Mexican Left." In *Mexico: Assessing Neo-Liberal Reform*, edited by M. Serrano. London: Institute of Latin American Studies, University of London.

———. 2001. "Lessons from Mexico." *Journal of Democracy* 12, no. 2: 151–6.

Womack, John. 1999. *Rebellion in Chiapas: An Historical Reader*. New York: The New Press.

World Bank. 2000. *World Development Report 1999/2000: Entering the 21st Century.* Washington, D. C.: The World Bank.

———. 2001a. *Mexico Data Profile.* Available online at http://devdata.worldbank. org/external/CPProfile.asp?SelectedCountry=MEX&CCODE=MEX&CNA ME=Mexico&PTYPE=CP.

———. 2001b. *World Development Report, 2000/2001: Attacking Poverty.* Oxford: Oxford University Press.

———. 2002. *Transition: The First Ten Years. Analysis and Lessons for Eastern Europe and the Former Soviet Union.* Washington, D. C.: The World Bank.

Youngers, Coletta A. 2002. "Drugs, Democracy and Collateral Damage: U.S. Drug Control in the Andes," Washington, D.C.: WOLA.

Zabludoff, Sidney J. 1997. "Colombian Narcotics Organizations as Business Enterprises." *Transnational Organized Crime* 3, no. 2: 20–49.

Zakaria, Fareed. 1997. "The Rise of Illiberal Democracy." In *Foreign Affairs* 76, no. 6: 22–43.

Zamarripa, Roberto. 2003. "Tolvanera/Atisbos." *Reforma,* June 16.

Zirnite, Peter. 1998. "The Militarization of the Drug War in Latin America." *Current History* 97, no. 168: 166–73.

Index